# THE BARE ESSENTIALS

## English Writing Skills

**Sarah Norton**
*Centennial College*

**Brian Green**
*Niagara College*

**Michèle Aina Barale**
*University of Colorado*

**Holt, Rinehart and Winston, Inc.**
*Fort Worth Chicago San Francisco Philadelphia*
*Montreal Toronto London Sydney Tokyo*

**Library of Congress Cataloging in Publication Data**

Norton, Sarah.
The bare essentials.

1. English language—Grammar—1950– I. Green, Brian. II. Barale, Michèle Aina. III. Title.
PE1112.N67 1983 808′.042 82-15537
ISBN 0-03-059821-4



Address Editorial Correspondence to:
301 Commerce Street
Fort Worth, Texas 76102



Printed in the United States of America

1 2 3 4 090 12 11 10 9 8 7 6 5 4

Holt, Rinehart and Winston, Inc.
The Dryden Press
Saunders College Publishing

# THE BARE ESSENTIALS

## English Writing Skills

# Preface

We have designed this book for college students taking a first-semester or first-year writing course. The complete explanations, numerous exercises, and complete answers, however, make it as suitable for individualized, self-paced learning programs as it is for conventional composition classes.

As the title suggests, *The Bare Essentials* covers only those points of grammar, usage, and mechanics that are indispensable to clear expository writing: organization of ideas, sentence structure, grammar, spelling, diction, and punctuation. The rules we present are applicable to all kinds of writing; principles with limited applications—research and documentation principles, for instance—are not discussed. This book teaches the basic skills, leaving the teacher free to supplement the text according to the special needs of the class or the specific objectives of the course.

Each "essential" is presented in a discrete unit. A glance at the table of contents will show that we have arranged the units in what might be called the "order of visibility" of composition errors—starting with spelling and ending with organization and diction—but the instructor may introduce the units in any order. For example, we like to teach unit 5 immediately after unit 1. The chapters within a unit should, however, be covered in the order in which they appear.

We believe that students can learn to write clear, error-free prose if they understand the principles involved, master the principles through practice with given sentences, and then apply the principles in their own writing. And they have to want to learn. Thus, we begin most chapters with a few words about the practical significance of the material. A short, nontechnical explanation of the writing principle appears next, followed by examples. Where the material is complex, we've broken it down into several easy-to-follow steps. Most of each chapter is devoted to practice exercises of gradually increasing difficulty, and the student is directed to do as many as necessary to master the rule. Taken sometimes from student work, sometimes from professional writing, the exercises are all designed to appeal to the interests of college students. In fact, we have given the entire book an informal tone, to engage and motivate the student. Each unit ends with a writing assignment that tests the student's mastery of all the principles in the unit, and other writing assignments are sprinkled throughout the book.

Several features of the book make it especially helpful and easy to use. First, the student can do most of the exercises right in the book. Second, the answers are printed on detachable pages at the back of the book, so students can easily correct their own work, getting immediate feedback about their errors. Third, a Progress Chart allows students to keep track of their errors as writing assignments are returned to them. Finally, on the inside of the back cover is a Revision Guide, which can be used both as a checklist for revision and rewriting and as a subject index to the book. Instructors may wish to duplicate the Revision Guide, attach it to a student's paper, and use it to guide and explain grading.

We wish to express our appreciation to those who read and taught sections of the book in its evolutionary stages, especially Paul G. Bator, Oakland University; Lawrence Borzumato, Ulster County Community College; Robert Christopher, Ramapo College; W. Michael Clippinger, Indiana Vocational Technical College; V. Kay Colbert, North Georgia College; Carol Sweedler-Brown, San Diego State University; and Jean Wilkinson, Los Angeles Pierce College. In particular, we thank Carol Baxter, who advised us, encouraged us, and helped us revise much of the manuscript.

*Sarah Norton*

*Brian Green*

*Michèle Aina Barale*

# Contents

## UNIT ONE



## UNIT TWO



## UNIT THREE

## UNIT FOUR

## Punctuation 141



## UNIT FIVE

## Organizing Your Writing 171



## UNIT SIX

## Beyond the Bare Essentials 203

## Appendices 221

# Introduction

## Why You Need This Book

*Who needs to write well, anyway? If I get a factory or general labor job, I won't ever need to write, and if I'm in management, a secretary will fix all my mistakes.*

College Student

*We can train a person on the job to do the specific tasks we require in about two weeks . . . maximum. What we need you people at the colleges to do is teach them to communicate—with other workers, with their supervisors—orally and in memos, reports, and letters.*

President of Steel-
Fabricating Firm Speaking
to the Technical Faculty
of a Community College

*You look at the guys who move up in this industry. They're the ones who can write intelligently and who can read and understand other people's writing. Hard work helps, and so does being the owner's nephew . . . but you've got to be able to read and write reasonably well to move past manual labor—and the guys who can't do it know that better than anyone. Ask them.*

Former Mining
Industry Employee

To an employer, any employee is more valuable if he or she is able to write correctly and clearly. No one can advance very far in a career without the ability to construct understandable sentences. It's that simple. Fairly or unfairly, employers and others will judge your intelligence and ability on the basis of your use of English. If you want to communicate effectively and earn respect, both on and off the job, you need to be able to write clearly.

That's the bad news. The good news is that *anyone who wants to* can learn to write acceptable English. All that is needed from you, really, is *car-*

*ing*. If you care enough—about what others think of you, about advancement in a career—then you'll put out the effort necessary, whether that means looking up spelling, rereading what you've written, or doing all the exercises in this book twice!

# How to Use this Book

In each chapter we do three things: explain a point, illustrate it with examples, and provide exercises to help you master it. The exercises are arranged in groups of ten-item sets that get more difficult as you go along. By the end of the last set in a chapter you should have a good grasp of the skill.

Here's how to proceed:

1. Read the explanation. Do this even if you think you understand the point being discussed.
2. Study the examples carefully.
3. Now turn to the exercises. If you've found an explanation easy and think that you have no problems with the skill, try an exercise set (ten sentences) near the end of the group of exercises following the explanation. If you get all ten sentences right, do one more set. If you complete that set correctly too, skip the rest and go on to the next point. Skip ahead only if you're really confident, though.

   If you don't feel confident, don't skip anything. Start with the first set and work through all the exercises until you're sure you understand the point.
4. *Always check your answers to one exercise (ten sentences) before going on to the next.* If you ignore this instruction, we can't help you. Only if you check after every ten sentences can you avoid repeating your mistakes and possibly reinforcing your error.
5. When you discover a mistake, go back to the explanation and examples and study them again. Make up some examples of your own to illustrate the rule. When you're sure you understand, continue with the exercises.

Finally, on the inside back cover you'll find the Revision Guide. Use it to check over your papers before handing them in. There's also a Progress Chart (appendix B) to help you keep track of errors in your writing and to record your improvement. Use both. This book is meant to be a practical tool, not a theoretical reference. Apply what you learn in the lessons to the writing assignments we've included and to all the writing you do. Explanations can identify writing problems and show you how to solve them; exercises can give you practice in eliminating errors, but only writing and revising bring real and lasting improvement.

# THE BARE ESSENTIALS

## English Writing Skills

# UNIT ONE

# Spelling

1 Three Suggestions for Quick Improvement

2 Sound-Alikes, Look-Alikes, and Spoilers

3 The Apostrophe

# Chapter 1

# Three Suggestions for Quick Improvement

We will deal with spelling first because, of all the errors you might make in writing, spelling is the one that is noticed by everyone, not just English teachers. No piece of writing that is full of misspellings can be classified as good. Misspellings can cause misunderstanding, as when the communications teacher promised his students a course with "a strong *vacational* emphasis." (Those students who weren't misled wondered what he was doing teaching communications.)

Sometimes misspellings cause confusion. Take this sentence, for example:

> Mouse is a desert with a base of wiped cream.

It takes a few seconds to "translate" the sentence into a definition of *mousse*, a dessert made with whipped cream.

Most often, though, misspellings are misleading in that they spoil the image you want to present. You want, naturally, to be seen as intelligent, careful, and conscientious. But if your writing is riddled with spelling errors, your reader will think you careless, uneducated, or even stupid. It is not true, by the way, that intelligence and the ability to spell go hand in hand. It *is* true, though, that people generally think they do. So, to prevent both confusion and embarrassment, it is essential that you spell correctly.

There are three things you can do to improve your spelling almost instantly:

| 1. Buy and use a good dictionary. |
|---|

A good dictionary is the one indispensable tool of the writer. You will need it *every time* you write. Most of your doubts about spelling can be answered if you take the time to check in your dictionary. The time you spend looking up words will not be wasted; your rewards will be the increased accuracy of your writing and the increased respect of your reader. Two useful dictionaries are *The American Heritage Dictionary of the English Language* and *Webster's New World Dictionary.* Both are available in easy-to-carry paperback editions that are convenient for school, home, and office use.

If you wonder how it's possible to look up a word that you can't spell, look at the two dictionaries we've recommended. At the front of each is a "Guide to the Dictionary," and in the guide is a chart showing the common spellings for all the sounds in the English language. If you know only how to pronounce a word, the chart will help you find its spelling.

| 2. Ask a good speller. |
|---|

Every family, every office, in fact every group of any kind tends to have one person whom everyone else asks for help in spelling. Most good spellers are secretly proud of their talent and pleased to demonstrate it. Don't be afraid to ask. Start your own skills exchange!

| 3. Learn three basic spelling rules. |
|---|

English spelling is frustratingly irregular, and no rule holds true in *all* cases. But there are three simple rules that do hold for most words, and mastering these rules will help you avoid many common errors.

Before learning the three rules, you need to know the difference between **vowels** and **consonants.** The vowels are **a**, **e**, **i**, **o**, and **u** (and sometimes **y**). All the other letters are consonants.

## Rule 1: Dropping the Final *e*

The first rule tells you when to drop the final, silent *e* when adding an ending to a word.

> *Drop* the final silent *e* when adding an ending beginning with a vowel.
> *Keep* the final, silent *e* when adding an ending beginning with a consonant.

Keeping the rule in mind, look at these examples:

| Endings Beginning with a Vowel | Endings Beginning with a Consonant |
|---|---|
| *-ing:* amuse + ing = amusing | *-ment:* amuse + ment = amusement |
| *-ed:* live + ed = lived | *-ly:* live + ly = lively |
| *-able:* like + able = likable | *-ness:* like + ness = likeness |
| *-ible:* force + ible = forcible | *-ful:* force + ful = forceful |
| *-er:* use + er = user | *-less:* use + less = useless |

### EXERCISES

Combine each word with the ending to form a new word. When you have finished, check your answers in the back of the book. (Answers begin on p. 240. You can tear them out if you want to.) If you miss even one answer, go over the rule and the examples again to find out why. If you get all the answers to exercises 1 and 2 correct, skip ahead to exercise 4.

### Exercise 1

1. sure + ly = __________
2. like + ing = __________
3. believe + able = __________
4. arrange + ment = __________
5. move + ing = __________
6. bare + ly = __________
7. radiate + or = __________
8. experience + ing = __________
9. absolute + ly = __________
10. use + ing = __________

## Exercise 2

1. safe + ly = ____________
2. argue + ing = ____________
3. size + able = ____________
4. accelerate + or = ____________
5. extreme + ly = ____________
6. improve + ment = ____________
7. reduce + ing = ____________
8. use + able = ____________
9. immediate + ly = ____________
10. require + ing = ____________

## Exercise 3

1. sincere + ly = ____________
2. cohere + ence = ____________
3. value + able = ____________
4. guide + ance = ____________
5. settle + ing = ____________
6. ice + y = ____________
7. complete + ly = ____________
8. purchase + ing = ____________
9. collapse + ible = ____________
10. dispense + ing = ____________

## Exercise 4

Add *e* in the blank space wherever it's needed to complete the spelling of these words. If no *e* is needed, leave the space blank.

1. bor_____ing
2. mov_____ment
3. scarc_____ly
4. unus_____able
5. car_____ful
6. advertis_____ment
7. excus_____able
8. provid_____ing
9. sens_____ible
10. improv_____ment

## Exercise 5

Add *e* in the blank space wherever it's needed.

1. saf____ty
2. rang____ing
3. reduc____ible
4. balanc____ing
5. entir____ly
6. insur____ance
7. definit____ly
8. car____less
9. collaps____ible
10. distanc____ing

## Exercise 6

Now make up sentences of your own, using all of the words you got wrong in exercises 1 through 5.

## Exceptions to Rule 1

1. Three common words do not follow the rule. Here they are:

argue + ment = argument
nine + th = ninth
true + ly = truly

2. There is one more exception to rule 1: after soft *c* (as in *notice*) and soft *g* (as in *change*), keep the final, silent *e* when adding an ending beginning with *a* or *o*. Here are two examples:

notice + able = noticeable
outrage + ous = outrageous

## Rule 2: Doubling the Final Consonant

The second rule tells you when to double the final consonant when adding an ending to a word.

> When adding an ending beginning with a vowel (such as *-able, -ing, -ed,* or *-er*), double the final consonant of the root word if the word
> 1. ends with a *single* consonant preceded by a *single* vowel AND
> 2. is stressed on the last syllable.

Notice that a word must have *both* characteristics for the rule to apply. Let's look at a few examples.

| | | |
|---|---|---|
| **begin + er** | ends with a single consonant *(n)* preceded by a single vowel *(i)* and is stressed on the last syllable *(begín),* so the rule applies, and we double the final consonant: | **beginner** |
| **control + ed** | ends with a single consonant *(l)* preceded by a single vowel *(o)* and is stressed on the last syllable *(contról),* so the rule applies: | **controlled** |
| **drop + ing** | ends with a single consonant *(p)* preceded by a single vowel *(o)* and is stressed on the last syllable (there is only one: *dróp*), so the rule applies: | **dropping** |
| **appear + ing** | ends with a single consonant *(r)* preceded by *two* vowels *(ea),* so the rule does not apply, and we do not double the final consonant: | **appearing** |
| **turn + ed** | ends with *two* consonants *(rn),* so the rule does not apply: | **turned** |
| **open + er** | ends with a single consonant *(n)* preceded by a single vowel *(e)* but is *not* stressed on the last syllable *(ópen),* so the rule does not apply: | **opener** |

(In words such as *equip, quit,* and *quiz,* the *u* should be considered part of the *q* and not a vowel. These words then follow the rule: *equipping, quitter,* and *quizzed.*)

## EXERCISES

Combine each word with the ending to form a new word. Check your answers to each set of ten before going on. If you make no mistakes in exercises 7 and 8, skip ahead to exercise 11. If you make even one mistake, do exercises 9 and 10.

---

### Exercise 7

1. ban + ing = ____________
2. stop + ing = ____________
3. admit + ed = ____________
4. nail + ing = ____________
5. stir + ed = ____________
6. jump + er = ____________
7. equip + ing = ____________
8. write + ing = ____________
9. map + ing = ____________
10. interrupt + ed = ____________

---

### Exercise 8

1. swim + er = ____________
2. begin + ing = ____________
3. drop + ed = ____________
4. train + ing = ____________
5. red + er = ____________
6. appear + ance = ____________
7. plan + ed = ____________
8. happen + ing = ____________
9. stop + er = ____________
10. insist + ed = ____________

---

### Exercise 9

1. suffer + ing = ____________
2. quiz + ed = ____________
3. permit + ing = ____________
4. ship + ed = ____________
5. meet + ing = ____________
6. compel + ing = ____________
7. crop + ed = ____________
8. tip + ing = ____________
9. program + er = ____________
10. quarter + ed = ____________

---

---

## Exercise 10

1. prefer + ing = __________
2. omit + ed = __________
3. transfer + ing = __________
4. develop + ing = __________
5. control + er = __________
6. occur + ed = __________
7. put + ing = __________
8. forget + able = __________
9. bite + ing = __________
10. prefer + ed = __________

---

## Exercise 11

1. bid + able = __________
2. comfort + ing = __________
3. forget + ful = __________
4. accept + ed = __________
5. avail + able = __________
6. regret + ing = __________
7. mention + ed = __________
8. control + able = __________
9. disappear + ance = __________
10. defer + ed = __________

---

## Exercise 12

1. overlap + ed = __________
2. expel + ing = __________
3. bid + er = __________
4. acquit + ed = __________
5. appear + ing = __________
6. plan + ing = __________
7. develop + ed = __________
8. transfer + ed = __________
9. parallel + ed = __________
10. commission + er = __________

---

## Exercise 13

1. occur + ence = __________
2. exist + ence = __________
3. cohere + ence = __________
4. deter + ence = __________

5. interfere + ence = ________
6. subsist + ence = ________
7. differ + ence = ________
8. depend + ence = ________
9. recur + ence = ________
10. insist + ence = ________

---

When it comes to adding *-ence,* three words are especially troublesome. *Prefer, refer,* and *confer* all appear to require a doubled final consonant. But they don't, because, when you add *-ence,* the stress shifts to the *first* syllable of the word. So you write

| | | | | |
|---|---|---|---|---|
| prefér | preférring | preférred | but | *préference* |
| refér | reférring | reférred | but | *réference* |
| confér | conférring | conférred | but | *cónference* |

## EXERCISE

---

### Exercise 14

Make up sentences in which you use the words you got wrong in exercises 7 through 13.

---

## Rule 3: Words Containing *ie* or *ei*

There are almost a thousand common English words containing *ie* or *ei,* so remembering the rule that governs them is worthwhile. It helps to keep in mind that *ie* occurs roughly twice as often as *ei.*

The old rhyme tells you most of what you need to know to spell these words:

> Write *i* before *e,* except after *c*
> Or when sounded like *ā,* as in *neighbor* and *weigh.*

If you remember this rhyme, you'll have no difficulty in spelling words like *belief, piece, ceiling, receive,* and *freight.*

Unfortunately, the rhyme covers only two of the cases in which we write *e* before *i:* after *c,* and when the syllable is pronounced with a long *ā* sound. So an addition to the rule is necessary:

> If short ĕ or long ī is the sound that is right,
> Write *e* before *i,* as in *their* or in *height.*

This rule covers words such as *Fahrenheit, seismic, heir,* and *leisure* (pronounce it to rhyme with *pleasure*). *Either* and *neither* can be pronounced "eye-ther" and "nye-ther," so they too require *ei.*

There are, of course, exceptions. This silly sentence contains the most common ones:

The *friend* of a *weird species* of *sheik seized caffeine, codeine,* and *protein.*

## EXERCISES

Fill in the blanks with *ie* or *ei.* After you finish each set, check your answers.

---

### Exercise 15

1. br____f
2. cash____r
3. rec____ve
4. p____rce
5. rel____f
6. retr____ve
7. c____ling
8. bel____ve
9. dec____tful
10. hyg____ne

---

### Exercise 16

1. th____f
2. p____ce
3. gr____f
4. conc____ve
5. pr____st
6. front____r
7. chandel____r
8. conc____t
9. perc____ve
10. Fahrenh____t

## Exercise 17

1. Each w____ner w____ghed three ounces.

2. The fr____ght yard was under police surv____llance.

3. She gave me a rec____pt for ____ght dollars.

4. There is no rel____f from his conc____t.

5. Elizabeth II now r____gns; Prince Charles is her h____r.

## Exercise 18

1. I ordered chow m____n and a st____n of beer.

2. N____ther of us knows how to use a G____ger counter.

3. Our n____ghbor has offered to hire our n____ce.

4. I dropped the horse's r____ns and fell out of the sl____gh.

5. It is conc____vable that ____ther one could do the job.

## Exercise 19

1. I gr____ved when Dracula struck a v____n.

2. It is th____r bel____f that too much prot____n is unhealthy.

3. That spec____s of ape grows to a h____ght of five feet.

4. The police s____zed the rec____vers of for____gn gold.

There are three or four more spelling rules we could explain here, but we won't—for two reasons. First, there are many exceptions to the remaining "rules" for English spelling. And, second, you don't need to memorize more rules *if you use your dictionary*. Now is the time to read the "Guide to the Dictionary" in the front of your dictionary. Reading it won't be very entertaining, but it will be well worth your while. The guide outlines the kinds of information given for each word in the dictionary and explains the abbreviations and symbols that are used. You will discover, for example, that you don't need to memorize long lists of irregular plurals: your dictionary provides the irregular plurals of the nouns you look up. It also gives the irregular forms of verbs, adjectives, and adverbs. (If you've forgotten how *regular* plurals, verb forms, adjectives, and adverbs are formed, the guide will remind you.) Your dictionary will also tell you how to add various endings to root words and even where you can divide a word when you need to hyphenate it at the end of a line. Take half an hour to read the guide in your dictionary; then do the following exercises.

## EXERCISES

Use your dictionary to do these exercises. Check your answers to each set of ten before going on to the next.

---

### Exercise 20

Write the plural form of each word.

1. hero ______________
2. history ______________
3. bus ______________
4. ghetto ______________
5. life ______________
6. crisis ______________
7. sheep ______________
8. phenomenon ______________
9. nucleus ______________
10. appendix ______________

---

### Exercise 21

Combine each root word with the ending given.

1. lonely + ness = ______________
2. copy + ed = ______________
3. crazy + ness = ______________
4. easy + er = ______________
5. pretty + est = ______________
6. reply + s = ______________

7. reply + ing = __________

8. thirty + eth = __________

9. unnecessary + ly = __________

10. traffic + ing = __________

## Exercise 22

Using hyphens, show where each word could be divided at the end of a line. (Some words can be divided in two or more places—for example, *ice-break-er.*)

1. letter __________
2. consists __________
3. patients __________
4. management __________
5. process __________
6. shipping __________
7. naphtha __________
8. through __________
9. distribution __________
10. success __________

# Chapter 2

# Sound-Alikes, Look-Alikes, and Spoilers

Using a dictionary, asking a good speller for help, and applying the three spelling rules will make an immediate improvement in your spelling. By following two additional suggestions you can further increase your spelling accuracy, but the skills involved will take longer to master. First, learn to tell apart words that are often confused because they sound or look alike. Second, learn to spell the words that most people find difficult—words we have called Spelling Spoilers. Don't try to master all of these words at once. Instead, memorize a few each week, and review them frequently. In two or three months you could be one of the people poor spellers turn to for help!

## Sound-Alikes and Look-Alikes

Some of your spelling troubles are probably caused by your using words that either sound or look like the words you really want. Careful pronunciation sometimes helps to correct this problem. For example, if you pronounce the words *accept* and *except* differently, you'll be less likely to confuse them in your writing. It is also useful to make up memory aids to help yourself remember the difference between words that sound alike but have very different meanings.

**accept**
**except**

*Accept* means "take." It is always a verb. ***Except*** means "excluding."

Everyone *except* Brian *accepted* my explanation.

**advice**
**advise**

The difference in pronunciation makes the difference in meaning clear. *Advise* (rhymes with *wise*) is a verb. *Advice* (rhymes with *nice*) is a noun.

I *advise* you not to listen to free *advice.*

**affect**
**effect**

*Affect* is a verb meaning "influence." *Effect* is a noun meaning "result." If you can substitute *result,* then *effect* is the word you need. (Occasionally *effect* can be a verb—meaning "bring about"—but you probably won't need to use it that way.)

Learning about the *effects* of caffeine *affected* my coffee-drinking habits.

**a lot**
**allot**

*A lot* (often misspelled *alot*) should be avoided. Use *many* or *much* instead. *Allot* means "distribute" or "assign."

He still has ~~a lot of~~ many problems, but he's coping ~~a lot~~ much better.

The teacher will *allot* the assignments according to the students' interests.

**are**
**our**

*Are* is a verb. *Our* shows ownership.

Nathaniel Hawthorne and Herman Melville *are* two of America's best-known novelists.

Jimmy Carter was one of *our* Presidents.

**choose**
**chose**

Pronunciation gives the clue here. *Choose* rhymes with *booze* and means "select." *Chose* rhymes with *rose* and means "selected."

Please *choose* a topic.

I *chose* film making.

**coarse**
**course**

*Coarse* means "rough, unrefined." For all other meanings use *course.*

That sandpaper is too *coarse.*

You'll enjoy the photography *course.*

Of *course* you'll do well.

**complement**
**compliment**

A *complement* completes something. *A compliment* is a gift of praise.

A glass of wine would be the perfect *complement* to the meal.

Some people are embarrassed by *compliments.*

**conscience**
**conscious**

Your *conscience* is your sense of right and wrong. *Conscious* means "aware" or "awake"—able to feel and think.

After Katy cheated on the test, her *conscience* bothered her.
Katy was *conscious* of having done wrong.
The injured man was *unconscious* for an hour.

**consul**
**council**
**counsel**

A *consul* is a government official stationed in another country. A *council* is an assembly or official group. Members of a council are *councilors. Counsel* can be used to mean both "advice" and "to advise."

The American *consul* in England was very helpful.
The Women's Advisory *Council* meets next month.
Maria gave me good *counsel.*
She *counseled* me to hire a lawyer.

**desert**
**dessert**

A *désert* is a dry, sandy place. As a verb, *desért* means "leave behind." *Dessért* is "double good," the kind of food you'd like two servings of, so give it *two s's.*

Las Vegas is a city in the middle of a *desert.*
My neighbor *deserted* her husband and children.
*Dessert* is my favorite part of the meal.

**dining**
**dinning**

You'll spell *dining* correctly if you remember the phrase "wining and dining." You'll probably never use *dinning.* It means "making a loud noise."

The children are in the *dining* room.
We are *dining* out tonight.
The sounds from the disco next door were *dinning* in my ears.

**does**
**dose**

Pronunciation provides the clue. *Does* rhymes with *buzz* and is a verb. *Dose* rhymes with *gross* and refers to a quantity of medicine.

John *does* drive fast, *doesn't* he?
My grandmother gave me a *dose* of cod liver oil.

**forth**
**fourth**

*Forth* means "forward" or "onward." ***Fourth*** contains the number **four,** which gives it its meaning.

Please stop pacing back and *forth.*
The Dallas Cowboys won their *fourth* game in a row.

**hear**
**here**

***Hear*** is what you do with your **ears.** *Here* is used for all other meanings.

Now *hear* this!
Ray isn't *here.*
*Here* is your assignment.

**it's**
**its**

*It's* is a shortened form of *it is.* The apostrophe takes the place of the *i* in *is.* If you can substitute *it is,* then *it's* is the form you need. If you can't substitute *it is,* then *its* is the correct word.

*It's* really not difficult. (*It is* really not difficult.)
The book has lost *its* cover. ("The book has lost *it is* cover" makes no sense, so you need *its.*)

**later**
**latter**

***Late**r* refers to time and has the word ***late*** in it. *Latter* means "the second of two" and has two *t's.* It is the opposite of *former.*

It is *later* than you think.
You take the former, and I'll take the *latter.*

**loose**
**lose**

Pronunciation is the key to these words. *Loose* rhymes with *goose* and means "not tight." *Lose* rhymes with *ooze* and means "misplace" or "be defeated."

A *loose* electrical connection is dangerous.
Burt Reynolds never *loses* a fight, a game, or a girl.

**miner**
**minor**

A ***mine**r* works in a **mine.** *Minor* means "lesser" or "not important." For example, a *minor* is a person of less than legal age.

Liquor can be served to *miners,* but not if they are *minors.*
For me, spelling is a *minor* problem.

**moral**
**morale**

Again, pronunciation provides the clue you need. *Mória l* refers to the understanding of what is right and wrong. *Morále* refers to the spirit or mental condition of a person or group.

People often have to make *moral* decisions.
The low *morale* of the workers prompted the strike.

**peace**
**piece**

***Pea**ce* is what we want on **earth.** *Piece* means "a part or portion of something," as in "a **pie**ce of **pie**."

Everyone hopes for *peace* in the Middle East.
A *piece* of the puzzle is missing.

**personal**
**personnel**

*Person**al*** means "private." *Personnel* refers to the group of people working for a particular employer or to the office responsible for maintaining employees' records.

The letter was marked "*Personal* and Confidential."
We are fortunate in having hired highly qualified *personnel.*
Nellie works in the *Personnel* Office.

**principal**
**principle**

*Principal* means "main." A *principle* is a rule.

A *principal* is the main administrator of a school.
Oil is Texas' *principal* industry.
The *principal* and the interest totaled more than I could pay. (In this case, the principal is the main amount of money.)
One of the teacher's *principles* is to refuse to accept late assignments.

**quiet**
**quite**

If you pronounce these words carefully, you won't confuse them. *Quiet* has two syllables; *quite* has only one.

The librarian asked us to be *quiet.*
We had not *quite* finished our homework.

**stationary**
**stationery**

*Stationary* means "fixed in place." *Stationery* is writing paper.

Did you want a portable or a *stationary* computer?
Please order a new supply of *stationery.*

**than**
**then**

Th*an* is used in comparisons. Pronounce it to rhyme with *can. Then* refers to time and rhymes with *when.*

Juan is a better speller *than* I.
He made his decision *then.*
Ted withdrew from the competition; *then* he realized the consequences.

**their**
**there**
**they're**

*Their* indicates ownership. *There* points out something or indicates place. It includes the word ***here,*** which also indicates place. *They're* is a shortened form of *they are.* (The apostrophe replaces the *a* in *are.*)

It was *their* fault.
*There* are two weeks left in the term.
You should look over *there.*
*They're* late, as usual.

**too**
**two**
**to**

The *too* with an extra *o* in it means "more than enough" or "also." *Two* is the number after one. For all other meanings use *to.*

He thinks he's been working *too* hard. She thinks so, *too.*
There are *two* sides to every argument.
The *two* women knew *too* much about each other *to* be friends.

**were**
**where**
**we're**

If you pronounce these three carefully, you won't confuse them. *Were* rhymes with *fur* and is a verb. *Where* is pronounced "wear," includes the word ***here,*** and indicates place. *We're* is a shortened form of *we are* and is pronounced "weer."

You *were* joking, *weren't* you?
*Where* did you want to meet?
*We're* on our way.

**who's**
**whose**

*Who's* is a shortened form of *who is* or *who has*. If you can substitute *who is* or *who has* for the *who's* in your sentence, then you are using the right spelling. Otherwise, use *whose*.

*Who's* coming to dinner? (*Who is* coming to dinner?)
*Who's* been sleeping in my bed? (*Who has* been sleeping?)
*Whose* calculator is this? ("*Who is* calculator" makes no sense, so you need *whose*.)

**woman**
**women**

Confusing these two is guaranteed to irritate your women readers. *Woman* is the singular form; compare *man*. *Women* is the plural form; compare *men*.

A *woman's* place is wherever she chooses to be.
The *women's* movement promotes equality between *women* and men.

**you're**
**your**

*You're* is a shortened form of *you are*. If you can substitute *you are* for the *you're* in your sentence, then you're using the correct form. If you can't substitute *you are*, use *your*.

*You're* welcome. (*You are* welcome.)
Unfortunately, *your* hamburger got burned. ("*You are* hamburger" makes no sense, so *your* is the word you want.)

## EXERCISES

Choose the correct word in each pair. If you don't know an answer, go back and reread the explanation. Check your answers after each set of ten questions (answers begin on p. 244). When you get five sets entirely correct, you may skip ahead to exercise 11.

---

## Exercise 1

1. Unemployment is having an (affect effect) on the kinds of (coarses courses) college students choose.
2. (Are Our) offer was not (accepted excepted).
3. Fresh fruit is a better (desert dessert) (than then) cake.
4. When (your you're) traveling abroad, (losing loosing) your ticket is a nightmare.
5. It was so (quite quiet) that you could (hear here) a pin drop.
6. He is the one (who's whose) (conscience conscious) ought to be troubled.

7. Alex, the (forth fourth) child, was nine years younger (then than) his sister.
8. Don't buy expensive luggage; (its it's) bound to get scratched during (its it's) travels.
9. The S.P.C.A. will (advice advise) you on what kind of dog to (chose choose).
10. (Does Dose) the (dining dinning) room serve fish and chips?

---

## Exercise 2

1. If a (principal principle) is always a rule, is a (principal principle) always a pal?
2. Finally, on the (forth fourth) try, I (choose chose) the right key.
3. We all enjoyed the dinner, (accept except) for the (desert dessert).
4. (Your You're) acting as if you had a guilty (conscience conscious).
5. If you aren't (quiet quite), I won't be able to (here hear) him.
6. In all my courses (except accept) English, I'm having only (miner minor) problems.
7. If they (loose lose) this game (to two too), the (moral morale) of the team will suffer.
8. Let your (conscience conscious) be (your you're) guide.
9. A (stationary stationery) engine is one that is fixed in (its it's) place.
10. (Does dose) the average (woman women) really worry about "yellow wax build-up"?

---

## Exercise 3

1. Did you (hear here) that Henry Kissinger is expected to speak (hear here) next week?
2. When the (stationary stationery) was delivered, we found (to too two) printing errors in the letterhead.
3. It's not whether you win or (loose lose); (its it's) how you play the game.
4. In (your you're) opinion, (miners minors) shouldn't be allowed to drive, let alone drink.
5. Would you like a (peace piece) of pie for (desert dessert)?
6. The penniless minister was pleased to (accept except) a grant from the (Counsel Council) on Religion and International Affairs.
7. The (coarse course) fabric spoiled the (affect effect).
8. All I want for Christmas is (peace piece) and (quite quiet).
9. (Whose Who's) afraid of (woman's women's) liberation?
10. A long (peace piece) of rope swung back and (forth fourth) in the breeze.

---

## Exercise 4

1. He (deserted desserted) his unit and (than then) fled to Chicago.
2. (Were We're Where) can I find a (quite quiet) place to study?
3. Of the (to too two) proposals, the (later latter) seems preferable.
4. We found the (consul council counsel) to be a man of (principal principle).
5. (A lot of, Allot of, Many) people take up jogging to try to (loose lose) weight.
6. (Your You're) supposed to swallow four teaspoons as (your you're) daily (does dose).
7. I thought I had mastered the "*i* before *e*" (principal principle), but (than then) they told me about the exceptions.
8. (Its It's) (later latter) than you think.
9. The thieves came back (later latter) and took everything (accept except) the radio.
10. It's no longer (quiet quite) so unusual for a (woman women) to be elected to public office.

## Exercise 5

1. They plan to (a lot allot) $1500 for the redecoration of their (dining dinning) room.
2. Let there be (peace piece) in (are our) time.
3. Each year, an increasing number of (woman women) (desert dessert) their families.
4. (Were We're Where) do you think (were we're where) going to get the money?
5. I found it impossible to remain (stationary stationery), so I walked rapidly back and (forth fourth).
6. I (hear here) (your you're) sorry you (choose chose) this (coarse course).
7. Do you think children (are our) (conscience conscious) of (there their they're) parents' sacrifices for them?
8. The learning process is greatly (affected effected) by student (moral morale).
9. He is a person (whose who's) (advice advise) I value.
10. Inflation and unemployment are the (principal principle) concerns of Americans; world (peace piece) is considered almost a (miner minor) problem in comparison.

## Exercise 6

1. Prolonged unemployment (affects effects) one's (moral morale).
2. A (complement compliment) is sometimes more welcome (than then) a kiss.
3. Following your (advise advice), I applied to the bank for a (personal personnel) loan.
4. As a coal (miner minor), he (does dose) run an increased risk of developing lung disease.
5. I suggest that (there their they're) behavior can hardly be described as (moral morale).
6. If I (hear here) one more complaint, (your you're) going to stay home.
7. (Whose Who's) been using my (personal personnel) (stationary stationery)?
8. If I had to (chose choose) between the two, I'd follow the (later latter) (coarse course) of action.
9. Two helpings of (desert dessert) should be (quiet quite) sufficient.
10. (To Too Two) many people don't look (were we're where) they're going.

## Exercise 7

1. I would like to have (desert dessert) as the first (coarse course).
2. (Your You're) going to have to follow the dictates of your own (conscious conscience).
3. Surely (its it's) a question of (principal principle).
4. The student asked the guidance counselor to (advice advise) her on a (personal personnel) matter.
5. The young musician gratefully (accepted excepted) our (complements compliments).
6. Some (miners minors) have little difficulty in convincing a bartender that (their there they're) of age.
7. She (choose chose) to work in the (dining dinning) room of the Holiday Inn.
8. Judging by the pinging sounds I (hear here), I'd say (your you're) car needs a tune-up.
9. I'd rather write an essay (than then) do an oral report in front of (are our) whole class.
10. The salt was (to too two) (coarse course) (to too two) pass through the holes of the shaker.

## Exercise 8

1. Moments after (its it's) takeoff, the plane banked (to too two) sharply (to too two) the right.
2. The company president (choose chose) to recommend the establishment of an advisory (consul council counsel).
3. Check with the (Personal Personnel) Department first; (than then) hire legal (consul council counsel).
4. If I'd been given a chance to (choose chose), I'd never have selected this (coarse course).
5. If he (does dose) that again, it will (affect effect) his chances for promotion.
6. The Security (Council Counsel) will announce (its it's) decision (later latter) this month.
7. My (personal personnel) opinion is that (woman women) are poor drivers.
8. Whenever I receive a (complement compliment), I feel a little self-(conscience conscious).
9. As a member of the (consul council counsel), she was often asked for (advice advise).
10. The purple sequins on her handbag (complement compliment) her pink satin pants (affectively effectively).

## Exercise 9

1. I don't understand (quiet quite) what (your you're) getting at.
2. I do not intend to (choose chose) the one (who's whose) application was late.
3. (Hear Here) the moose stopped and lowered (it's its) head.
4. (A lot of Many Much) college (personal personnel) suffer from low (moral morale).
5. It's (to too two) bad, but (were we're where) too tired to go.
6. If you could remember the rules, (than then) (your you're) troubles would be over.
7. The camel's (coarse course) hair protects it from the (desert dessert) sun.
8. Until I reached home, I was not (conscience conscious) of the drug's (affect effect).
9. Each state establishes (its it's) own minimum wage, (does dose) it not?
10. The impressionist painters were particularly (conscience conscious) of the (affects effects) of light on the landscape.

## Exercise 10

1. I made the turn and (than then) saw the sign: "No left turn; buses (accepted excepted).
2. If you let the dog run (loose lose), you must (accept except) the consequences.
3. (Whose Who's) turn is it to find the (complement compliment) of the angle?
4. We were (to too two) late for dinner but in time for (desert dessert).
5. I accept your (advice advise) for the sound (council consul counsel) it is.
6. (Their There They're) are many children who believe the tooth fairy will come if they (loose lose) a tooth.
7. A (stationary stationery) store is (were we're where) you'll find carbon paper.
8. The (miner minor) skirmish before the game had the (affect effect) of making us determined to win.
9. Edmund Burke believed manners were more important (than then) (morales morals).
10. State colleges are governed by a (consul council counsel) (who's whose) function is to (advice advise) the Board of Education.

## Exercise 11

Your own writing is the best test of your spelling accuracy. Write ten sentences using sound-alikes and look-alikes. Try to use those that cause you the most difficulty.

## Exercise 12

Your turn again. Write a short paragraph on any topic you choose. In your paragraph, use at least five of the sound-alikes and look-alikes you have had trouble with. Refer to the explanations, if necessary, and don't forget to use your dictionary!

## Spelling Spoilers

Here is a list of words that are frequently misspelled. Have someone dictate the list to you. Circle the ones you misspell, and memorize them, a few at a time. Try to learn ten each week. Review your list often, until you have mastered every word. Making up memory aids for especially troublesome words will help you conquer them. Here are some examples to get you started:

| | |
|---|---|
| **accommodate:** | It means "make room for," and the word itself makes room for two *c*'s and two *m*'s. |
| **business:** | Busi**n**ess is no **sin.** |
| **environment:** | The word *env**iron**ment,* like the earth, has **iron** in it. |
| **friend:** | He is a fri**end** to the **end.** |
| **grammar:** | Poor gram**mar** will **mar** your writing. |

| | | |
|---|---|---|
| absence | finally | procedure |
| accommodate | forty | proceed |
| achievement | friend | professor |
| acknowledge | gauge | psychology |
| across | government | recommend |
| adolescence | grammar | relevant |
| among | guarantee | repetition |
| answer | guidance | restaurant |
| argument | height | rhythm |
| beginning | hoping | ridiculous |
| business | hypocrisy | safety |
| careful | immediately | schedule |
| category | independent | separate |
| clothes | laboratory | shining |
| committee | license | similar |
| conscious | likely | somewhat |
| criticism | loneliness | speech |
| definitely | lonely | studying |
| dependent | maintenance | succeed |
| desperate | marriage | superintendent |
| development | mentally | surprise |
| disappear | necessary | technique |
| disappoint | ninety | thorough |
| discipline | ninth | tragedy |
| dissatisfied | occasionally | truly |
| doesn't | omission | unnecessary |
| eighth | opinion | until |
| embarrassed | opportunity | unusual |
| environment | paid | usually |
| exercise | parallel | vacuum |
| existence | perform | Wednesday |
| explanation | planned | writing |
| extremely | possess | written |
| familiar | prejudice | |
| February | privilege | |

## EXERCISE

---

### Exercise 13

Make up sentences containing the words you misspelled when the list of Spelling Spoilers was dictated. Underline the Spelling Spoiler(s) in each sentence. (If you do this exercise once a week, you will master the list very quickly.)

---

One final suggestion. You may find that, despite all your efforts, there are a few words you just cannot spell correctly. The solution? Either write them out on the inside cover of your dictionary or look in your dictionary or a thesaurus to find synonyms (different words with the same or similar meanings), and use those instead. Two thesauruses are available in inexpensive paperback editions: *Roget's Thesaurus* and Soule's *Dictionary of English Synonyms.*

# Chapter 3

# The Apostrophe

Although it is very easy to use correctly, the apostrophe is one of the most misused gadgets in English. In fact, correct use of apostrophes is one of the best indicators of a careful writer. One large corporation gives prospective employees a five-part grammar test, and three of the sections test the applicant's ability to use the apostrophe correctly. Clearly this employer doesn't consider the apostrophe a frill.

In many sentences, an apostrophe is needed to enable the reader to understand what you're trying to say. Here's an example:

> The teacher began class by calling the students names.
>
> The teacher began class by calling the students' names.

The apostrophe is used for two distinct purposes: to indicate contraction and to indicate possession.

## Contraction

The rule about where to put apostrophes in contractions is one of the rare rules to which there are no exceptions. It *always* holds.

> When two words are shortened into one, and a letter (or letters) is left out, the apostrophe goes in the place of the missing letter(s).

| | |
|---|---|
| they are → they're | you would → you'd |
| there is → there's | cannot → can't |
| we are → we're | is not → isn't |
| we will → we'll | who is, who has → who's |
| it is, it has → it's | will not → won't *(Note the slight spelling variation here.)* |

## EXERCISES

Check your answers to each set of ten before going on to the next. Answers for this chapter begin on p. 246.

---

### Exercise 1

Make these sets of words into contractions.

1. there is ________________
2. did not ________________
3. they will ________________
4. it is ________________
5. do not ________________
6. it will ________________
7. it has ________________
8. we are ________________
9. you are ________________
10. he is ________________

---

### Exercise 2

Make these sets of words into contractions.

1. she will ________________
2. we have ________________
3. I am ________________
4. will not ________________
5. who is ________________
6. should not ________________
7. they are ________________
8. who has ________________
9. you will ________________
10. has not ________________

---

## Exercise 3

Place apostrophes correctly in these words.

1. cant
2. youre
3. theyll
4. wouldnt
5. whos
6. wont
7. itll
8. theyre
9. weve
10. youve

## Exercise 4

Correct these sentences by placing apostrophes where needed.

1. Theyll have to stay home because theyre still sick.
2. Its been a long time since theyve had a good holiday.
3. Were many miles from where we were then.
4. Youre not going to try your luck again, are you?
5. Its been a long time since someone wholl stand up for what is right has run for office.
6. Youre going to class because its good for you; youll never get far unless youve got your education.
7. Lets see if theyre up to the standards weve set.
8. Well have to do better if were to succeed.
9. Theyve finally done what shes suggested.
10. Since youve been to Europe, weve adopted two more children.

## Exercise 5

If you've had no difficulty with exercises 1 through 4, skip this exercise and go on to "Possession." If you have had problems, review the rule for contraction, study your errors carefully to be sure you understand why you were wrong, and do exercise 5. Then check your answers.

Make the bracketed words into contractions.

1. (Who is) the girl (I have) been seeing you with?
2. (There is) a faster way to get there, but (we have) missed the turn.
3. (It has) been impossible to talk to you because (you have) already made up your mind.
4. (I have) found (they are) not very friendly unless (there is) a chance of making some money.
5. Hollywood is the center of our motion-picture industry, but (you

will) be surprised to learn that it (is not) the home of my favorite movie stars.
6. We (could not) get here faster; (I am) not very good at reading maps.
7. Sam (will not) be a good accountant as long as (he is) unwilling to work after hours.
8. Money has been my biggest problem, but (I have) also had difficulties with my health, as (you are) aware.
9. (You will) find that his favorite food is fish; (he is) a fairly normal cat.
10. (We are) all here, but (we will) have to wait until (he is) sure we (have not) brought someone who (does not) belong.

---

## Possession

The apostrophe also shows ownership or possession: *'s* is added to the *owner* word.

the book's cover (The cover belongs to the book.)
the students' names (The names belong to the students.)
an arm's length (The length is of, or belonging to, an arm.)

As you can see, possession does not have to be literal. The owner does not have to be a person or thing; ideas or concepts can be owners, too.

day's work (the work of, or belonging to, a day)
hour's pay (the pay of, or belonging to, an hour)
danger's thrill (the thrill of danger)
Saturday's child (the child of Saturday)

When you want to show possession, *first identify the owner word;* then apply this simple rule.

> 1. Add *'s* to the owner word, regardless of what letter it ends in.
> 2. If the resulting word ends in a double or triple *s*, erase the last one, leaving the apostrophe in place.

Examples:

| | |
|---|---|
| car + 's = car's | clerks + 's = clerks'~~s~~ |
| ball + 's = ball's | Dickens + 's = Dickens'~~s~~ |
| women + 's = women's | Pam + 's = Pam's |
| boss + 's = boss'~~s~~ | Les + 's = Les'~~s~~ |

It doesn't matter whether the owner word is singular or plural; the rule is the same.

There are several exceptions to the possession rule. The following words show possession by their spelling and don't need the *'s*.

| | | |
|---|---|---|
| my | her | its |
| mine | hers | whose |
| your | our | their |
| yours | ours | theirs |
| his | | |

As you learned in chapter 2, in the section on sound-alikes and look-alikes, four of these words are often confused with contractions that sound like them. The possessives are at the left in the following list, the contractions at the right. Remember, when you need to decide which word to use, you can separate the contraction into its two words and try them out in the sentence. Better yet, you can memorize these words.

| | | |
|---|---|---|
| their: | they own something | they're = they are |
| your: | you own something | you're = you are |
| whose: | "who" owns something | who's = who is, who has |
| its: | it owns something | it's = it is, it has |

*They're* going to try *their* luck at cards.
*You're* losing *your* hair.
*Who's* been sleeping in *whose* bed?
*It's* obvious the car has a hole in *its* muffler.

## EXERCISES

### Exercise 6

Make the following words possessive (owner words).

1. wagon ____________
2. sea ____________
3. everybody ____________
4. love ____________
5. Alice ____________
6. horse ____________
7. men ____________
8. Ross ____________
9. class ____________
10. agents ____________

## Exercise 7

If you got any of the words in exercise 6 wrong, go back over the possession rule. Make sure you fully understand what you're doing, because the exercises are going to get harder. When you're satisfied you know the rule and how to apply it, make these words possessive.

1. saleswoman ______________
2. nurses ______________
3. it ______________
4. candy ______________
5. someone ______________
6. Jones ______________
7. Niagara Falls ______________
8. women ______________
9. stewardess ______________
10. lady ______________

## Exercise 8

Make the following words possessive.

1. you ______________
2. Bess ______________
3. they ______________
4. children ______________
5. babies ______________
6. history ______________
7. one ______________
8. actress ______________
9. chairmen ______________
10. ladies ______________

## Exercise 9

Make the words in parentheses possessive.

1. He gave one (month) notice before leaving (they) office.
2. All of the (children) work was better than (you).
3. The (dog) collar was around (it) neck.
4. (George) hobby is spending his (wife) money.
5. In (it) purest form, gold is very soft, and a (jeweler) joy to work with.

6. (Phyllis) essay was on (Moses) Laws.
7. (Fishermen) time is wasted if (they) luck is bad.
8. When the (spray) effect wore off, our (trees) trunks became infested with beetles.
9. Use of the American (Indians) oil wells is monitored by the (government) representatives.
10. After a (moment) pause, I accepted a (week) pay instead of the time off I was entitled to.

---

## Exercise 10

Correct these sentences by adding apostrophes where necessary. This is the last exercise on possession, so be sure you understand possession before going on to the next exercises.

1. Hikers equipment is on special during the weeks sale at Browns Sporting Goods.
2. Womens liberation is a touchy topic for Gails sister, whos lost a job to a man.
3. The waitress tip ended up in the busboys pocket.
4. Virtue is its own reward, according to people whose consciences are clear.
5. The mens room is down the hall, but its door isn't marked.
6. Gordie Howes records may eventually fall, but his careers achievements will never be surpassed.
7. Thousands of mourners who visit Elvis Presleys grave annually prove that they take literally his song "Love Me Tender."
8. Its coat shone like gold in the suns dying rays.
9. Pornographers books are not chosen by our schools curriculum planners.
10. Mens and womens traditional roles are being questioned as this generations leaders refuse to take any of yesterdays values for granted.

---

## REVIEW EXERCISES

The following exercises will test and reinforce your understanding of both contraction and possession.

## Exercise 11

Choose the correct word from those in parentheses. Check your answers before going on.

1. (Its It's) been a long time since (its it's) last overhaul, but I think (its it's) all right for another (week week's weeks') driving.
2. (They're There Their) your new relatives, so (its it's) silly not to try to get along with them.
3. (Your You're) in real trouble if the (police's polices') check turns up anything on (your you're) record.
4. (Betty's Bettys') dream is to make a career of her part-time work at (Children's Childrens') Aid.
5. (Who's Whose) going to win the game is (anybodys' anybody's) guess.
6. (They're Their There) real triumph is in achieving (they're their there) goals in spite of the handicaps that (they're their there) facing.
7. (Its It's) been a long time since (your you're) (son's sons') wife had her baby.
8. (Todays Today's Todays') music is returning to the (melodies melodies') and themes of (its it's) roots.
9. When (your you're) smiling, (its it's) as though the people you meet have known you all (they're their there) lives.
10. The (boys boy's boys') won the (cheaters cheater's) money back in (Gords' Gord's) (fathers father's fathers') poker game.

## Exercise 12

Correct the following sentences where necessary.

1. I dont think were as far from the fire wardens station as you're calculations indicate.
2. Can't you admit your wrong and apologize for all they're trouble?
3. Their were six of them there, but Mikes friend was'nt afraid, because he knew Mikes reputation for getting out of tight spot's.
4. You shouldnt cheat, even if there not looking at your paper.
5. A turtles life can exceed one hundred years, while a mayflys life is only one day.
6. Food is so expensive, its hard to provide for you're family.
7. Marty's brother went to work for CBS at they're New York studio's.
8. Summers heat gradually fades into autumns cool, which then becomes winters biting cold.

9. We're lucky that you're able to control their quarrels; otherwise, wed have nothing but fighting all night long.
10. Amos first rule was to treat others the way youd want them to treat you.

---

## Exercise 13

Make words 1 through 5 possessive. Give the contraction for words 6 through 10.

1. boys ______________________ 6. they are ______________________

2. knife ______________________ 7. who is ______________________

3. audience ______________________ 8. you are ______________________

4. it ______________________ 9. it is ______________________

5. secretaries ______________________ 10. could not ______________________

Now write five sentences, each containing one of the possessives and one of the contractions. Example:

The *boys'* shorts are so flimsy that *they're* falling apart.

---

## Exercise 14

Make words 1 through 5 possessive. Give the contraction for words 6 through 10.

1. gentlemen ______________________ 6. will not ______________________

2. typist ______________________ 7. it has ______________________

3. anyone ______________________ 8. there is ______________________

4. enemy ______________________ 9. has not ______________________

5. enemies ______________________ 10. should not ______________________

Now write five sentences, each containing one of the possessives and one of the contractions.

---

## Exercise 15

For working this far, you deserve a reward: this exercise consists of a collection of old jokes.[1] Correct the misplaced and omitted apostrophes.

1. A Hollywood star, famous for his capacity for overdrinking, told his new lady love: "Ive put you're picture in the one spot I'm sure to see it every night: under the table."
2. A regular patron at Shnops bar reports that he and his girl can't seem to agree on wedding plans. "She wants a big church wedding with usher's and bridesmaid's and I just don't want to get married."
3. Winston Churchill once was asked if he knew any professional women. He answered promptly, "Ive never met any amateur one's."
4. Discouragement: watching you're secretary yawn while typing one of you're most amusing letters.
5. A Carolina genius has perfected a new baby food thats half orange juice and half garlic. Its secret is it not only makes the baby healthier, but easier to find in the dark.
6. Theres one bus driver on the Madison Avenue route whose hung one of those shrunken head's over his coin box. He explains to curious passengers, "He wouldnt move to the rear of the bus."
7. A frugal Vermonter complains that his grandfather displayed the first dollar he earned in a frame that cost ten cents. Now the frames worth a dollar and the dollars worth a dime.
8. Short-haired girl to long-haired boy: "Of course Daddy doesn't mind our being alone together every night. He thinks your a girl."
9. "Im in real trouble," a man confessed to an analyst. "I cant rid myself of the conviction that Im a dog." "Jiminy!" exclaimed the analyst. "How long has this been going on?" The man answered, "Since I was a puppy."
10. In Las Vegas, the owners of the famous Caesars Palace are very annoyed with the kid whose opened an orange juice stand nearby. He's calling it Squeezers Palace.

---

[1]Adapted from Bennett Cerf, *The Sound of Laughter* (Garden City, N.Y.: Doubleday, 1970). 

# UNIT TWO

# Sentence Structure

# Chapter 4

# Cracking the Sentence Code

There is nothing really mysterious or difficult about the sentence itself; you've been speaking sentences successfully since you were two. The difficulty arises when you go to write—not sentences, oddly enough, but paragraphs. Almost all college students, if asked to write ten sentences on ten different topics, could do so without an error. But if those same students were to write paragraphs, sentence fragments and run-on sentences would creep in—errors that confuse or annoy readers.

The solution to fragment and run-on problems has two parts:

> Be sure every sentence you write
> 1. sounds right
>
> and 2. has a subject and a verb.

Your ear is the best instrument with which to test your sentences. If you read your sentences aloud, you'll probably be able to tell by the sound whether they are complete, clear, and satisfactory. A complete sentence is one that makes sense by itself.

Read these sentences aloud:

Windsurfing is one of the world's newest sports.

Although windsurfing is still a young sport.

The second "sentence" doesn't sound right, does it? It does not make sense on its own and is in fact a sentence fragment.

Testing your sentences by reading them aloud won't work if you read your paragraphs straight through from beginning to end. The trick is to read from end to beginning. That is, read your last sentence aloud, and *listen* to it. If it sounds all right, then read aloud the next-to-last sentence, and so on, until you have worked your way back to the first sentence you wrote.

Now, what do you do with the ones that "sound funny"? Before you can fix them, you need to be able to "decode" each sentence to find out whether it has a subject and a verb. The subject and the verb are the bare essentials of the sentence; every sentence you write must have both. (The only exception is the *command,* in which the subject is understood rather than expressed. Consider this command: "Put your signature here." The subject *you* is understood.)

## Finding Subjects and Verbs

A sentence is about *someone* or *something.* That someone or something is the **subject.** The word (or words) that tells what the subject *is* or *does* is the **verb.** The verb will express some sort of action, or condition, or occurrence.

Find the verb first. One way is by finding the word or group of words whose form can be changed to indicate a change in time. In the sentence

The quarterback has called the play.

*has called* (in the past) can be changed to *is calling* (present) or *will call* (future), so *has called* is the verb.

Once you have found the verb, find the subject, by asking *who* or *what* the verb is referring to.

Look at these examples. We have underlined the subjects once and the verbs twice.

Jean helped me.
(Helped expresses an action and is the verb.
Who or what helped? Jean helped, so Jean is the subject.)

Finding verbs is relatively easy.
(Is expresses a condition and is the verb.
Who or what is [easy]? Finding, which is the subject.)

How you do it remains a mystery to me.
(Remains expresses a condition and is the verb.
Who or what remains [a mystery]? How you do it, which is the subject.
Notice that the subject can be more than one word.)

Teddy bears were named after President Theodore Roosevelt.
(Were named expresses an occurrence and is the verb.
Who or what were named? Teddy bears.)

Their rehabilitation program seems successful.
(Seems expresses a condition and is the verb.
Who or what seems [successful]? Program.)

## EXERCISE

---

### Exercise 1

Find the subject and the verb in each of the following sentences. Underline the subject with one line and the verb with two. When you have finished, check your answers on p. 251. If you make even one mistake, carefully reread "Finding Subjects and Verbs." Be sure you understand this material thoroughly before you go on.

1. Alan met a bear.
2. A bear met Alan.
3. The bear was bulgy.
4. Sad to say, the bulge was Alan.
5. Grizzlies are famous for their unpredictability.
6. Meeting bears unexpectedly is clearly risky.
7. According to an old myth, bears never run downhill.
8. Believe me. They do.
9. Females with cubs are known to be especially vicious.
10. How to defend oneself presents a real problem.

---

Usually the subject comes before the verb in a sentence, but not always. Occasionally we find it after the verb:

Back to the refreshment stand for the fourth time stumbled the weary father.
(Who or what stumbled? The father.)

At the bottom of the page, in red ink, was my grade.
(Who or what was? My grade.)

In sentences beginning with *There* + some form of the verb *to be,* or with *Here* + some form of the verb *to be,* the subject is always found after the verb.

There are three good reasons for learning to write well.
(Who or what are? Reasons.)

There will be a test next week.
(Who or what will be? A test.)

Here are the solutions to last week's problem set.
(Who or what are? Solutions.)

In questions the subject often follows the verb:

Are you sure about this?
(Who or what are? You.)

Is he late again?
(Who or what is? He.)

But notice that in questions beginning with *who, whose, what,* or *which,* the subject and verb are in "normal" order:

Who met the bear?
Whose belly was bulgy?

What happened to Alan?
Which grizzly ate Alan?

## EXERCISES

Find the subject and the verb in each of the following sentences. Underline the subject with one line, the verb with two. Check your answers to each set of ten sentences before you go on.

---

## Exercise 2

1. Donald Duck first appeared in comics in 1938.
2. After Mandarin Chinese, the English language has the most speakers in the world.
3. Mark Twain is the pen name of Samuel Langhorne Clemens.
4. Are you from Detroit?
5. In Norway, drinking drivers are jailed for three weeks.
6. No exceptions are made.
7. Crime is the product of a diseased society.
8. Over there is the San Diego Zoo, with its famous orangutans and wildebeests.
9. To the devoted distance runner, jogging is almost a religion.
10. Just out of reach under the bed crouched the frightened cat.

---

## Exercise 3

1. Money, like manure, does no good until it is spread.
2. Here are the steps to follow.
3. Coca-Cola was created in 1886, at its home plant in Atlanta.
4. Whose idea was this, anyway?
5. Drive carefully.
6. Study makes the eyes weak and the brain strong.
7. Turn it down!
8. Directly behind us, on Colonial Road, lives the mayor.
9. According to an old Eskimo proverb, love comes after marriage.
10. Only in Mexico is the Volkswagen Beetle still available for purchase.

## Exercise 4

1. Doing grammar exercises is boring.
2. A man's best friend is his dog—better even than his wife. (Eskimo proverb)
3. Were they happy with their choice?
4. In the playground were thirty-four screaming children.
5. Here are the files you asked for.
6. Are you still angry with me?
7. In April each year, on Patriot's Day, the Boston Marathon is held.
8. Replacing ceramic tiles is messy, but not difficult.
9. Please stop at the next corner.
10. The boardwalk in Atlantic City, New Jersey, extends for more than five miles.

## More about Verbs

The verb in a sentence may be a single word, as in most of the exercises you've just done, or it may be a group of words. **Helping verbs** are often added to main verbs, so that an idea can be expressed precisely. The words *shall, should, may, might, can, could, must, ought, will, would, have, do,* and *be* are helping verbs.

> The complete verb in a sentence consists of the main verb + any helping verbs.

Here are a few of the forms of the verb *write*. Notice that in questions the subject may come between the helping verb and the main verb.

You may write now.
He certainly can write!
We should write home more often.
I shall write tomorrow.
He could have written yesterday.
She is writing her memoirs.
Did he write to you?
He had written his apology.
You ought to write to him.
We will have written by then.
I will write to the editor.
The proposal has been written.
Orders should have been written.
Could you have written it in French?

One verb form, in particular, always takes a helping verb. Here is the rule:

> A verb ending in *-ing* MUST have a helping verb (or verbs) before it.

Here are a few of the forms an *-ing* verb can take:

I am writing the report.
You will be writing a report.
He should have been writing it.
Is she writing the paper for him?
She must have been writing all night.
You are writing illegibly.
I was writing neatly.
Have you been writing on the wall?

Beware of certain words that are often confused with helping verbs:

> Words such as *not, only always, sometimes, never, ever,* and *just* are NOT part of the verb.

These words sometimes appear in the middle of a complete verb, but they are modifiers, not verbs. Do not underline them:

I have just won the lottery!
He is almost always chosen first.
Most people do not welcome unasked-for advice.

## EXERCISES

Underline the subject once and the complete verb twice. Correct each set of ten sentences before you go on to the next.

### Exercise 5

1. He has tried very hard.
2. You should have been paying attention.
3. Should we write the report now?
4. In the Grand Canyon, the Desert View Watchtower overlooks the Painted Desert.
5. Where is the nearest gas station?
6. We do not want to leave.
7. Which one do you want?
8. Old men will always think young men fools.
9. The baby has just fallen asleep.
10. Back and forth, lazily but without stopping, swam the shark.

### Exercise 6

1. The whole country is covered with hip-deep snow for several months.
2. Why would anyone want to go over the falls in a barrel?
3. Alex Haley in 1965 was becoming strongly aware of his roots.
4. Never again will I agree to ride with you!
5. A person may forgive an injury, but not an insult.
6. There have been at least two notices.
7. You can become addicted to coffee.
8. How long did you stay in the Okefenokee Swamp?
9. Have you ever been to the Everglades?
10. Only recently have women been interested in auto mechanics.

### Exercise 7

1. By the year 2000, gasoline made from coal will be commercially available.
2. At the end of August, I will have been working here for twelve years.
3. Are George Washington's wooden teeth displayed at the Smithsonian Institution?
4. The wise man will take everything seriously except himself.

5. Dodge City, Kansas, was once termed "the wickedest city" in America.
6. Joe Hall is always being discovered by some critic or producer, only to be promptly forgotten.
7. Could anyone here have done it better?
8. Have you ever been caught cheating on a test?
9. Very little is known about lycanthropy, except by werewolves.
10. Aren't you glad to be finished?

---

## More about Subjects

Very often, groups of words called **prepositional phrases** come before the subject in a sentence or between the subject and the verb. When you're looking for the subject in a sentence, prepositional phrases can trip you up unless you know this rule:

> The subject of a sentence is never in a prepositional phrase.

You have to be able to identify prepositional phrases so that you will know where *not* to look for the subject. A prepositional phrase is a group of words that begins with a preposition and ends with the name of something or someone (a noun or a pronoun). Often a prepositional phrase will indicate the direction or location of something. Here are some prepositional phrases:

about the book
above the book
according to the book
after the meeting
against the wall
along the hall
among the books
among them
around the office
before lunch
behind the desk
below the window
beside the book
between the desks
by the book
concerning the memo
despite the book
down the hall
except the staff
for the manager
from the office
in the book
inside the office
into the elevator
in front of the door
like the book
near the wall
on the desk
onto the floor
of the typist
over a door
to the staff
through the window
under the book
until the meeting
up the hall
with a book
without the book
without them

When you're looking for the subject in a sentence, you can make the task easier by crossing out any prepositional phrases. For example,

The keys ~~of the typewriter~~ should be cleaned frequently.
What should be cleaned? The keys (not the typewriter).

~~In case of an emergency~~, one ~~of the group~~ should go ~~to the nearest ranger station for help~~.
Who should go? One (not the group).

## EXERCISES

First cross out the prepositional phrase(s) in each sentence. Then underline the subject once and the verb twice. Check your answers to each set of ten sentences before going on. When you get three sets entirely correct, skip ahead to exercise 13.

---

### Exercise 8

1. A bird in the hand is worth two in the bush.
2. Most of us plan to go on Saturday.
3. Many of your answers are unreadable.
4. Do you want either of them?
5. Meet me at twelve in the cafeteria.

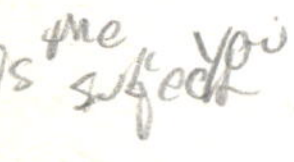

6. A couple of hamburgers should be enough.
7. A dozen brands of video recorder are now on the market.
8. There is a movie about cloning on television tonight.
9. After eight hours of classes, the thought of collapsing in front of the TV set is very appealing.
10. One episode of "The Gong Show" is more than enough.

---

### Exercise 9

1. A stitch in time saves nine.
2. For many students, lack of money is probably the most serious problem.
3. In the middle of May, after the end of term, the Intercollegiate Arm-Wrestling Championships will be held.
4. One strand of fiber optics can carry both telephone and television signals.
5. During the second week of term, the class will be taken on a tour of the resource center.
6. Contrary to your expectations, and despite the rumors, your instructor does not bite.
7. On Callisto, one of Jupiter's thirteen moons, snow may "fall" up, not down.
8. At Millhaven Penitentiary, a prisoner blinded himself last week in an effort to escape.

9. One of the most expensive movies made in the 1930s was *King Kong.*
10. In similar circumstances, most of us would probably have accepted his help.

---

## Exercise 10

1. By this time, you may be tired of the notion of Superman.
2. The happiness of every country depends upon the character of its people.
3. Above my desk hangs someone else's diploma.
4. During the course of the discussion, several of us went to sleep.
5. In the summer and on weekends, he works on his log cabin with his wife.
6. The "short side" of a goalie is the side closer to the post.
7. New steps should be taken to encourage the flow of capital into small businesses.
8. After waiting for more than an hour, we finally left without you.
9. So far only two of your answers to the questions have been incorrect.
10. One of the country's most distinguished reporters will speak on the responsibilities of the press.

---

## Exercise 11

1. On the average, people on the West Coast, especially in California, are taller than those in the East.
2. By waiting on tables, babysitting, and doing other jobs, I manage to make ends meet.
3. The pile of books and papers on your desk is about as neat as a tossed salad.
4. Almost no one in television news bothers to analyze the issues.
5. But for you, we would be finished with this meeting by now.
6. No book about famous smokers would be complete without a mention of Winston Churchill, Sigmund Freud, and Mark Twain.
7. Despite Chou En-lai's wishes to the contrary, the Chinese plan to build a memorial to him.
8. A daily intake of more than 600 mg. of caffeine can result in headaches, insomnia, and heart palpitations.
9. Six to ten cups of coffee will contain 600 mg. of caffeine.
10. Despite its strong taste, espresso contains no more caffeine than regular coffee.

---

## Exercise 12

1. On the floor next to the computer sat the frazzled technician with his head in his hands.
2. In the dog world, poodles on an average bite more people than do Doberman pinschers.
3. Within a week, please give me your report on the pyrazine anion project.
4. In the spring, parked in front of his TV set, Barry trains for the Stanley Cup playoffs.
5. Government programs to encourage investment in small-business ventures have failed in the past few years.
6. In the Arctic wastes of Ungava, there is a mysterious stone structure in the shape of a giant hammer standing on end.
7. There is no obvious explanation for its presence in this isolated place.
8. According to archeologist Thomas E. Lee, it may be a monument left by Vikings in their travels west from Greenland.
9. Here, on an island called Pamiok, are the ruins of what may have been a Viking long house.
10. If so, then, centuries before Columbus' "discovery" of America, the Vikings were in what is now northern Quebec.

## Exercise 13

Write ten sentences of your own. Cross out all the prepositional phrases, and underline the subject once and the complete verb twice.

## Multiple Subjects and Verbs

So far you have been working with sentences containing only one complete subject and one complete verb. Sentences can, however, have more than one subject and verb. Here is a sentence with a multiple subject:

> Lexington and Concord are suburbs of Boston.

This sentence has a multiple verb:

> He elbowed and wriggled his way along the aisle of the bus.

And this sentence has a multiple subject and a multiple verb:

> The psychiatrist and the intern leaped from their chairs and seized the patient.

The elements of a multiple subject or verb are usually joined by *and* (but sometimes by *or*). Multiple subjects and verbs may contain more than two elements, as in the following sentences:

> Clarity, brevity, and simplicity are the basic qualities of good writing.
>
> I finished my paper, put the cat outside, took the phone off the hook, and crawled into bed.

## EXERCISES

Find and underline the subjects once and the verbs twice. Be sure to underline all the elements in a multiple subject or verb. Check your answers after completing each set of ten sentences.

### Exercise 14

1. Jack and Jill went up the hill.
2. Georgie Porgie kissed the girls and made them cry.
3. Jack and Jill went up the hill and fetched a pail of water.
4. Cotton and soy beans are staple crops.
5. I tried and tried but didn't succeed.
6. Jim or Brian will go next.
7. The two canoeists and their dog were missing for four days.
8. Alan Alda now writes, directs, and acts—in that order.
9. Wait ten minutes and then phone again.
10. Reading aloud and singing are good vocal exercises.

### Exercise 15

1. Misspellings can create misunderstanding and cause embarrassment.
2. About fifteen years ago, the *Durham County Register* printed an article about a British military leader.
3. In the article, the old soldier was highly praised but unfortunately was described as "battle-scared."
4. Furious, the soldier called the paper and demanded an apology.
5. The writer and the editor soothed the old man and promised to publish a retraction.
6. In the retraction, the paper apologized for the error and explained, "What we really meant, of course, was 'bottle-scarred.'"
7. "Drive slowly and see our city; drive fast and see our jail."
8. Good drivers obey all traffic regulations and never lose their heads.

9. Do as you wish, but be here on time.
10. Come-by-Chance, Blow-me-Down, Run-by-Guess, and Jerry's Nose are places in Newfoundland, Canada.

---

## Exercise 16

1. "Take only pictures. Leave only footprints." (Sign posted in Banff National Park)
2. Jan and I studied for more than a week but failed the exam anyway.
3. In the pond were two goldfish, an old green tennis ball, and a couple of broken bottles.
4. He worked and saved all his life and died miserable and alone.
5. Everybody but me went to camp or spent a few weeks at a cottage.
6. Among the many kinds of cheese made in Wisconsin are cheddar, Swiss, and Muenster.
7. Shoe companies, book publishers, and equipment manufacturers are all profiting from the jogging boom.
8. We drove the car from Seattle to Portland and then went by bus to San Francisco.
9. The politicians of our time attempt in vain to change the world but seldom try to change themselves.
10. According to the paper, the government will create more jobs, train more tradespeople, support local industry, and push for a higher rate of tourism.

---

## Exercise 17

Here's a challenging review exercise to test your subject- and verb-finding ability.[1] Find and underline the subjects once and the verbs twice. Be sure to underline all elements in a multiple subject or verb.

1. For the women in the solitude of their isolated shanties . . . the heat and scarcity of water made life somewhat more disagreeable and difficult.
2. For them there was no such thing as change nor anything even vaguely resembling a holiday season.
3. Families must be fed after some fashion or other, and dishes washed three times a day, three hundred and sixty-five days in the year.
4. Babies must be fed and washed and dressed and "changed" and

[1]The sentences in this exercise have been taken from Edith Summers Kelley, *Weeds* (Carbondale, Ill: Southern Illinois University Press, 1972), pp. 194–195.

rocked when they cried and watched and kept out of mischief and danger.

5. Fires must be lighted and kept going as long as needed for cooking, no matter how great the heat.
6. Cows must be milked and cream skimmed and butter churned.
7. Hens must be fed and eggs gathered and the filth shoveled out of the henhouses.
8. Diapers must be washed, and grimy little drawers and rompers and stiff overalls and sweaty work-shirts and grease-bespattered dresses and kitchen aprons and filthy, sour-smelling towels and socks stinking with the putridity of unwashed feet and all the other articles . . . of a farm woman's family wash.
9. Floors must be swept and scrubbed and stoves cleaned and a never-ending war waged against the constant encroachment of dust, grease, stable manure, flies, spiders, rats, mice, ants, and all the other breeders of filth . . . continually at work in country households.
10. These activities, with the occasional variation of Sunday visiting, made up the life of the women. . . .

---

# Chapter 5

# Still More About Verbs (For Those Who Need It)

Every verb has four forms:

1. the **base form:** used by itself or with *can, may, might, shall, will, could, would, should, must;*
2. the **past tense form:** used by itself;
3. the **-ing form:** used with *am, is, are, was, were;*

and 4. the **past participle form:** used with *have, has, had* or with *am, is, are, was, were.*

These forms are the **principal parts** of a verb. Here are some examples:

| Base | Past Tense | -ing Form | Past Participle |
|---|---|---|---|
| walk | walked | walking | walked |
| learn | learned | learning | learned |
| seem | seemed | seeming | seemed |
| enjoy | enjoyed | enjoying | enjoyed |

To use verbs correctly, you must know their principal parts. Knowing two facts will help you. First, your dictionary will give you the principal parts of certain verbs (irregular ones). Just look up the base form, and you'll find the past tense and the past participle beside it, usually in parentheses. If the past tense and past participle are *not* given, the verb is **regular.** So, the second thing you need to know is how to form the past tense and the past participle of regular verbs: by adding *-ed* to the base form. The examples listed above—*walk, learn, seem,* and *enjoy*—are regular verbs.

Many of the most common verbs are **irregular.** Their past tense and past participle are formed in a variety of ways. Following is a list of the principal parts of some of the most common irregular verbs. (We have not included the *-ing* form because it never causes any difficulty. It is always made up of the *base form* + *ing.*)

### The Principal Parts of Irregular Verbs

| **Base** (Use with *can, may, might, shall, will, could, would, should, must.*) | **Past Tense** | **Past Participle** (Use with *have, has, had* or with *am, is, are, was, were.*) |
|---|---|---|
| be (am, is, are) | was, were | been |
| bear | bore | borne |
| become | became | become |
| begin | began | begun |
| bid (offer to pay) | bid | bid |
| bite | bit | bitten |
| blow | blew | blown |
| break | broke | broken |
| bring | brought | brought |
| build | built | built |
| burst | burst | burst |
| buy | bought | bought |
| catch | caught | caught |
| choose | chose | chosen |
| come | came | come |
| cost | cost | cost |
| deal | dealt | dealt |
| dive | dived/dove | dived |
| do | did | done |
| draw | drew | drawn |
| drink | drank | drunk |
| drive | drove | driven |
| eat | ate | eaten |
| fall | fell | fallen |
| feel | felt | felt |
| fight | fought | fought |
| find | found | found |
| fling | flung | flung |
| fly | flew | flown |
| forget | forgot | forgotten/forgot |

### The Principal Parts of Irregular Verbs (*continued*)

| **Base** (Use with *can, may, might, shall, will, could, would, should, must.*) | **Past Tense** | **Past Participle** (Use with *have, has, had* or with *am, is, are, was, were.*) |
|---|---|---|
| forgive | forgave | forgiven |
| freeze | froze | frozen |
| get | got | got/gotten |
| give | gave | given |
| go | went | gone (*not* went) |
| grow | grew | grown |
| hang (suspend) | hung | hung |
| hang (put to death) | hanged | hanged |
| have | had | had |
| hear | heard | heard |
| hide | hid | hidden |
| hit | hit | hit |
| hold | held | held |
| hurt | hurt | hurt |
| keep | kept | kept |
| know | knew | known |
| lay | laid | laid |
| lead | led | led |
| leave | left | left |
| lend | lent | lent |
| lie | lay | lain |
| lose | lost | lost |
| make | made | made |
| mean | meant | meant |
| meet | met | met |
| pay | paid | paid |
| put | put | put |
| ride | rode | ridden |
| ring | rang | rung |
| rise | rose | risen |
| run | ran | run |
| say | said | said |
| see | saw (*not* seen) | seen |
| sell | sold | sold |
| set | set | set |
| shake | shook | shaken |
| shine | shone | shone |
| sing | sang | sung |
| sit | sat | sat |
| sleep | slept | slept |
| slide | slid | slid |
| speak | spoke | spoken |

### The Principal Parts of Irregular Verbs (*continued*)

| **Base** (Use with *can, may, might, shall, will, could, would, should, must.*) | **Past Tense** | **Past Participle** (Use with *have, has, had* or with *am, is, are, was, were.*) |
|---|---|---|
| speed | sped | sped |
| spend | spent | spent |
| stand | stood | stood |
| steal | stole | stolen |
| strike | struck | struck |
| swear | swore | sworn |
| swim | swam | swum |
| swing | swung | swung |
| take | took | taken |
| teach | taught | taught |
| tear | tore | torn |
| tell | told | told |
| think | thought | thought |
| throw | threw | thrown |
| wear | wore | worn |
| win | won | won |
| wind | wound | wound |
| write | wrote | written |

## EXERCISES

In the blank, write the correct form (either the past tense or the past participle) of the verb shown to the left of the sentence. Do not add or remove helping verbs. Answers begin on p. 256.

### Exercise 1

1. become After much practice, the team ____________ better at scoring.
2. bring The subject should have been ____________ up at last week's meeting.
3. have If only we could have ____________ your advice last month!

4. sing — I ______________ my heart out, but the audience didn't seem to appreciate my efforts.
5. fling — Ignoring the "Fragile" sticker, the clerk ______________ the parcel into the chute.
6. freeze — A blast of icy air ______________ them in their tracks.
7. get — We have ______________ out of shape during the winter.
8. lend — To help the young couple get started, we ______________ them our tools.
9. swing — Stiffly he ______________ from the saddle.
10. lay — After spending an hour reading, she ______________ the book down and went to bed.

---

## Exercise 2

1. lead — She ______________ them through several back alleys and down a narrow street they had never seen before.
2. lose — Before long they were aware that they had ______________ their way.
3. say — Neither of them ______________ anything, afraid of making her angry.
4. sleep — After several hours of traveling, they stopped and ______________.
5. swim — Back on the trail again, she brought them to a river that both of them had ______________ when they were small.

6. tell — After they crossed, she ____________ them that the journey was half over.

7. throw — By this time, they were so tired that her next suggestion ____________ them into a panic.

8. steal — She wanted them to smuggle across the border a car she had ____________.

9. ride — Despite their fear, they ____________ with her as far as the customs building.

10. write — After the adventure, they agreed to publish the journal they had ____________.

---

The sentences in exercises 3 through 10 require both the past tense and the past participle of the verb shown at the left. Write the required form in each blank. Do not add or remove helping verbs.

---

## Exercise 3

1. wear — We ____________ the same thing we had ____________ to last year's masquerade.

2. build — The house was ____________ in a matter of days by the same men who ____________ my uncle's house so quickly five years ago.

3. slide — Otters had ____________ for years in the same spot where we now ____________ our canoe into the water.

4. blow — The wind ____________ so hard this time that it ripped apart a shed that had already been ____________ down.

5. bear — Politely we ____________ his complaining, until we could not have ____________ it another minute.

6. hit — When he learned what had happened, Bugsy ____________ Florrie harder than she'd ever been ____________ before.

7. ride — Having ____________ a cow once, I wouldn't mind if I never ____________ one again.

8. spend — I ____________ more on his present than I have ____________ on my mother over the whole year.

9. win — When I ____________ the contest, I was delighted, for I had never ____________ anything before.

10. tell — Sandie ____________ her dog to lie down; she should have ____________ it to play dead.

---

## Exercise 4

1. wind — Mary ____________ the clock, not knowing that Peter had ____________ it the night before.

2. tear — Jerome ____________ the sheet into strips; when the sheet was all ____________, he tied the strips together and escaped through the window.

3. lie — The cat ____________ defiantly right where the dog had ____________ all morning.

4. bite — He ____________ his nails whenever he was nervous; as a result his fingernails were ____________ to the quick.

5. grow The vine ____________ until it had ____________ over the window and onto the roof.

6. have I ____________ a funny feeling that I had been ____________.

7. burst The little boy ____________ into tears when he saw that his balloon had ____________.

8. run With Mr. McGregor chasing him, Peter ____________ faster than he'd ever ____________ before.

9. make The kite you ____________ flies better than mine, which was ____________ in China.

10. bring Visitors from Chile ____________ us a copper tray, not knowing that we had ____________ one back ourselves.

---

## Exercise 5

1. bid Lewis ____________ $200 for the ceramic bear with a clock in its stomach; luckily, someone else had already ____________ $225.

2. ring The bell is supposed to be ____________ every half hour, but the last time it ____________ was at nine o'clock.

3. see I would not believe that you ____________ a Sasquatch if I hadn't ____________ it too.

4. break The talks were ______________ off yesterday, just after Zimbabwe ______________ diplomatic ties with South Africa.

5. fight At our last meeting, we ______________ over the same issues that we have ______________ over for years.

6. keep The snow ______________ falling, which meant that the children had to be ______________ indoors.

7. put He ______________ his paper in the pile in which the other students had ______________ theirs.

8. write I finally ______________ to my parents, who complained that I should have ______________ weeks ago.

9. throw Carlos ______________ the ball that his sister had ______________ over the fence.

10. take Before anyone else could have ______________ it, I ______________ the last piece of cake.

---

## Exercise 6

1. think I ______________ she would have ______________ to ask you to dinner while your roommate was away.

2. begin We had just ______________ to unpack the lunch when the rain ______________.

3. feel When I had my tonsils out, I ______________ worse than I had ever ______________ before.

4. buy   We ______________ twenty lottery tickets, which was more than we'd ______________ the year before.

5. do   We ought not to have ______________ it, but we ______________ it anyway.

6. give   For my birthday, Uncle Herbert ______________ me the tie I had ______________ him for Christmas.

7. pay   We ______________ what they asked for the car, but it was more than I thought we should have ______________.

8. lend   I ______________ her the money, even though I had ______________ her ten dollars a week earlier.

9. go   After everyone else had ______________ , I ______________ home.

10. hurt   It ______________ me to learn that you had been ______________ by my careless remark.

---

## Exercise 7

1. come   When Ann ______________ to the door, we could see we had ______________ earlier than she had expected.

2. rise   I ______________ from my bed to see if the sun had ______________ .

3. leave   We ______________ at midnight; otherwise we would have been the only ones ______________ to clean up.

4. speed Having ____________ home from school, Jimmy ____________ off to the park on his bike.

5. teach I have ____________ you all I know, but you ____________ me very little in return.

6. fall The old man slipped and ____________ on the sidewalk, right where I had ____________ the day before.

7. choose Despite the fact that we ____________ carefully, I'm afraid that we have ____________ the wrong man for the job.

8. hear I ____________ a slightly different story from the one you had ____________.

9. fly The plane we ____________ in looked old enough to have been ____________ by the Wright brothers.

10. strike A visit to the island ____________ us as a good idea, but when we got there, we found the same idea had ____________ about two thousand other people as well.

---

## Exercise 8

1. hold Knowing that I could not have ____________ on much longer, Gerry ____________ me as tightly as he could.

2. steal Chuck ____________ a motorcycle that had been ____________ from Kenny the month before.

3. swing Her hair ____________ out behind her as she was ____________ round by her partner.

4. hide Biggs ____________ his money in the rented garage where Roy had ____________ the van.

5. say She ____________ she would do it, but she's ____________ so before, hasn't she?

6. draw As the master of ceremonies ____________ the winning tickets, I prayed that my number would be ____________.

7. meet I'm sure I ____________ Ruth for the first time yesterday, but she insists we have ____________ before.

8. swear She ____________ she would never tell anyone, and I have ____________ to give her a black eye if she does.

9. forgive Lucie ____________ Ralph, but he has not yet ____________ her.

10. lay Jim ____________ his passport on the official's desk, where all the others had been ____________ .

---

## Exercise 9

1. drive Laura had already ____________ to the airport twice that day, but she cheerfully ____________ us anyway.

2. mean I ____________ what I said, but no insult was ____________ by the remark.

3. hang The butcher ____________ the beef for three weeks before he cut it, but, judging by its toughness, it should have been ____________ for at least five weeks.

4. deal — In that game, I __________ the cards face up, and play began when five cards had been __________ to each player.

5. find — Today I __________ not a single ball, although at times I have __________ a dozen or more.

6. lead — Since Terry had __________ his campers to the beach, I __________ mine to the mountain.

7. know — I had not __________ that you __________ of this place.

8. forget — My wife __________ our anniversary again; this is the third year in a row she's __________ it.

9. sell — We __________ most of the stuff at the garage sale. The TV set was the first thing to be __________.

10. speak — I __________ to Barb about her having __________ so thoughtlessly to you.

---

## Exercise 10

1. hang — The judge sentenced the man to be __________ by the neck until dead, and they __________ him the next morning.

2. stand — We __________ in line for two hours; we couldn't have __________ any longer.

3. lose — You __________ control of the ball, and we have __________ the game as a result.

4. get — Brian ____________ one of the best grade-point averages any student has ever ____________ at his college.

5. sleep — Julie ____________ for ten hours and would have ____________ longer if we had let her.

6. freeze — I ____________ the meat, as you asked me to, but I'm sure it's been ____________ before.

7. shakc — Aftcr I had ____________ the money out of the envelope, I ____________ the envelope once more to be sure I had got it all.

8. set — Greg ____________ the jack in place, but it was not ____________ straight.

9. swim, dive — After not having ____________ or ____________ for years, we ____________ and ____________ all afternoon in the Jacksons' pool.

10. eat, drink — They ____________ and ____________ until they could have ____________ and ____________ no more.

# Chapter 6

# Solving Sentence-Fragment Problems

Any group of words that is punctuated as a sentence but that does not have a subject or a complete verb is a **sentence fragment.** Fragments are perfectly appropriate in conversation and in some kinds of writing, but normally they are unacceptable in college, technical, and business writing. You've already learned how to spot a sentence fragment: read the words aloud, and check to see whether the subject or the verb (or both) is missing. Let's look at a few examples:

> Now, as always, are greatly influenced by the current fashion.
> (Who or what are influenced? The sentence doesn't tell you. The subject is missing.)
>
> Historians attempting to analyze America's role in WW II.
> (Part of the verb is missing. Remember that a verb ending in *-ing* must have a helping verb in front of it.)
>
> For the treatment of the common cold.
> (Subject and verb are both missing.)
>
> Regarding the student we discussed last week.
> (Subject and verb are both missing.)

Now, what do you do with the fragments you've found?

> To change a sentence fragment into a complete sentence, add whatever is missing: a subject, a verb, or both.

You may need to add a subject:

Now, as always, some people are greatly influenced by the current fashion.

You may need to add part of a verb:

Historians are attempting to analyze America's role in WW II.

Sometimes it's better to change the form of the verb:

Historians attempt to analyze America's role in WW II.

You may need to add both a subject and a verb:

Many people use Vitamin C for the treatment of the common cold.

And sometimes you need to add more than just a subject and a verb:

I have written to the Registrar regarding the student we discussed last week.

Don't let the length of a fragment fool you. You may think that if a string of words is long, it must be a sentence. Not so. No matter how long the string of words is, if it doesn't have both a subject and a verb, it is not a sentence. Here is an example:

Here and there a pride of lions, staring with mild disdain at the intruding tourists who drive slowly through the wildlife park in comfortable cars with closed windows.

Do you know what's missing? Can you change the fragment into a sentence?

## EXERCISES

Read each "sentence" aloud. Put *S* before each complete sentence and *F* before each sentence fragment. Make each fragment into a complete sentence by adding whatever is missing: a subject, a verb, or both. After you complete each set of ten sentences, check your answers. If you get three sets of ten entirely correct, you may skip the rest. Answers begin on p. 258.

---

### Exercise 1

1. _______ About sentence fragments.
2. _______ To hear about your decision to quit school.
3. _______ Glad to do it for you.
4. _______ Falling asleep in class, after working all night.

5. ______ The poker players meeting in the cafeteria.
6. ______ Nobody seems very enthusiastic.
7. ______ Concert attendance down because of high ticket prices.
8. ______ Learning of the proposed increase in bus fares.
9. ______ Having saved for just such an emergency.
10. ______ Feeling very pleased with myself, I bought 200 tickets.

---

## Exercise 2

1. ______ Enough to last for an entire semester.
2. ______ Turtles being both cheap and easy to train.
3. ______ Never cared for them, frankly.
4. ______ Learning how to write a computer program.
5. ______ The accomplishments of Charlie Chaplin in films.
6. ______ Pete Rose, formerly of the Cincinnati Reds.
7. ______ Do you really think so?
8. ______ Many of whom have seen the film dozens of times.
9. ______ Employees paid only for the work they do.
10. ______ Never put off until tomorrow what you can put off until next week.

---

## Exercise 3

1. ______ As you can see, procrastination is my downfall.
2. ______ Will Kermit ever love Miss Piggy?
3. ______ The reason being he loves horror films.
4. ______ When you feel you have no friends.
5. ______ Unable to locate your account number.
6. ______ The instructions that were given us before the test.
7. ______ Hope that you are feeling better.
8. ______ The ability to learn from mistakes.
9. ______ That, together with her attitude of superiority to the rest of us.
10. ______ The Chinese word for chopsticks being *fai-tze,* which means "small utensil for eating."

---

## Exercise 4

1. ______ To suffer for his carelessness and his neglect of his family.
2. ______ A Fleetwood Mac is a hamburger shaped like a Cadillac.
3. ______ Making the team being the most important achievement of his life.
4. ______ Unless you know what is more than enough.

5. _______ As always, with your wishes in mind.
6. _______ The child developing a habit that is most irritating.
7. _______ Now finish it.
8. _______ Not letting me finish, he turned away.
9. _______ Another boring Saturday night, watching television and eating popcorn.
10. _______ A little learning is a dangerous thing.

---

## Exercise 5

1. _______ Unless you have a better suggestion.
2. _______ He is charming and intelligent but no talent.
3. _______ The trial of John W. Hinckley, Jr. began on April 27, 1982.
4. _______ His Honor Judge Milton Byers presiding.
5. _______ For you don't need even a high school diploma.
6. _______ The Australian government's physical fitness program, "Life—Be in It."
7. _______ Not having to punch a clock every morning at 8:15 and every afternoon at 4:00.
8. _______ To qualify a verb with an adjective?
9. _______ Elderly people sometimes told that they look back upon a pleasant but unreal past.
10. _______ As more Americans between the ages of one and fourteen die from accidents rather than disease.

---

# Independent and Dependent Clauses

A group of words containing a subject and a verb is a clause. There are two kinds of clauses. An **independent clause** is one that makes complete sense on its own. It can stand alone, as a sentence. A **dependent clause,** as its name suggests, cannot stand alone as a sentence; it *depends* on another clause to make complete sense.

Dependent clauses are easy to recognize, because they begin with words such as these:

**Dependent Clause Cues**

| | | |
|---|---|---|
| after | if | until |
| although | in order that | what, whatever |
| as, as if | provided that | when, whenever |
| as soon as | since | where, wherever |

## Dependent-Clause Cues (*continued*)

| | | |
|---|---|---|
| as long as | so that | whether |
| because | that | which, whichever |
| before | though | while |
| even if, even though | unless | who, whom, whose |

Whenever a clause begins with one of these words or phrases, it is dependent.

> A dependent clause must be attached to an independent clause. If it stands alone, it is a sentence fragment.

Here is an independent clause:

I am a poor speller.

If we put one of the dependent-clause cues in front of it, it can no longer stand alone:

Because I am a poor speller

We can correct this kind of fragment by attaching it to an independent clause:

Because I am a poor speller, I have chained my dictionary to my wrist.

### EXERCISES

Put an *S* before each clause that is independent and therefore a sentence. Put an *F* before each clause that is dependent and therefore a sentence fragment. Underline the dependent-clause cue in each sentence fragment.

### Exercise 6

1. ______ Although I tried hard.
2. ______ Before you buy one.
3. ______ Since he quit school.
4. ______ Whichever decision we make.
5. ______ Where he had always wanted to go.

6. _______ As I told you last week.
7. _______ If you meet me at noon.
8. _______ As soon as they get here, let's leave.
9. _______ What they think.
10. _______ I worked quickly so that I could leave early.

---

## Exercise 7

1. _______ After the game was over.
2. _______ Whatever Lola wants.
3. _______ Even if I did agree to go with you.
4. _______ Because I have too much homework.
5. _______ Who seems to be very worried about you.
6. _______ Unless you can pass a simple spelling test.
7. _______ The people who finish before the time is up.
8. _______ Although unhappy with your choice, I won't interfere.
9. _______ When you move to a new apartment.
10. _______ Since September, my weight has not changed.

---

## Exercise 8

1. _______ Unfortunately, when the time came to collect the money.
2. _______ Which team will win, do you think?
3. _______ Since I believe she's doing the best she can.
4. _______ If you miss the next class, too.
5. _______ Provided that the company is pleased with your work.
6. _______ Even though the car hasn't had a tune-up in two years.
7. _______ Before the college accepted me, I worked as a babysitter.
8. _______ While the cat's away.
9. _______ Luckily, the horse that we bet on.
10. _______ Occasionally, so that you don't get lonely.

---

## Exercise 9

1. _______ All those who are late coming back from lunch.
2. _______ The instructions that were in the box were in Italian.
3. _______ So that I might get by.
4. _______ What he thinks doesn't matter.
5. _______ Where you left them yesterday, I guess.
6. _______ Now and then, since my boss is away.
7. _______ Whatever does Lola want?
8. _______ In a situation like this, whichever decision you make.

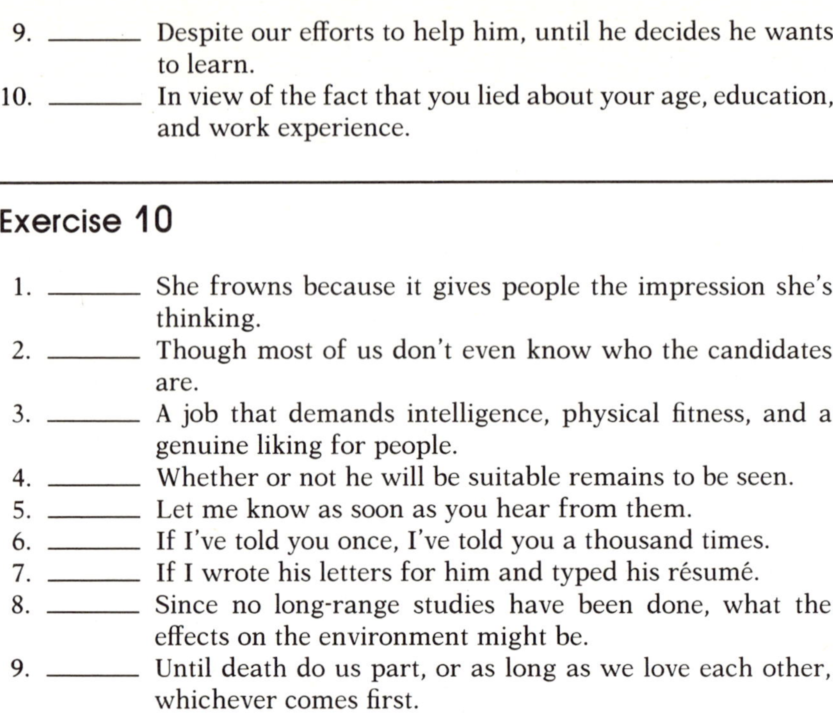

9. _______ Despite our efforts to help him, until he decides he wants to learn.
10. _______ In view of the fact that you lied about your age, education, and work experience.

---

## Exercise 10

1. _______ She frowns because it gives people the impression she's thinking.
2. _______ Though most of us don't even know who the candidates are.
3. _______ A job that demands intelligence, physical fitness, and a genuine liking for people.
4. _______ Whether or not he will be suitable remains to be seen.
5. _______ Let me know as soon as you hear from them.
6. _______ If I've told you once, I've told you a thousand times.
7. _______ If I wrote his letters for him and typed his résumé.
8. _______ Since no long-range studies have been done, what the effects on the environment might be.
9. _______ Until death do us part, or as long as we love each other, whichever comes first.
10. _______ When the jockey approached the table where the three men sat indulging in quantities of food—food rich in both taste and calories.

---

Most sentence fragments are dependent clauses punctuated as sentences. Fortunately, this is the easiest kind of fragment to recognize and fix. All you need to do is join the dependent clause either to the sentence that comes before it or to the one that comes after it—whichever linkage makes better sense.

One final point: if you join your clause fragment to the independent clause that follows it, you must separate the two clauses with a comma (see chapter 17, p. 155).

Read the following example to yourself; then read it aloud (remember, last sentence first).

> Washington is a magnificent state. Although I was born and brought up there. I still wonder at the beauty of its mountains and coast.

The second "sentence" sounds incomplete, and the dependent-clause cue at the beginning of it is the clue you need to identify it as a sentence fragment. You could join the fragment to the sentence before it, but then you would get "Washington is a magnificent state, although I was born and brought up there"—which doesn't make sense. Clearly the fragment should be joined to the sentence which follows it, like this:

Washington is a magnificent state. Although I was born and brought up there, I still wonder at the beauty of its mountains and coast.

## EXERCISES

---

### Exercise 11

Correct the sentence fragments in exercises 6 through 10. Make each fragment into a complete sentence by adding an independent clause either before or after the dependent clause. Remember to punctuate correctly: if a dependent clause comes at the beginning of your sentence, put a comma after it. When you have completed this exercise, exchange with another student and check each other's work.

---

### Exercise 12

Below are ten independent clauses. Make each into a dependent clause by adding one of the dependent-clause cues. Then add an independent clause to make a complete sentence. Example:

He felt very nervous.

Add a dependent-clause cue:

*Although* he felt very nervous.

Now add an independent clause:

Although he felt very nervous, *he gave a good speech.*

1. You will succeed.

___

2. She does as she is told.

___

3. I don't think so.

___

4. We hope to win this one.

_______________

5. There were five left.

_______________

6. Something always goes wrong.

_______________

7. I am usually lucky.

_______________

8. He watched very carefully.

_______________

9. For those in the service industries, the future looks bright.

_______________

10. Some say that the solutions to all our problems will be found in technology. _______________

_______________

_______________

## Exercise 13

Using the following dependent-clause cues, write ten dependent clauses of your own. Then make each into a complete sentence by adding an independent clause. Watch your punctuation!

1. as soon as _______________
2. even if _______________
3. before _______________
4. since _______________

5. whenever ________________________________________

6. while ___________________________________________

7. unless __________________________________________

8. what ___________________________________________

9. whose __________________________________________

10. that ___________________________________________

__________________________________________________

# Chapter 7

# Solving Run-on Problems

Just as a sentence can lack certain elements and thus be a fragment, so can it contain too many elements. A sentence with too much in it is a **run-on.** Run-ons most often occur when you write in a hurry or when you're disorganized and not thinking clearly. If you think about what you want to say and proceed slowly and carefully, you shouldn't have any problems with them.

There are two varieties of run-on sentence: the comma splice and the true run-on.

## The Comma Splice

As the name suggests, the **comma splice** occurs when two complete sentences (independent clauses) are joined together, with only a comma between them. Here's an example:

> That dog's obedient, she's been well trained.

Two sentences, each complete and able to stand on its own, have been "spliced" together with a comma. The comma is insufficient punctuation for the job.

> The easiest way to fix a comma splice is to replace the comma with a semicolon.

That dog's obedient; she's been well trained.

To be sure you understand how to use semicolons correctly, study chapter 18, pages 162–163.

> Another way to fix a comma splice is to add an appropriate linking word between the two clauses.

Two types of linking words will work.

1. You can insert one of these words: *and, but, or, nor, for, so, yet.* These should be preceded by a comma:

That dog's obedient, for she's been well trained.

2. You can insert one of the dependent-clause cues listed on p. 71:

That dog's obedient because she's been well trained.

> The third way to fix a comma splice is to make the run-on sentence into two short sentences.

That dog's obedient. She's been well trained.

In all three of these solutions, you replace the comma with a word or punctuation mark strong enough to come between two independent clauses.

## EXERCISES

---

### Exercise 1

Correct the following sentences where necessary. Then check your answers. (Answers begin on p. 261.) If you find that you're confused about when to use a semicolon and when to use a period, be sure to read p. 162 before going on.

1. Kevin is lazy, Allan is no better.
2. Stop me if you've heard this one, there was this bus driver on his first day at work.

3. I'd like to help, but I have my own problems to worry about.
4. Ronnie says he likes hiking, but he never goes very far, maybe that's because he has asthma.
5. Just because the train was two hours late, you shouldn't have lost your temper like that.
6. It bothers me to see her playing cards all the time, she could easily fail her classes.
7. Denise was transformed, overnight she had turned from a plain-looking student into a sex symbol.
8. Fall is my favorite time of year, the colors are beautiful.
9. A fine mess this is, I'll never forgive you for getting me into this situation.
10. Carefully backing the car onto the road, she fought her nervousness and concentrated on driving.

---

## Exercise 2

If you enjoy puns, you'll like this exercise.[1]

1. Last Saturday we had a great idea, we went to see Dracula and then went out for a bite.
2. Two silkworms were once having a race, however, they ended up in a tie.
3. Some of the convicted Watergate defendants are writing their memoirs, they will be able to use their pen names.
4. The rematch race between the tortoise and the rabbit was extremely close, it was won by a hare.
5. Jobs in a garbage-collecting service are usually fairly secure, business is always picking up.
6. Garbage collectors have a tendency to be depressed most of their working careers, they're often down in the dumps.
7. Jewelers who repair watches for a living put in extremely long hours, they're always working over time.
8. Under a display of stuffed animals in a gift shop in Florida is a sign that reads, "Please do not feed the animals, they are already stuffed."
9. The elephants at the circus in town are planning to go on strike, supposedly, they are tired of working for peanuts.
10. A man called a veterinarian to look at his son's pony because it sounded sick, the vet found the pony to be all right, it was just a little hoarse.

---

[1]Adapted from Harvey C. Gordon, *PUNishment: The Art of Punning, or How to Lose Friends and Agonize People* (New York: Warner Books, 1980). Reprinted by permission

## Exercise 3

1. Mark Twain once said that giving up smoking was no problem at all, he had done it himself, dozens of times.
2. I picked up my new car on Wednesday, one week later, it was recalled for a safety check.
3. Cats are too independent for my taste, I much prefer dogs, who can be counted on to be there when you need them.
4. Very few movies are rated G anymore, many parents are unhappy with this trend.
5. Americans are fascinated by science, they regard it with both wonder and fear.
6. Samuel Johnson wrote the first dictionary of the English language, a task that took him seven years and ruined his health.
7. San Francisco's new symphony hall is shaped like a horseshoe, the international symbol for good luck, perhaps its shape will prove to be a good omen.
8. Frankly, I don't think very highly of Joan, since she is bad-tempered and lazy, I doubt she'll make a good gym teacher.
9. We would be wise to make up our minds what we want, peace or war, then to get ready for what we want.
10. On the banks of the Mississippi River, in the city of St. Louis, stands a monumental arch designed by Eero Saarinen, more than 600 feet high, sheathed in gleaming plates of steel, it is called the Gateway Arch.

## The Run-On Sentence

In the true **run-on sentence**, too many ideas are shoved together into one sentence. In general, a sentence should convey no more than two ideas. There is no hard-and-fast rule about how many clauses you may have in a sentence, but more than two independent clauses can result in a sentence that's hard to read and even harder to understand.

> There were still twelve people at the party, but after Janice went home, we decided it was time to leave, so we collected our coats and said good-bye to the others, and, after a careful drive home at 30 mph, we drank coffee and stayed up until three the following morning discussing the evening's events.

It's obvious that the storyteller who created this monster got carried away with enthusiasm for the tale and just scribbled everything down without much thought. Take your time and keep your reader in mind, and you probably won't make this sort of error. If you do find run-on sentences in your writing, however, follow this rule:

> Revise run-on sentences by breaking them up into shorter sentences.

There were still twelve people at the party, but after Janice went home, we decided it was time to leave. So we collected our coats and said goodbye to the others. After a careful drive home at 30 mph, we drank coffee and stayed up until three the following morning discussing the evening's events.

## EXERCISES

---

### Exercise 4

Using the four types of corrections you've learned in this chapter, make these sentences easier to read. There is more than one right way of fixing these; just be sure your resulting sentences are easy to read and make sense. The answers we've provided are only suggestions.

1. *Ordinary People* is one of my favorite films because it seems so true to life, and I'm thinking of reading the book.
2. People tend to forget that a complete education involves the body as well as the mind, and in most high schools physical education isn't taken seriously, while at college there is even less emphasis on athletics except for support of a few varsity teams, but all this might change if the Department of Education changed its policy.
3. When The Band split up, my favorite group became The Eagles, but I don't listen to music much anymore because my stereo's broken, and I haven't got a summer job, so I can't afford to have it fixed.
4. Bruce hates alarm clocks and refuses to keep one in his apartment, he's the guy who used to go out with my sister.
5. It's always best to tell the truth, because one lie leads to another, eventually you'll get caught.
6. They took up sailing last year, we haven't seen them since.
7. I'm tired, and I guess you must be, too, so let's just finish this last one and then turn in, and we can get an early start tomorrow and polish off the rest before noon so we can have the rest of the day to ourselves.
8. Foolish people are those who, through ignorance or stupidity, refuse to believe there's anything they don't know, but when a situation comes along that they aren't familiar with, and they don't know how to act, they just plow ahead without a care, and usually they end up making the situation worse and adding to their richly deserved reputation as fools.

9. I think there are many components of a sense of humor, one is the ability to see the absurd in normal situations, and another is the very rare gift of being able to see oneself as an object of fun or ridicule, almost no one has the latter ability to any degree.
10. The American political system is really very straightforward and simple, if you think about it, because we have several levels of government, each with its own powers and jurisdictions and each responsible to its constituents, but difficulties arise when jurisdictions overlap or aren't clearly defined.

---

## Exercise 5

1. Why did he do it, he knew he couldn't get away with it.
2. Jasmine isn't going with them, though she wants to, as far as I know, she wasn't even asked.
3. You asked me for my opinion of that group, so here it is, the lead vocalist can barely carry a tune and her voice is so thin she can scarcely be heard even with a microphone, and the drummer seems always to be about half a beat behind, and looks as though he's half asleep, but the keyboard man isn't bad.
4. Anything else wouldn't have worked, we were sure we had done the right thing, even though the outcome wasn't quite what we had expected.
5. Although some people believe that the existence of psychic phenomena such as ESP, precognition, and poltergeists cannot be questioned, I am not yet convinced.
6. It's a good thing he likes you, he could be a very dangerous enemy, you know that as well as I do.
7. No one else was up, I walked out of the house and down to the beach, the shore was empty and silent, except for the soft sounds of the waves.
8. Several students I know have no interest in school and play cards or watch TV most of the time rather than study and would prefer to be out working and feel that they are accomplishing something worthwhile.
9. In many cities, there is an acute shortage of rental housing, and landlords are under little competitive pressure to hold rents down, so rents are likely to be high, and the ever-increasing cost of renting compounds the problems facing those on welfare, or on fixed incomes, or with low-paying jobs, and these are the people who have no choice but to rent, they can never hope to own their own homes.
10. We have little choice but to depend on science and technology to find solutions to the energy crisis, perhaps through the utilization

of new energy sources such as fusion, solar power, and geothermal energy, and to the problems of nuclear and chemical pollution, as well as to the new problems that are being caused by advances in genetic engineering.

---

## Exercise 6

Correct the following sentences to eliminate comma splices, run-ons, and fragments. Your answers may differ somewhat from ours.

1. Considering my background in the field, my high level of achievement since the completion of my education, and the fact that my uncle is the sales manager of the company.
2. Thinking that I was being hilarious, I tried another joke.
3. Writing true comedy is not easy, in fact few disciplines are more demanding.
4. When I was shown the evidence that was being presented against him and realized the hopelessness of his case.
5. It concerns me to see him on trial with such a lawyer, he could easily lose a case he should win.
6. The thought was there, just the same, that doesn't help if no action was taken.
7. He shoots!
8. Isaac Asimov, the well-known science fiction writer.
9. Insincerity is his most notable character trait, and obesity his most notable physical characteristic.
10. Fishing for perch on a bright spring day from the dock near his summer cottage.

---

## Exercise 7

Again, eliminate comma splices, run-ons, and fragments. Our answers to this exercise make up a story, but yours may differ somewhat.

1. Although he was a wonderful dancer.
2. He had very large feet, these enormous growths did not permit him to be as graceful as he wished.
3. One day, as he sat dreaming in the park.
4. We must try to understand the emotional suffering of a man who was doomed to have the largest feet in America, if we cannot at least be sympathetic the burden may well be too much for him to bear, for he will be spiritually, not to mention physically, alone forever.
5. On his journey to Europe he encountered severe difficulties, he per-

severed, however, and, after many embarrassing experiences, arrived in France.

6. Claiming that his feet would be an asset to the wine industry.
7. The people cheered as he approached, he was a genuine marvel.
8. On his ninth day of work in the wine vats he met with trouble, a jealous coworker had put a banana skin among the grapes, he had hidden it just where the ambitious grape masher would be sure to slip on it.
9. He slipped and fell, injuring his back seriously, but his life was not ruined.
10. A kindly passerby rushed him to the hospital, there he was attended by an efficient nurse who won his heart, and he married her as soon as he was released from the hospital, and they were very happy, and not one of their children had large feet.

---

## Exercise 8

Correct the sentence fragments, comma splices, and run-ons in the following passage, then compare your version with the author's original version in the answer section.[2]

It is loosely estimated that some 3,000,000 Americans belong to about 1,000 religious cults. The largest of which bear names like the Unification Church, the Divine Light Mission, the Hare Krishna, and the Way. Each of which has temples or branches in most major cities. . . . Just why is it that such groups can command almost total dedication and obedience from their members? Their secret is simple, they understand the need for community, structure, and meaning. For these are what all cults peddle.

For lonely people, cults offer, in the beginning, indiscriminate friendship. Says an official of the Unification Church, "If someone's lonely, we talk to him or her, there are a lot of lonely people walking around." The newcomer is surrounded by people offering friendship and beaming approval, many of the cults require communal living. So powerfully rewarding is this sudden warmth and attention that cult members are often willing to give up contact with their families and former friends, to donate their life's earnings to the cult, to forego drugs and even sex in return.

But the cult sells more than community, it also offers much-needed structure, cults impose tight constraints on behavior, they demand and create enormous discipline. Some apparently going so far as to impose that discipline through beatings, forced labor, and their own forms of ostracism or imprisonment. Psychiatrist H. A. S. Sukhdeo . . . concludes, "Our society is so free and permissive, and people have so many options to choose from. That they cannot make their own decisions effectively. They want others to make the decisions. And they will follow."

---

[2]Adapted from Alvin Toffler, *The Third Wave* (New York: Bantam Books, 1981), pp. 374–375. 

## Exercise 9

Write a letter to a friend who will soon be attending your school. Describe your experiences and provide any advice you think will be useful when your friend begins classes next year. Check your letter carefully to eliminate spelling and apostrophe errors and to make sure your sentences are correctly constructed. Watch especially for fragments and run-ons.

# Chapter 8

# Solving Modifier Problems

The thieves were caught before much of the loot could be disposed of by the police.

Coughing, sputtering, and leaking all over the road, we helped Sonny push the old Ford into the nearest service station.

At the age of five, the barber cut Jamie's hair, which curled to his shoulders nearly for the first time.

These sentences show what can happen to your writing if you aren't sure how to use modifiers. A **modifier** is a word or group of words that adds information about another word in a sentence. In the examples above, the underlined words are modifiers. Used correctly, modifiers describe or explain or limit another word, making its meaning more precise. Used carelessly, however, modifiers can cause confusion or, even worse, amusement. There's nothing more embarrassing than being laughed at when you didn't mean to be funny.

You need to be able to recognize and solve two kinds of modifier problems: misplaced modifiers and dangling modifiers.

## Misplaced Modifiers

Modifiers must be as close as possible to the words they apply to. Usually a reader will assume that a modifier modifies whatever it's next to. It's important to remember this because, as the following examples show, changing the position of a modifier can change the meaning of your sentence.

I told Mr. Jones only what I had done. (I didn't tell him anything else.)

I told only Mr. Jones what I had done. (I didn't tell anybody else.)

Only I told Mr. Jones what I had done. (Nobody else told Mr. Jones.)

I told Mr. Jones what only I had done. (No one else did it.)

> To make sure a modifier is in the right place, ask yourself, "What does it apply to?" and put it beside that word.

When a modifier is not close enough to the word it refers to, it is said to be misplaced. A **misplaced modifier** can be *a single word in the wrong place:*

The supervisor told me they needed someone who could type badly.

Is some company really hiring people to do poor work? Or does the company urgently need a typist? Obviously, the modifier *badly* belongs next to *needed:*

The supervisor told me they badly needed someone who could type.

> Be especially careful with these words: *almost, nearly, just, only, even, hardly, merely, scarcely.* Put them right before the words they modify.

*Misplaced:* I almost ate the whole thing.

*Correctly placed:* I ate almost the whole thing.

*Misplaced: Heaven's Gate* was the dullest movie I've ever seen nearly.

*Correctly placed: Heaven's Gate* was nearly the dullest movie I've ever seen.

A misplaced modifier can also be *a group of words in the wrong place:*

Scratching each other playfully, we watched the monkeys.

The modifier, *scratching each other playfully,* is too far away from the word it is supposed to modify, *monkeys.* In fact, it seems to modify *we,* making the sentence ridiculous. We need to rewrite the sentence:

We watched the monkeys scratching each other playfully.

Look at this one:

I worked for my father, who owns a sawmill during the summer.

*During the summer* applies to *worked* and should be closer to it:

During the summer, I worked for my father, who owns a sawmill.

Notice that a modifier need not always go right next to what it modifies; it should, however, be as close as possible to it.

Occasionally, as in the examples above, the modifier is obviously out of place. The writer's intention is clear, and the sentences are easy to correct. But sometimes modifiers are misplaced in such a way that the meaning is not clear, as in this example:

Lucy said on her way out she would give the memo to John.

Did Lucy *say* it on her way out? Or is she going to *deliver the memo* on her way out? To avoid confusion, we must move the modifier and, depending on which meaning we want, write either

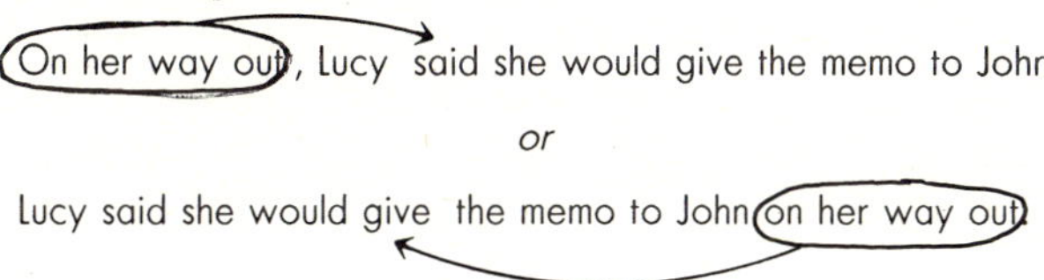


## EXERCISES

Some of the sentences in these exercises contain misplaced modifiers. Rewrite the sentences as necessary, positioning the modifiers correctly. Check your answers to each set of ten before going on. (Answers begin on p. 266.) If you get the first two sets entirely correct, skip ahead to exercise 4.

---

### Exercise 1

1. Unless they're French or Italian, some people never go to movies.

_______________

2. Tony bought plants for his aquarium that cost $6.50.

_______________

3. They nearly decided to pay me $245 a week.

_______________

4. I will ask you only one more time.

_______________

5. Wearing two left shoes and a funny little flowered hat, we laughed at the antics of the clown. ________________

________________

6. I hate parties where food is served to the guests on little paper plates. ________________

________________

7. The shawl was what Valerie had been looking for exactly.

________________

8. Bonita came back before I could escape in a rage.

________________

9. There just is enough time left.

________________

10. Mr. Harrison told us on Tuesday there would be a test.

________________

________________

## Exercise 2

1. Barbara Walters convinced John Dean he should talk with difficulty. ________________

________________

2. Two suitable jobs only were advertised.

________________

3. This course can be completed by anyone who has learned English grammar in six weeks. ________________

________________

4. The obituary column lists the names of people who have died recently for a small fee. ______________________________

______________________________________________

5. The lead guitarist played professionally before coming to Chicago in Europe. ______________________________

______________________________________________

6. The shawl was exactly what Valerie had been looking for in the window. ______________________________

______________________________________________

7. Every week they told me to come back and check the notice board.

______________________________________________

8. Parents want to know what their children are doing in school for their own satisfaction. ______________________________

______________________________________________

9. The cause of the accident was a little guy in a small car with a big mouth. ______________________________

______________________________________________

10. Anyone who has spent a night lost in the woods can identify with the frightening picture Thoreau has painted easily. ____________

______________________________________________

______________________________________________

## Exercise 3

1. Some games depend very much on the decisions of officials such as hockey. ______________________________

______________________________________________

2. He almost watched television all night.

______________________________________________

3. Clint Eastwood tried to persuade the other actors to follow his proposal eagerly. ______________________________________________

______________________________________________

4. Stir the flour into the butter in the saucepan with the wooden spoon. ______________________________________________

______________________________________________

5. As someone who is concerned about fitness, you really should stop smoking. ______________________________________________

______________________________________________

6. On tonight's show, Raymond Giles, the well-known interior designer, will be discussing how to design an efficient kitchen with Julia Child.

______________________________________________

______________________________________________

7. He took a stand against a tree while waiting for the bear with only an old black powder rifle. ______________________________________________

______________________________________________

8. I passed the security guard and two workmen walking to class.

______________________________________________

9. One possible solution would be to try studying, something you haven't done before. ______________________________________________

______________________________________________

10. Government subsidies would act as an incentive to the student who is preparing for a career properly administered. ____________

________________________________________

________________________________________

## Exercise 4

Make up three sentences containing misplaced modifiers; then correct them.

________________________________________

## Dangling Modifiers

A **dangling modifier** occurs when there is *no appropriate word in the sentence* for the modifier to apply to. With no appropriate word to modify, the modifier *seems* to apply to whatever it's next to, often with ridiculous results:

After four semesters of hard work, my parents rewarded me with a car.

(This sentence seems to say that the parents are going to school.)

Jogging along the sidewalk, a truck swerved and nearly hit me.

(The *truck* was jogging along the sidewalk?)

Dangling modifiers are trickier to fix than misplaced ones; you can't simply move danglers to another spot in the sentence. There are, however, two ways in which you can fix them. One way requires that you remember this rule:

> When a modifier comes at the beginning of a sentence, it modifies the subject of the sentence.[1]

This means that you can avoid dangling modifiers by choosing the subjects of your sentences carefully. All you have to do is make sure the subject is an appropriate one for the modifier to apply to. Using this method, we can rewrite our two examples by changing the subjects:

After four semesters of hard work, I got my reward. My parents bought me a car.

Jogging along the sidewalk, I was nearly hit by a swerving truck.

[1]Adverbial modifiers are exceptions to this rule, but they won't give you any trouble. Example:

Quickly she did as she was told.

Another way to correct a dangling modifier is by changing it into a dependent clause:

> After I had completed four semesters of hard work, my parents rewarded me with a car.
>
> As I was jogging along the sidewalk, a truck swerved and nearly hit me.

Sometimes a dangling modifier comes at the end of a sentence:

> McDonald's would be a good place to go, not having much money.

Can you correct this sentence? Try it; then look at footnote 2, below.

Here is a summary of the steps to follow in solving modifier problems:

1. Ask "What does the modifier apply to?"
2. Be sure there is a word *in the sentence* for the modifier to apply to.
3. Put the modifier as close as possible to the word it applies to.

## EXERCISES

Most of the sentences in exercises 5 and 6 contain dangling modifiers. Make corrections by changing the subject of the sentence to one the modifier can appropriately apply to. There is no one "right" way to correct each sentence; our answers are only suggestions.

### Exercise 5

1. As a college English teacher, dangling modifiers upset me.

2. Having finished the bedroom, the kitchen was next to be painted.

3. Turning to the Appendix, the example I quoted is in the third paragraph.

[2]Here are two suggestions:

1. *Add a subject:* Not having much money, I thought McDonald's would be a good place to go.
2. *Change the dangler to a dependent clause:* McDonald's would be a good place to go since I don't have much money.

4. The surface must be sanded smooth before applying varnish.

______________________________________________

5. Upon entering, the store was completely empty.

______________________________________________

6. Even as a very small boy, being a Harlem Globetrotter was Louis' ambition. ______________________________________________

______________________________________________

7. Raging uncontrolled for two days, the Napa Valley grape crop was ravaged by a fire set by an arsonist. ______________________________________________

______________________________________________

8. It's understandable that, being only 4′10″, Maria isn't fond of "short people" jokes. ______________________________________________

______________________________________________

9. Looking over his shoulder, the car slowly backed up.

______________________________________________

10. In very cold weather, the engine should be thoroughly warmed up before attempting to drive. ______________________________________________

______________________________________________

## Exercise 6

1. After changing the tire, the jack should be released.

______________________________________________

2. The next question is whether to order beer or wine, having decided on pizza. ______________________________________________

______________________________________________

3. After waiting for you for an hour, the evening was ruined.

_______________________________________________

4. Nicknamed "Old Faithful," Yellowstone National Park's most popular geyser shoots an immense cloud of steam into the air approximately once an hour. ______________________________

_______________________________________________

_______________________________________________

5. Most of the spare keys, after spending $9 on them, have been lost.

_______________________________________________

6. Julie and Jessie are completely different when comparing their personalities and interests. ______________________________

_______________________________________________

7. Having completed the beginning, the ending is the next most important part of the essay. ______________________________

_______________________________________________

8. Once having shot and killed a bear in her kitchen, Lynne has a well-deserved reputation for courage. ______________________________

_______________________________________________

9. After having been isolated for so long, the world seemed to the paroled man to be spinning at a hectic pace. ______________________________

_______________________________________________

10. After shoveling the walks, the driveway, and the sidewalk, it snowed another four inches. ______________________________

_______________________________________________

_______________________________________________

## Exercise 7

Correct the dangling modifiers in exercise 5 by changing them into dependent clauses.

## Exercise 8

Correct the dangling modifiers in exercise 6 by changing them into dependent clauses.

## Exercise 9

Correct the misplaced and dangling modifiers in exercises 9 through 11 in any way you choose. Our answers are only suggestions.

1. Being made of very thin crystal, the dishwasher breaks the glasses as fast as I can buy them. ______________________________

   _______________________________________________

2. The menu featured artichoke hearts deep-fried in mayonnaise.

   _______________________________________________

3. As a college student constantly faced with stress, the pressure is intolerable. ______________________________

   _______________________________________________

4. His socks were full of holes which were long and red.

   _______________________________________________

5. Although not a churchgoer, respect for others is an important part of my philosophy. ______________________________

______________________________

6. After deciding whether the wine should be blended, sugar is added.

______________________________

7. Environmental groups protested the damage done by oil slicks from coast to coast. ______________________________

______________________________

8. The sign in the restaurant window read, "Our Establishment Serves Tea in a Bag Just Like Mother." ______________________________

______________________________

9. Animals are loved by many people, especially when small.

______________________________

10. Having broken its wings, they took the seagull to the S.P.C.A.

______________________________

______________________________

## Exercise 10

1. Although he lives fifty miles away, he nearly manages to come to every class. ______________________________

______________________________

2. We went to the party that Sandie gave for Lucille's promotion on a motorcycle. ______________________________

______________________________

3. The lion was recaptured before anyone was mauled or bitten by the trainer. ______________________________________________

______________________________________________

4. After reading the assigned material, an emotional discussion took place. ______________________________________________

______________________________________________

5. I saw the Queen and her entourage arrive through a plate-glass window. ______________________________________________

______________________________________________

6. Having ruled out the other two engines, the Wankel is the one we'll choose. ______________________________________________

______________________________________________

7. Swimming isn't a good idea if cold or polluted.

______________________________________________

8. Pet-lover Doris Day will interview William Shatner and his dog Spock, who is also a pet owner. ______________________________

______________________________________________

9. I learned about Joan's having a baby in last week's letter.

______________________________________________

10. The person who is successful in most cases has a large vocabulary.

______________________________________________

______________________________________________

## Exercise 11

1. After completing the study of staffing requirements, an assistant to the personnel manager will be hired. ______________________________

______________________________________________

2. The Historical Society that was studying the matter last week submitted its report. ______________________________

______________________________________________

3. Our English teacher explained how to skim and scan on Monday.

______________________________________________

4. Left over from last week's party, our guests didn't find the meal very appetizing. ______________________________

______________________________________________

5. Employees who are late frequently are dismissed without notice.

______________________________________________

6. Having forgotten to pick me up twice this week, I'm quitting Jim's car pool. ______________________________

______________________________________________

7. The switch is attached to the wall with screws just like the wall plate. ______________________________

______________________________________________

8. The thieves were caught before much of the loot could be disposed of by the police. ______________________________

______________________________________________

9. Coughing, sputtering, and leaking all over the road, we helped Sonny push the old Ford into the nearest service station. ________

________________________________________________

10. At the age of five, the barber cut Jamie's hair, which curled to his shoulders nearly for the first time. ____________________

________________________________________________

________________________________________________

# Chapter 9

# The Parallelism Principle

When writing about items in a series, you must be sure all the items are **parallel;** that is, they must be written in the same grammatical form.

> I like camping, fishing, and to hike.

The items in this list are not parallel. Two end in *-ing,* but the third *(to hike)* is the infinitive form of the verb. To correct the sentence, you must make all the items in the list take the same grammatical form—either

> I like to camp, to fish, and to hike.
>
> *or*
>
> I like camping, fishing, and hiking.

> Correct faulty parallelism by giving the items in a series the same grammatical form.

One way to tell whether all the items in a list are parallel is to picture (or actually write) the items in list form, one below the other. That way, you can make sure that all the elements are the same—that they are all words, or phrases, or clauses.

| **Not Parallel** | **Parallel** |
| --- | --- |
| Sharon is kind,<br>considerate, and<br>likes to help. | Sharon is kind,<br>considerate, and<br>helpful. |
| I support myself by tending bar,<br>piano, and<br>shooting pool. | I support myself by tending bar,<br>playing piano, and<br>shooting pool. |
| Her upbringing made her neat,<br>polite, and<br>an obnoxious<br>person. | Her upbringing made her neat,<br>polite, and<br>obnoxious. |
| Gordon tries to do what is right,<br>different, and<br>make a profit. | Gordon tries to do what is right,<br>what is different, and<br>what is profitable. |
| With his sharp mind,<br>by having the boss as his uncle, and<br>few enemies,<br>he'll go far. | With his sharp mind,<br>the boss as his uncle, and<br>few enemies.<br>he'll go far.<br>*or*<br>Having a sharp mind,<br>the boss as his uncle, and<br>few enemies,<br>he'll go far. |

As you can see, achieving parallelism is partly a matter of developing an ear for the sound of a correct list. Practice, and the exercises in this chapter, will help. Once you have mastered parallelism in your sentences, you will be ready to develop ideas and arguments in parallel sequence and thus to write well-organized, clear paragraphs, letters, and essays. All this will be discussed in a later unit ("Organizing Your Writing"); we mention it now only to show you that parallelism, far from being a "frill," is a fundamental part of good writing.

## EXERCISES

Correct the following sentences where necessary. As you work through these exercises, try to spot faulty parallelism and correct it from the sound of the sentences, before you examine them closely for mistakes. Check your answers to each set of ten before going on. Answers begin on p. 270.

## Exercise 1

1. The three main kinds of speech are demonstrative, informative, and the kind persuading someone of something.
2. The single mother faces many problems. Two of the most difficult are supporting her household and sole parent to her child.
3. He advised me to take two aspirins and that I call him in the morning.
4. Books provide us with information, education, and they're entertaining to read.
5. To make your court appearance as painless as possible, prepare your case thoroughly, and maintaining a pleasant, positive attitude.
6. The apostrophe is used for two purposes: contraction, and it shows possession.
7. Swiftly and with skill the woman gutted and scaled the fish.
8. I am overworked and not paid enough.
9. You need to develop skill and strategy and be agile to be a good tennis player.
10. The two main responsibilities of a corrections officer are security and controlling the inmates.

## Exercise 2

1. A part-time job can develop your decision-making skills, your sense of responsibility, and you feel more self-confident and independent.
2. The three keys to improving your marks are study, you must work hard, and bribing the teacher.
3. I couldn't decide whether I should become a chef or to study data processing.
4. The recent increase in teenage suicides can be attributed primarily to two causes: the widespread lack of strong religious beliefs and there are no strict moral codes either.
5. A course in logical reasoning will help him to evaluate what he reads and in making sound decisions.
6. When you're buying a new car, you should look at more than just the size, style, and how much it costs. The warranty, how much it costs to run, and trade-in value should also be taken into consideration.
7. Mrs. Hunter assigns two hours of homework every night, and we're expected to do an essay each week.
8. The two most important characteristics of a personal work space are how neat and well organized it looks, and the privacy.
9. Playing with small construction toys is beneficial to young children

because it develops their fine motor skills, encourages concentration and patience, and their creative imagination is stimulated.

10. My supervisor told me that my performance was generally satisfactory but to improve my writing.

---

## Exercise 3

1. The role of the health instructor is to teach preventive medicine, care of the sick, and how to go about rehabilitating the injured.
2. The most common causes of snowmobile accidents are mechanical failure, the weather conditions might be poor, and the driver careless.
3. The portable classrooms are ill-equipped, poorly lighted, and there isn't any heat.
4. The advantages of a thesis statement are that it limits your topic, the contents of the paper are made very clear, and you show how your paper will be organized.
5. Unemployment deprives the individual of purchasing power, and the country's national output is reduced.
6. A good nurse is energetic, tolerant, sympathetic, and can be relied upon.
7. The money spent on space exploration should be used to provide aid to the underdeveloped countries, and medical research could be funded.
8. The best house cats are quiet, clean, affectionate, and should be somewhere else.
9. Springtime brings out some interesting emotions along with the flowers and leaves: a new appreciation for the beauty of nature, and members of the opposite sex are newly admired.
10. You can conclude a paper with a summary of main points, by posing a question, or you could end with a quotation.

---

## Exercise 4

Make the following lists parallel. In each case there's more than one way to do it, because you can make your items parallel with any item in the list. Therefore, your answers may differ from ours. Here's an example:

| | | |
|---|---|---|
| *wrong:* | stick handling | score a goal |
| *right:* | stick handling | goal scoring |
| | *or* | |
| *right:* | handle the stick | score a goal |

1. *wrong:* mechanically | by using your hands

   *right:* ______________________________

2. *wrong:* nursing | being a pilot

   *right:* ______________________________

3. *wrong:* achieve her goals | finding true happiness

   *right:* ______________________________

4. *wrong:* sense of humor | wealthy | intelligent

   *right:* ______________________________

5. *wrong:* daily exercise | wholesome food | getting a checkup regularly

   *right:* ______________________________

6. *wrong:* a good cigar | drinking a glass of brandy | conversation with friends

   *right:* ______________________________

7. *wrong:* speed | comfortable | good cornering

   *right:* ______________________________

8. *wrong:* look for bargains | quality should be chosen | value

   *right:* ______________________________

9. *wrong:* security | valuable | safety

   *right:* ______________________________

10. *wrong:* tanned golden brown | skimpy bathing suit | big boyfriend

    *right:* ______________________________

______________________________

## Exercise 5

Create a sentence for each of the parallel lists you developed in exercise 4. Example:

His stick handling was adequate, but his goal scoring was pitiful.

## Exercise 6

Write a short paper on a topic you choose or on a topic assigned by your teacher. When you have completed your work, read it over carefully. Check your spelling. Check your sentence structure by reading your work aloud, from last sentence to first. Be sure to correct any unclear modifiers and errors in parallelism before handing in your paper.

You might like to try one of these topics:

1. Why a specific television commercial pleases (or irritates) you.
2. What makes your favorite restaurant the best in town.
3. How to be boring.
4. How the world would be different if everyone had a tail.
5. What you would wish for if you were granted one wish, and why.

# UNIT THREE

# Grammar

# Chapter 10

# Subject-Verb Agreement

Errors in grammar are like flies in soup: they don't usually affect meaning any more than flies affect flavor, but they are distracting. They must be eliminated if you want your reader to pay attention to what you say rather than how you say it.

One of the most common grammatical problems is failure to make the subject and verb in a sentence agree with each other. Here is the rule for subject-verb agreement:

> Singular subjects take singular verbs.
> Plural subjects take plural verbs.

Remember that *singular* words concern one person or thing . . .

The lion roars. Jerry runs. His plan fails.

. . . and *plural* words concern more than one person or thing:

The lions roar. Tom and Jerry run. Their plans fail.

The rule for subject-verb agreement will cause you no problem at all as long as you make sure that the word the verb agrees with is really the subject.

To see how a problem can arise, look at this example:

One of the boys write graffiti.

The writer forgot that the subject of a sentence is never in a prepositional phrase. The verb needs to be changed to agree with *one:*

One of the boys writes graffiti.

If you're careful about identifying the subject of your sentence, you'll have no trouble with subject-verb agreement. To sharpen up your subject-finding ability, review chapter 4, "Cracking the Sentence Code." Then do the following exercises.

## EXERCISES

### Exercise 1

Identify the subject in each sentence. Answers begin on p. 272.

1. Over there are an ostrich and a penguin, two birds that cannot fly.
2. Unfortunately, large numbers of Americans are bored by politics.
3. The World Disco Dancing Championships are held in December.
4. Where are the invoices I asked for?
5. Do the volcanoes on the Hawaiian Islands erupt frequently?
6. In order to compete with television, the print media are offering more service features.
7. One of the most adaptable creatures on earth, the cockroach might very well outlive man.
8. There are few advantages to being a waitress in a college cafeteria.
9. Is there anything easier than the rule for subject-verb agreement?
10. The pressures of homework, part-time work, and nagging parents have forced many students to drop out of school.

### Exercise 2

Rewrite each of the sentences, following the procedure shown in the example. Example:

They are to let us know when they are able to fill the order.
He is to let us know when he is able to fill the order.

1. He tells me he is unwilling to work overtime.

   They ______________________________

2. That policy change affects the entire program.

   Those ______________________________

3. Her paper is late because she's been ill.

   Their papers ______________________________

4. The union leader complains that his lot is not a happy one.

   The union leaders ______________________________

5. They do their best work when they are unsupervised.

   He ______________________________

6. They insist on having their way.

   She ______________________________

7. Each of Cinderella's sisters was horrid in her own way.

   Both ______________________________

8. This man's wife isn't doing him any good.

   Those ______________________________

9. The peanut farmer stands to lose money unless he diversifies his crops.

   The peanut farmers ______________________________

10. Everyone who deposits $50 has his or her name entered in the draw.

    All those ______________________________

---

## Exercise 3

Rewrite each sentence, following the procedure shown in the example. Example:

Jellybeans are my favorite snack.
My favorite snack is jellybeans.

1. Laurie's only interest is motorcycles.

   Motorcycles ______________________________

2. What he spends most of his money on is clothes.

   ______________________________

3. Cigarettes are the one luxury I allow myself.

   ______________________________

4. Long hours of practice were the reason for our success.

   ______________________________

5. What America needs now is strong leadership and more jobs.

   ______________________________

6. The reason for his failure was too many absences from class.

   ______________________________

7. Disputes over wages and benefits are often the cause of strikes.

   ______________________________

8. Multiple subjects and multiple verbs are what I find difficult.

   ______________________________

9. Something that takes a lot of my time is math assignments.

   ______________________________

10. My little brother's constant interruptions are the reason I didn't finish the assignment. ______________________________

    ______________________________

    ______________________________

So far, so good. You can find the subject, even when it's hiding on the far side of the verb or nearly buried under a load of prepositional phrases. You can match up singular subjects with singular verbs, and plural subjects with plural verbs. Now let's take a look at a few of the complications that make subject-verb agreement into such a disagreeable problem.

## Six Special Cases

Some subjects are tricky: they look singular but are actually plural, or they look plural when they're really singular. There are six different kinds of these slippery subjects, all of them common, and all of them likely to trip up the unwary writer.

**1. Multiple subjects joined by *or, either . . . or, neither . . . nor, not . . . but.*** All the multiple subjects we've dealt with so far have been joined by *and* and have required plural verbs, so agreement hasn't been a problem. But watch out when the two or more elements of a multiple subject are joined by *or, either . . . or, neither . . . nor,* or *not . . . but.* In these cases, *the verb agrees in number with the nearest subject.* That is, if the subject closest to the verb is singular, the verb will be singular; if the subject closest to the verb is plural, the verb must be plural, too.

Neither the president nor the senators are responsible.

Neither the senators nor the president is responsible.

### EXERCISE

---

### Exercise 4

Circle the correct verb. For 9 and 10, make up two sentences of your own.

1. Not the electricity but the telephones (was were) knocked out during the storm.
2. Either "Miss" or "Ms." (is are) fine with me.
3. Squash, tennis, or racquetball (is are) better for you than backgammon or poker.
4. Either Joan or you (is are) at fault.
5. Not Beacon Hill but Friendly's hamburgers (is are) what I miss most about Boston.
6. The oil company informed me that neither they nor their representative (is are) responsible for the damage to my car.
7. Neither the book nor the movies based on it (was were) worth the money I spent on them.
8. According to a recent survey, not sexual incompatibility but dis-

agreements over children (cause causes) the most strain in a marriage.

9. Either ______________________ or ______________________ .

10. Not ______________________ but ______________________ .

---

**2. Subjects that look multiple but really aren't.** Don't be fooled by phrases beginning with such words as *with, like, as well as, together with, in addition to, including.* These phrases are NOT part of the subject of the sentence. Cross them out mentally; they do not affect the verb.

My typing teacher, ~~as well as my counselor~~, has advised me to switch programs.

Obviously, two people were involved in the advising; nevertheless, the subject (teacher) is singular, and so the verb must be singular, too (has advised).

All my courses, ~~including chemistry~~, are easier this term.

If you mentally cross out the phrase "including chemistry," you can easily see that the verb (are) must be plural to agree with the plural subject (courses).

## EXERCISE

---

## Exercise 5

Circle the correct verb. Then make up two sentences of your own.

1. Bruce Springsteen, with the E-Street Band, (is are) playing in Omaha tomorrow night.
2. Clark Kent, like Lois Lane and Jimmy Olsen, (work works) at the *Daily Planet.*
3. My accounting assignment, not to mention my psychology and English homework, (is are) enough to drive me to drink.
4. The Modified American Plan, including transfers and some meals, (is are) still more than I can afford.
5. Every year, at the start of the football season, Lucy, together with Sally, Linus, and Snoopy, (trick tricks) Charlie Brown.
6. My brother, as well as my parents, (want wants) me to move out.
7. The food he serves, along with the drinks he mixes, (is are) delicious.
8. This play, in addition to the ones she wrote in her youth, (is are) guaranteed to put you to sleep.

9. ______________ , like ______________ , ______________ .

10. ____________ , together with ____________ , ____________ .

---

**3. Words ending in *one, thing,* or *body.*** When used as subjects, the following words are always singular, requiring the singular form of the verb:

| | | |
|---|---|---|
| everyone | everything | everybody |
| anyone | anything | anybody |
| someone | something | somebody |
| no one | nothing | nobody |

The last part of the word is the tip-off here: every*one*, any*thing*, no*body*. If you focus on this last part, you'll remember to use a singular verb with these subjects. Usually these words are troublesome only when modifiers crop up between them and their verbs. For example, no one would write "Everyone are here." The trouble starts when you sandwich a bunch of words between the subject and the verb. You might, if you weren't on your toes, write this: "Everyone involved in implementing the company's new policies and procedures are here." Obviously, the meaning is plural: several people are present. But the subject (every*one*) is singular in form, so the verb must be *is*.

## EXERCISE

---

## Exercise 6

Circle the right verb. Then make up two sentences of your own.

1. Everybody on the fourth and fifth floors (was were) questioned by Hercule Poirot.
2. No one who had seen the murderer (was were) found.
3. Everyone, including the landlady's husband, (believe believes) the superintendent did it.
4. Anyone with information leading to an arrest (is are) entitled to a reward.
5. So far, no one but Miss Marple (seem seems) like to try to claim the money.
6. Everything she has discovered, including the clue of the blood-stained letters, (is are) to be revealed tonight.
7. Until then, absolutely nothing in the victim's rooms (is are) to be touched.
8. Nobody (dare dares) question Miss Marple's explanation of the crime.

9. Something ______________________________.

10. Everybody ______________________________.

---

**4. *Each, either (of), neither (of).*** Used as subjects, these take singular verbs.

Either was suitable for the job.

Each wants desperately to win.

Neither of the stores is open after six o'clock. (Remember, the subject is never in a prepositional phrase.)

## EXERCISE

---

## Exercise 7

Circle the right verb. Then make up two sentences of your own.

1. Neither (deserve deserves) a promotion.
2. Either of those dates (is are) fine with me.
3. Neither of the proposals (interest interests) me.
4. Each of the contestants (hope hopes) to be chosen.
5. Either of the wrenches (work works) on that bolt.
6. I am sorry to say that neither (is are) ready to be used.
7. Each of their children (wants want) something different.
8. Neither of his excuses (is are) believable.

9. Either ______________________________.

10. Each ______________________________.

---

**5. Collective nouns.** A collective noun is a word naming a group. Some examples are *company, class, committee, team, crowd, group, family, audience, public,* and *majority.* When you are referring to the group acting as a *unit,* use a *singular* verb. When you are referring to the *members* of the group acting *individually,* use a *plural* verb.

The team is sure to win tomorrow's game. (Here *team* refers to the group acting as a whole.)

The team are getting into their uniforms now. (The separate members of the team are acting individually.)

## EXERCISE

---

### Exercise 8

Circle the correct verb. Then make up two sentences of your own.

1. The nuclear family (is are) the fundamental unit of society.
2. The class (prefer prefers) Frost to Stevens.
3. A majority of airlines now (provide provides) nonsmoking sections.
4. The budget committee (fight fights) among themselves continually.
5. (Has Have) this group reached a consensus?
6. Having waited for almost an hour, the crowd (was were) growing restless.
7. The office (give gives) a farewell party whenever anyone leaves.
8. Last night's audience (was were) delighted with *The Glass Menagerie.*

9. The company ______________________________.

10. The American public ______________________________.

---

**6. Units of money, time, mass, length, and distance.** These require singular verbs.

Four dollars is too much to pay for a hamburger.

Three hours is a long time to wait, and five miles is too far to walk.

One hundred fifty pounds is the weight of an average man.

## EXERCISES

---

### Exercise 9

Circle the correct verb. Then write two sentences of your own.

1. Three hours (seem seems) to pass very quickly when I'm at the movies.
2. Creators of this new diet claim that five pounds (is are) not too much to lose in one week.
3. Ninety-nine cents (seem seems) a fair price.
4. Four thousand dollars (is are) all I need for a fur coat.

5. If you are unprepared, three hours for an exam (seem seems) like an eternity.
6. Three inches (is are) the height of a satisfying sandwich.
7. Five dollars an hour for babysitting (is are) not bad.
8. Seven hours of classes (is are) too much for one day.

9. Eighteen years ________________________________________.

10. One hundred miles ____________________________________.

---

In exercises 10 through 12, correct the error in subject-verb agreement. Check your answers to each set of ten sentences before going on.

---

## Exercise 10

1. The whole committee are in favor of the project.
2. Anybody who really want to will succeed.
3. Over the last ten years, the number of couples who are living together has increased greatly.
4. Every one of the listed topics bore me.
5. The money and benefits available to professional football players are fabulous.
6. If there is no bubbles, then you have patched your tire successfully.
7. Neither Peter nor I is a very strong swimmer.
8. The lack of things to write about cause the headaches.
9. Farrah Fawcett, along with Dolly Parton and Lily Tomlin, have talent as well as beauty.
10. It's not only the cost but also the time wasted that make me unhappy.

---

## Exercise 11

1. The cause of all the noise and confusion were not immediately clear.
2. Tai Chi, like yoga, teaches you to relax.
3. Neither the university nor the community colleges appeals to me.
4. Only three hours of his lecture were interesting.
5. Everybody but witches love Halloween.
6. Four thousand pounds is simply too much for a four-cylinder engine to pull.
7. Every one of the applicants look good to me.
8. This afternoon the class are going to learn some propaganda techniques.

9. Neither the cat nor the dog were willing to help the little red hen, but everybody were eager to eat her bread.
10. Speculation does not occur when the balance of payments are in order.

---

## Exercise 12

1. A handful of companies dominate the American cereal industry.
2. The loss of men and materials were devastating to the enemy.
3. Have either of the teams won a series yet?
4. Experience in programing, together with a willingness to work hard and an ability to get along with others, are required.
5. For years the TV-watching majority has demanded the return of shows like "As the World Turns" and "Search for Tomorrow."
6. Ten years in prison seem like a very harsh penalty.
7. In any crowd of several hundred people, there are bound to be a handful or two of unruly boors.
8. Absolutely everyone, my girlfriend and my mother included, not to mention my closest friends, have advised me not to pursue my musical career.
9. It is not necessarily true that statements made about one identical twin applies with equal validity to the other.
10. Walt Disney's dream, embodied in part in two world-famous amusement parks, was to offer entertainment to "children" from 9 to 90. Disneyland, in California, and Disney World, in Florida, links the West with the East in enjoyment of that dream.

---

Complete the sentences in exercises 13 and 14 using present-tense verbs. After doing each set of ten sentences, check in the answer section to see whether your verbs should be singular or plural.

---

## Exercise 13

1. Neither my boss nor the receptionist ______________________________

2. Everybody with two or more pets ______________________________

3. Not the plasterer but the electricians ______________________________

4. A flock of birds ______________________________

5. Every one of his employees ______________________________

6. Two thousand pounds ______________________________

7. The entire book, including the index and the appendices, ________

______________________________________________

8. The lead guitarist, like the drummer, ____________________

9. Either rock or disco ______________________________

10. No one among the hundreds present ____________________

______________________________________________

## Exercise 14

1. The audience ______________________________

2. The bill, including tip and taxes, ____________________

3. Part of the cost ______________________________

4. Either Henry or his customers ____________________

5. A survey of fourteen consumers ____________________

6. Each of the band members ____________________

7. An hour and fifteen minutes ____________________

8. Wayne and Shuster, together with Harvey Korman, __________

______________________________________________

9. The minority ______________________________

10. Each and every one of you ____________________

______________________________________________

## Exercise 15

Write your own sentences, choosing your subjects as indicated and using present-tense verbs.

1. Use a collective noun as subject.

______________________________________________

2. Use a compound subject.

---

3. Use *no one* as your subject.

---

4. Use *everybody* as your subject.

---

5. Use *neither . . . nor*.

---

6. Use *not . . . but*.

---

7. Use a collective noun as singular subject.

---

8. Use a collective noun as plural subject.

---

9. Use your own height as subject.

---

10. Use a compound subject joined by *or*.

---

---

## Exercise 16

As a final check on your mastery of subject-verb agreement, correct the following sentences.

1. The comical antics of the Muppets captures the attention of young viewers.
2. The multitude of choices that are offered are extraordinary.

3. Everyone I know except my parents adore Mick Jagger.
4. The cost of new homes are rising every day.
5. My sense of fear and foreboding were irrational but very strong.
6. Every one of us, at one time or another, have expressed views on the subject.
7. Some people believe that violence and sex is evil.
8. For the dieter, all those luscious and fattening desserts on display is enough to drive one crazy.
9. There seems to be much drinking and partying going on next door.
10. The variety of shows available at the flick of a switch are practically limitless.
11. The controversy surrounding these matters lead to time-consuming debate.
12. A free press is one of the most important rights the people of a democratic society possesses.
13. When the channels for expressing conflicting opinions disappears, so does justice.
14. High mortgage rates, high real-estate prices, and low interest in gardening is causing young couples to put off buying homes.
15. But nobody, neither driver nor taxi user, neither police officer nor civic official, are happy about these latest reforms.

# Chapter 11

# Pronoun-Antecedent Agreement

The title of this chapter may be formidable, but the idea is really very simple. **Pronouns** are words that substitute for, or refer to, the name of a person or thing. The word that a pronoun substitutes for, or refers, to is called the **antecedent.**

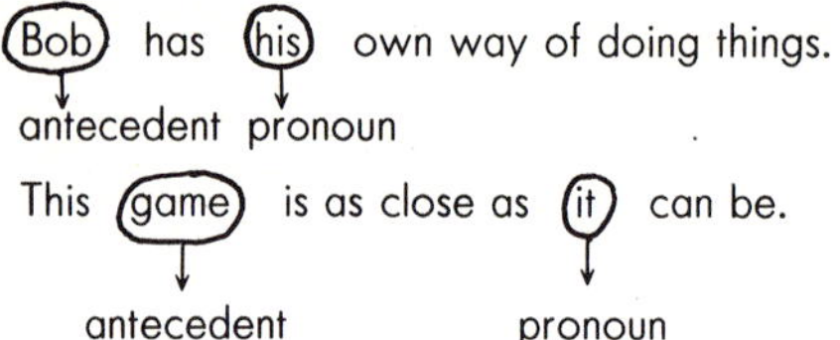


The basic rule to remember is this:

> A pronoun must agree with its antecedent.

You probably follow this rule most of the time without even realizing that you know it. For example, you would never write

Bob has *its* own way of doing things.

*or*

This game is as close as *he* can be.

because you know that these pronouns don't agree with these antecedents. There are three aspects of pronoun usage, however, that you need to be careful about. The first is how to use the relative pronouns—*which, that, who,* and *whom:*

> *Who* and *whom* are always used to refer to people.
> *That* and *which* refer to everything else.

The man *who* was hurt had to quit climbing.
The women *who* were present voted unanimously.
The cocker spaniel *that* I met looked hostile.
Her car, *which* is imported, is smaller than cars *that* are built here.
The man *whom* the committee had decided to hire refused the job.

By the way, if you aren't sure whether to use *who* or *whom,* you can often rewrite the sentence so that you don't need either one: "The man the committee had decided to hire refused the job."

## EXERCISE

---

### Exercise 1

Correct the following sentences where necessary. Answers begin on p. 276.

1. Is this the dog who bit the mail carrier that carries a squirt gun?
2. The path that I took led me past the home of a hermit, which lived all alone in the forest that surrounded our town.
3. The goal that came at 15:45 of the third period was scored by a player that I used to know at high school.
4. That can't be Janice O'Toole, the little girl that I used to bounce on my knee!
5. The building that we entered next was owned by the company who employed my father.
6. He is the man that I turn to whenever I feel depressed because of something my sister has said or done.
7. The open-concept office is one that makes sense to anyone who has worked in a stuffy little cubicle all day.
8. The four tests that we wrote today would have defeated anyone that wasn't prepared for them.
9. The wind whistled around the cabin, against whom they had

propped their skis while waiting to see whether the skiers which they had passed earlier could catch up.

10. An advantage of the open-concept office is that it lets you see which people are working hard and which are taking it easy. It also allows you to spot women that you'd like to meet.

---

The second tricky aspect of pronoun-antecedent agreement concerns words and phrases that you learned about in chapter 10—words and phrases ending in *-one, -body,* and *-thing:*

| | | |
|---|---|---|
| everyone | everybody | everything |
| anyone | anybody | anything |
| someone | somebody | something |
| no one | nobody | nothing |
| none | | |
| each (one) | | |
| every one | | |

In chapter 10, you learned that when these words are used as subjects, they are singular and take singular verbs. So it makes sense that the pronouns that stand for, or refer to, them must be singular.

> Antecedents ending in *-one, -body,* and *-thing* are singular and must be referred to by singular pronouns: *he, she, it, his, her, its.*

Everyone is expected to do *his* duty.
Each of the students must supply *his* or *her* own lunch.
Every mother deserves a break from *her* routine.
No one can truly say in *his* heart that *he* believes otherwise.

The his/her question deserves mention. Often you will see *his* and *he* used to indicate both sexes in sentences like the first and fourth above. If you find this usage upsetting, rewrite the sentences to avoid the problem.

We are all expected to do our duty.
No one can honestly believe otherwise.

It is wrong to write

Everyone is expected to do their duty.
No one can truly say in their heart that they believe otherwise.

Another problem involves sentences that are grammatically correct but sound awkward:

If anyone is at the door, he'll have to knock louder.
Everyone arrives on time, but he leaves early.

It is wrong to write

If anyone is at the door, they'll have to knock louder.
Everyone arrives on time, but they leave early.

So, in order to make the sentences sound better, you need to rewrite them. Here is one way:

Anyone who is at the door will have to knock louder.
Everyone arrives on time but leaves early.

In speech it has become acceptable to use plural pronouns with *-one, -body,* and *-thing* antecedents. Although these antecedents are singular and take singular verbs, often they are plural in meaning, and in conversation we find ourselves saying

Everyone clapped *their* hands with glee.
No one has to stay if *they* don't want to.

This rule bending is also used to avoid the *his/her* problem.

Someone lost *their* coat.

This usage may be acceptable in conversation; *it is not acceptable in written Standard English.*

## EXERCISE

---

## Exercise 2

Choose the correct word from the pair in parentheses. Check your answers before continuing.

1. No one I know would allow (his their) name to stand on the ballot.
2. Each of us prefers to answer the charges for (herself themselves).
3. Everyone wants to be considered an expert in (his their) own subject.
4. If we all try to do our best, each will find (his their) reward in a job well done.
5. Dogs and cats show (its their) affection for (its their) masters in vastly different ways.
6. All of the club members will have to contribute all (he they) can if no one is able to get (his their) parents to finance the trip.
7. Somebody is lying to cover up (his their) own guilt.

8. None of the pictures he took could be called great by (itself themselves), but together they made a stunning collection.
9. Each student must decide for (himself themselves) whether (he they) wants to be popular, successful, or happy, because it is unlikely that (he they) will be all three at once during the college years.
10. Ladies and gentlemen, whoever (he they) may be, must learn certain basic rules of behavior so that no one can criticize (him them) in later life for ignorance.

---

Avoiding the third difficulty with pronoun-antecedent agreement depends on your common sense and your ability to think of your reader. If you try to look at your writing from your reader's point of view, it is unlikely that you will break this rule:

> A pronoun must *clearly* refer to the correct antecedent.

The mistake that occurs when you fail to follow this rule is called **vague reference:**

Sam pointed to his brother and said that he had saved his life.

Who saved whom? Here's another:

Jackie felt that Helen should have been more careful with her car when she lent it to her because she was a good friend of her husband.

Who owns the car? Who has the husband?

In these sentences you can only guess about the meaning, because you don't know who is being referred to by the pronouns. You can make these sentences less confusing by using proper names more often and changing the sentences around. Try it on our examples.

Another type of vague reference occurs when a pronoun doesn't have an antecedent at all.

He loves watching fast cars and would like to do it himself someday.
(Do what?)

Bicycling is her favorite pastime, but she still doesn't own one.
(One what?)

How would you revise these sentences?

Be sure that pronouns have clear antecedents, with which they agree in number. That, in a nutshell (see "Clichés," p. 208), is the rule of thumb for pronoun-antecedent agreement.

# EXERCISES

## Exercise 3

Correct the following sentences where necessary. In some cases, a perfectly correct answer of yours will differ from the answer we've given. That's because the reference was so vague that the sentence could be understood in more than one way.

1. Max is a good skater, which he practices daily.
2. He didn't hear her cry for help, which was due to his wearing earplugs.
3. That Mr. Cohen would be Stephen's teacher never occurred to him.
4. It seemed that every time he looked at the donkey he brayed.
5. Management refused to allow a cost-of-living clause, which is why the union walked out.
6. He told his brother he would soon get a job.
7. Whenever Ann and Carol met, she acted in a very friendly way so that no one would suspect that she hated her.
8. Joe told Henry that he was losing his hair.
9. Matthew threw his calculator on the floor and dented it.
10. This letter is in response to your ad for a waitress and bartender, male or female. Being both, I wish to apply for the position.

## Exercise 4

Correct the following sentences where necessary. Check your answers before continuing.

1. Anyone that has finished all his homework by now can't have done it properly.
2. This is a beaten team; none of the players cares any more whether he performs well.
3. Everybody I know is going, even if they can't get a date.
4. Each of my roommates finally left to find an apartment of their own.
5. I'd like to meet someone that is tall, dark, handsome, and rich; in fact, they don't even have to be tall, dark, or handsome.
6. Here everybody is allowed to find their own path to success, according to what they consider success to be.
7. The book tries to prove that nobody can rise above their own level of ability without the help of friends.

8. Constant nagging would make anyone lose their mind unless they learned to ignore it.
9. Somebody that has many friends will have to go; they will need friends if they hope to return.
10. Everyone likes to think that they're unique, but each of us is their own idea of perfect, so in fact we are all the same.

---

## Exercise 5

Correct these sentences where necessary. Then check your answers.

1. Each of the cars has their own faults, but nobody else wants this one, so I'll take it.
2. Every child is a product of their environment as well as their parentage.
3. They will get help from no one, since everybody has left in her own car.
4. The men which made up the team agreed that everybody would have to complete their assignment.
5. Writing is what he does best, although he hasn't been able to complete one lately.
6. She'll put her to bed now because she is short-tempered.
7. Everyone must get in their places for the game to begin.
8. Anybody that is without a partner will have to be sure she finds one which is about her height.
9. Neither the jacket nor the pants fits the way it should.
10. He said he wasn't trying hard enough and that anyone who said he was would get a punch on their nose.

---

# Chapter 12

# Tense Agreement

Verbs are time markers. The different tenses are used to express differences in time:

I (was fired) two weeks ago; I (hope) I (will find) a new job soon.
past — present — future

Sometimes, as in the sentence above, it is necessary to use several different tenses in a single sentence to get the meaning across. But usually, whether you're writing a sentence, a paragraph, an essay, or a report, you will use *one tense throughout.* Normally you will choose either the past or the present tense. Here is the rule to follow:

> Don't change tense unless the meaning requires the change.

Readers like and expect consistency. If you begin a sentence with "I kicked and screamed and protested," the reader will tune in to the past-tense verbs and expect any other verbs in the sentence to be in the past tense, too. Therefore, if you finish the sentence with " . . . but he looks at me with those big blue eyes and gets me to take him to the dance," the reader will be abruptly jolted out of one time frame and into another. This sort of jolting is uncomfortable, and readers don't like it.

Shifting tenses is like shifting gears: it should be done smoothly and when necessary—never abruptly, out of carelessness, or on a whim. Avoid causing verbal whiplash: keep your tenses consistent.

*Wrong:* He kicked a stone from his path as he rambles up the winding driveway.

*Right:* He kicked a stone from his path as he rambled up the winding driveway.

*Also right:* He kicks a stone from his path as he rambles up the winding driveway.

*Wrong:* She hesitated but then began to climb the steps. Suddenly she hears a low groan.

*Right:* She hesitated but then began to climb the steps. Suddenly she heard a low groan.

*Also right:* She hesitates but then begins to climb the steps. Suddenly she hears a low groan.

## EXERCISES

Most of the following sentences contain unnecessary tense shifts. Use the first verb in each sentence as your time marker, and change the tense(s) of the other verb(s) in the sentence to agree with it. If you get exercise 1 entirely correct, skip ahead to exercise 4. Answers begin on p. 278.

---

### Exercise 1

1. He goes home and told her what happened.
2. He was so successful that he's offered a promotion.
3. The plane was chartered, the bags were packed, and the champagne is on ice.
4. The referee stands there, blinking, unable to believe what he was seeing.
5. The serviceman returned home from Southeast Asia for his furlough, but nobody in town seemed happy to see him.
6. As Castro stepped forward to speak, the crowd begins to clap, stamp, and whistle.
7. First you will fry the onions; then you brown the meat.
8. Mount Rushmore, South Dakota, was the site that Gutzon Borglum selects for his gigantic granite sculptures of George Washington, Thomas Jefferson, Abraham Lincoln, and Theodore Roosevelt.
9. "Safety colors" are bright and will attract immediate attention.
10. It was not until the sixteenth century, when Leonardo designs his flying machine, that flight begins.

---

## Exercise 2

1. Drill the holes for the speakers; then you'll cut a hole in the dashboard.
2. The coach went over the game and carefully analyzes the plays.
3. The Peter Principle states that every person will rise to his or her level of incompetence.
4. The couple next door had a boa constrictor that keeps getting loose.
5. He began by asking a rhetorical question that he proceeds to answer.
6. First he buys me chocolates when he knows I'm on a diet; then he embarrassed me by kissing me in front of everyone.
7. While our team suffered one defeat after another, the other teams rejoice.
8. The town seemed fast asleep as he drove along Main Street.
9. The new employee was too inexperienced to do the job in the time she's given.
10. If a player hits another player or knocks him down, he would get a warning.

## Exercise 3

1. Prejudice is learned and will be hard to outgrow.
2. I studied so hard for that test, and look at the reward I get!
3. If you will just keep your eyes and ears open, you learn something new every day.
4. After I had already put the car away, I realize Ann is still waiting for me at school.
5. The guard didn't say anything. He just stands there and stares at us.
6. If you would include an example here, the explanation is much easier to follow.
7. He kept trying to reach me for weeks, but he didn't know I've moved.
8. Her argument became silly when she goes on to suggest that watching television weakened the genes.
9. In the belief that playing pool was somehow good for his health, he plays at least two hours every day.
10. In the dead of night, while coyotes howled in the distance, someone—or some*thing*—is prowling in the dark recesses of the cave.

## Exercise 4

Correct the faulty tense shifts in the following passage.[1] When you're done, compare your paragraphs with the author's original version in the answer section.

The first time I began to sneeze, a friend tells me to go and bathe my feet in hot water and go to bed. I did so. Shortly afterward, another friend advises me to get up and take a cold shower. I do that also. Within the hour, another friend assures me that it was policy to "feed a cold and starve a fever." I had both. So I thought it best to fill myself up for the cold, then let the fever starve awhile.

I ate pretty heartily [I went to the restaurant of a man who has just opened for business that morning]; he waited near me in respectful silence untill I finish feeding my cold, when he inquires if the people about Virginia City are much afflicted with colds. I tell him I thought they were. He then goes out and takes in his sign.

I started down toward the office, and on the way encounter another bosom friend, who tells me that a quart of salt-water, taken warm, would come as near curing a cold as anything in the world. I hardly thought I had room for it, but I try it anyhow. The result was surprising. I believed I had thrown up my immortal soul. . . . If I have another cold in the head and no course left me but to take either an earthquake or a quart of warm salt-water, I would take my chances on the earthquake.

## Exercise 5

The following passage[2] is written in the present tense. Rewrite the passage, changing the verbs to the past tense. Your first sentence will begin "The fisherman returned after his day's outing. . . ." Compare your version with the one given in the answer section.

The fisherman returns after his day's outing with his two friends whom he has taken out for the day, to his summer cottage. They carry with them their rods, their landing net, and the paraphernalia of their profession. The fisherman carries also on a string a dirty looking collection of little fish, called by courtesy the "Catch." The fisherman's wife and his wife's sister and the young lady who is staying with them come running to meet the fishing party, giving cries of admiration as they get a sight of the catch. In reality they would refuse to buy those fish from a butcher at a cent and a half a pound. But they fall into ecstasies, and they cry, "Oh, aren't they beauties! Look at this big one!" The "big one" is about eight inches long . . . and looks . . . as if it had died of consumption.

[1]Adapted from Mark Twain, "Curing a Cold," in *The Complete Humorous Sketches and Tales of Mark Twain*, ed. Charles Neider (New York: Doubleday, 1961), pp. 25–26.

[2]Adapted from Stephen Leacock, *The Everlasting Angler*. Reprinted by permission of The Canadian Publishers, McClelland and Stewart Limited, Toronto.

# Chapter 13

# Person Agreement

There are three categories of "person" that you can use when you write or speak:

**first person:** I, we
**second person:** you (singular and plural)
**third person:** he, she, one, someone, they

Here is the rule for person agreement:

| Do not mix "persons" unless meaning requires it. |
| --- |

In other words, you must be consistent: if you begin a discussion in second person, you must use second person all the way through. Look at this sentence:

If *you* wish to succeed, *one* must work hard.

This is the most common error—mixing second-person *you* with third-person *one.* Here's another example:

*One* can live happily in Alaska if *you* have a very warm coat.

We can correct this error by using the second person throughout . . .

> *You* can live happily in Alaska if *you* have a very warm coat.

. . . or by using the third person throughout:

> *One* can live happily in Alaska if *one* has a very warm coat.
>
> *or*
>
> *One* can live happily in Alaska if *he* has a very warm coat.

These last three sentences raise two points of style that you should be aware of:

1. Although these three versions are equally correct, they sound somewhat different from one another. The second sentence, with its two *one*'s, sounds the most formal—even a little stilted. Don't overuse *one.* The sentence in the second person sounds the most informal and natural—like something you would say. The third sentence is between the other two in formality and is the one you'd be most likely to use in writing for school or business.

2. As we noted in chapter 11, the pronoun *he* is generally used to represent both sexes. If this usage bothers you, you can sometimes substitute *he or she:*

> A person can live happily in Alaska if he or she has a very warm coat.

But if *he or she* occurs too frequently, the sentence becomes very awkward:

> A student can easily pass this course if he or she applies himself or herself to his or her studies.

You can fix sentences like these by switching the *whole sentence* to plural:

> Students can easily pass this course if they apply themselves to their studies.

## EXERCISES

---

### Exercise 1

Choose the correct word from the brackets for each of the following sentences. Check your answers on p. 280 before continuing.

1. One who works hard will usually succeed, even if (you they he) may be without talent.
2. A great burden is lifted from one's shoulders by the realization that (you he they) will be accepted.
3. Any girl could be popular if (you one she) would use Beautifem Products!
4. You'd do better if (you one he) were to try harder.

5. If one reads the instructions, (you I one) will have no more difficulty.
6. Anyone who helps will get (your their his) reward.
7. No member of this team needs to feel that (you she) didn't try as hard as (you she) could.
8. A survey of the problem shows that (he it) could have been solved earlier if corrective measures had been taken.
9. When we came up for air, (you we he one) couldn't see land!
10. If you get pneumonia, (one you he) should rest completely and follow a doctor's orders.

---

Correct the following sentences where necessary. Check your answers to each set of ten before going on.

---

## Exercise 2

1. You mustn't upset the instructor if one wishes to leave class on time.
2. Anyone going to the class party can pick up your tickets now.
3. Men who don't think women are their equals may have to get used to living on your own.
4. Americans don't seem to realize that the situation may get out of hand if you don't vote wisely.
5. One must try to control your temper when you feel frustrated or angry.
6. When he pushed me into the water, I pulled him in after me.
7. Everyone is going to get what they deserve.
8. If one is convicted on that charge, a fine is the least of your worries.
9. After we had driven about 300 miles, you could feel the sleepiness begin to weight our eyelids.
10. One who is unable to cope with pressure must expect to be replaced when he has demonstrated his incompetence.

---

## Exercise 3

1. A great way to develop one's skills is to push yourself to the limit.
2. Everyone who wants more from life must stand up and shout your name as loudly as you can.
3. Americans who travel abroad should remember you're representing your country.
4. Following one's hunch can lead to disaster—or to an easy solution to your problem.

5. Once you have been elected to the Senate, one should always remember that he is in the public eye.
6. In this country, one receives more acclaim as a baseball player than you do as a symphony conductor.
7. Anyone who drives one of those things should be aware of the risk you're taking.
8. You'll never find a place to live that's perfect for your lifestyle, even if you search from here to Kalamazoo.
9. Can one really be happy if you don't own an electric pencil sharpener?
10. Why must people always want something they don't have, even when you have more than you'll ever need?

---

## Exercise 4

1. I enjoy living in the country, because there one doesn't have to deal with traffic or pollution, and you can always get to the city if you want to.
2. One never really knows whether she's joking or not, do you?
3. I collect art because you can always get your money back on the investment, and one can sometimes make a killing.
4. No one can help him, because if you try, one is quickly and rudely rebuffed.
5. Americans who vacation in Canada should take the opportunity to add to your collection of china at bargain prices.
6. A high school graduate who can't construct a proper sentence ought to be ashamed of yourself.
7. One can't go around picking up after one's sloppy relatives all day, can you?
8. When we left the hotel's air-conditioned comfort, the heat knocked you over.
9. Entomology may seem dull to one who doesn't know much about it, but to one who is fascinated by the unusual and the eccentric it can be a gold mine of wonderful facts.
10. An expert wine taster will find this a very acceptable vintage, and even one who knows little about wine will enjoy yourself with a bottle or two.

---

## Exercise 5

This exercise will test and reinforce your understanding of both tense agreement and person agreement. Correct the following sentences where necessary.

1. When you're bright, talented, and rich, one doesn't really have to try very hard to impress one's elders, especially if you were also handsome.
2. Two years ago, we went for a long canoe trip in Yosemite National Park. We are amazed by the beauty of the country, especially the spectacular mountains. You learn quickly why many artists have found inspiration there.
3. You can't beat a charcoal grill for preparing great hamburgers in the summertime. One got so tired of pan-fried meat patties all winter long.
4. Now that spring is here, we are looking forward to doing all the outdoor things that we missed in the winter. You really don't get out as much as one should when it's cold, but we were going to make up for that now.
5. You can't truly enjoy a sport unless you know the basic rules. How can one understand the game unless you know what's going on?
6. One mustn't push him too far, because he will either lose his temper or become hysterical, and that isn't what you want.
7. Our opinion is that there is not a better spot in town to meet for a quiet, inexpensive lunch. We get good service, which you don't find very often, and one finds the bill tolerable as well.
8. It was as though she had turned on a light: suddenly we all get the idea. You can't wait to get your hand in the air to tell the others what you had discovered.
9. Finally we were out of debt. Years of hard work and sacrifice had left one tired and somewhat bitter, but the feeling of accomplishment at that moment made you feel it was all worth it.
10. I can hardly believe I climbed it. Often one gets so tired that you want to give up.

---

## Exercise 6

Choose the right word from those in parentheses:

People who get married while (they're one is) still in college may have an especially hard time completing (your their one's) studies. If both spouses are in school, (they he or she one) may not have enough money for an apartment, and they may have to live with (one's your their) parents for a while. Students whose spouses work may find (oneself themselves himself) studying on weekends while (their his or her one's) spouses rest or socialize. The wife who supports a student husband, along with the husband who supports a student wife, may find that the responsibility weighs heavily on (him her them). Anyone in such a situation would be likely to feel at the end of (their your his) wits sometimes, so students whose marriages are shaky may find that (one is they are you are) having a very hard time of it and that (you their one's) schoolwork is suffering. On the other hand, these various demands may strengthen a marriage, and a student who marries may find that (their  one's  his or her) motivation to succeed at school has increased. Some married students may even find (themselves himself oneself) studying more, using the time (they he one) would otherwise have spent dating.

---

## Exercise 7

Think of the most important experience you've ever had. (If you don't like important, try thrilling or frightening.) Write an account of this experience, telling your story in the third person (that is, instead of using *I*, use *he* or *she*). When you've completed your work, reread it carefully. Check your spelling. Check your sentence structure. Check carefully subject-verb, pronoun-antecedent, tense, and person agreement.

---

# UNIT FOUR

# Punctuation

# Chapter 14

# The Question Mark

Everyone knows that a question mark follows an interrogative, or asking, sentence, but we all sometimes forget about it. Let this chapter simply serve as a reminder not to forget!

> The question mark is the end punctuation for all interrogative sentences.

The question mark gives the reader an important clue to the meaning of your sentence.

> There's more?

is vastly different in meaning from

> There's more!

and that difference is communicated to the reader by the punctuation alone.

The only time you don't end a question with a question mark is when the question is part of a statement.

> Are you going? (question)
> I asked whether you are going. (statement)

Do you know them? (question)
I wonder whether you know them. (statement)

## EXERCISES

---

### Exercise 1

Put a check next to the sentences that have correct end punctuation. Turn to p. 283 to check your answers before going on.

1. _______ Why do I have to be the one to go.
2. _______ Jim wanted to know whether the class picture is ready for the yearbook?
3. _______ Is there intelligent life on Mars?
4. _______ Some people wonder whether there is intelligent life on earth.
5. _______ Can't you make him be quiet?
6. _______ There is some question as to whether Jason is capable of passing typing?
7. _______ How do they get the whipped cream inside the cake without leaving a hole in the cake.
8. _______ If chess is such a good game, why do so few people play?
9. _______ There is still a chance, isn't there?
10. _______ If they get a new pitcher, they could have a winning season.

---

### Exercise 2

Put a check next to the sentences that have correct end punctuation. Check your answers before going on.

1. _______ Who's at the door?
2. _______ I'm a better actress than she is, don't you think?
3. _______ Haven't you done enough damage for one day.
4. _______ I question the fairness of the marking in this course?
5. _______ The others can do it, so why can't I?
6. _______ I wonder whether they will arrive on time.
7. _______ Jill asked about the price of a new car?
8. _______ If ever there was a time for action, it's now?
9. _______ Although I've talked it over with the teacher many times, and thought about it often, I still don't understand why sociology is so important in a business course?

10. ______ Have you ever considered all the different types of people you'll have to deal with every day in that line of work.

---

## Exercise 3

Supply the correct end punctuation for these sentences. Then check your answers.

1. I'd like to help, but I don't know what I could do
2. Kim will be in real trouble if you don't admit you were wrong
3. Why is there always a cop around when I'm speeding, but never when I need help
4. Cut the lawn this morning, or you'll have to stay home tonight
5. It's a tough way to make a living, isn't it
6. It's not so bad if you keep up to date and don't let the marking get you down
7. If there were a different course available, I'd take it
8. When will the weather clear up so we can start our trip
9. Can't we go any faster in this old wreck
10. Take a look around you sometime and see for yourself whether I'm right

---

# Chapter 15

# The Exclamation Mark

The exclamation mark can be a most valuable piece of punctuation for conveying your tone of voice to the reader. There is a distinct difference in tone between these two sentences:

> There's a man behind you.
>
> There's a man behind you!

In the first case, a piece of information is being supplied, possibly about the lineup at a grocery-store checkout counter. The second sentence might be a shouted warning about a mugger in the back seat of a car.

> Use an exclamation mark as end punctuation in sentences requiring extreme emphasis or dramatic effect.

The only way that the exclamation mark can have any punch or drama is if you use it sparingly. If you use an exclamation mark after every third sentence, how will your reader know when you really mean to indicate excitement? The overuse of the exclamation mark is a result of too much comic-book reading. The writers of comics use the exclamation mark after every sentence to try to heighten the impact of their characters' words. Instead, they've robbed their exclamation marks of all meaning.

Practically any sentence may have an exclamation mark after it, but remember that the punctuation changes the meaning of the sentence. Read the following sentences with and without an exclamation mark, and picture the situation that would call for each reading.

| | |
|---|---|
| He's gone | Don't touch that button |
| The room was empty | There she goes again |

## EXERCISES

### Exercise 1

Supply the correct end punctuation for these sentences. In many cases, the punctuation you use will depend on how you want the sentence to be read. Notice the extent to which different punctuation can change the meaning of a sentence. Answers are on p. 283.

1. Why is everything always so difficult for me
2. Why, it's my long-lost brother
3. I dare you
4. Could they have known about Carol and me before they saw us at the drive-in
5. There's another way
6. You aren't paying attention to what I'm saying, are you
7. Where Wilson goes, trouble is sure to follow
8. How he manages to get dates with such gorgeous women, I can't imagine
9. When you say there's going to be trouble, what do you mean
10. They descended on the newly opened department store with the battle cry, "Charge it"

### Exercise 2

Provide each of these sentences with appropriate end punctuation—an exclamation mark, question mark, or period.

1. Who can we turn to now that the deadline has passed
2. There's a fly in my soup
3. Help          Where are the lifeguards when you need them
4. I wonder where the twins went

5. Can't we go outside to play Absolutely not
6. The sky is falling
7. Where once there was hope, now there is only fear
8. Has the winner been declared Hooray
9. I can't believe it The thing actually flies
10. What good will that do Why don't you try another brand

---

# Chapter 16

# The Colon

The colon functions as an "introducer." When a statement is followed by a list or by one or more examples, the colon between the statement and what follows alerts the reader to what is coming.

> We have only two choices: for and against.
>
> There are three things I can't stand: brussels sprouts, cats, and Robert Redford's films.
>
> One person prevented her rise to wealth and fame: herself.

*The statement that precedes the colon must be a complete sentence (independent clause).* Therefore, a colon can never come after *is* or *are.* For example, the use of the colon in the sentence

> Two things I cannot stand are: cats and brussels sprouts.

is incorrect because the statement before the colon is not a complete sentence.

The colon, then, follows a complete statement and introduces a list or example that defines or amplifies something in the statement. The information after the colon very often answers the question "what?" or "who?"

There is a new danger to consider: (what?) inflation.

He peered into the clear water to see his favorite friend: (who?) himself.

The colon is also used after a complete sentence introducing a quotation.

Irving Layton is not fond of academic critics: "There hasn't been a writer of power and originality during the past century who hasn't had to fight his way to acceptance against the educated pipsqueaks hibernating in universities." [Layton, in a letter to *The Montreal Star*]

The use of the colon can be summed up as follows:

> The colon follows an independent clause and introduces one of three things: examples, a list, or a quotation.

## EXERCISES

### Exercise 1

Put a check next to the sentences that are correctly punctuated. Check your answers on p. 284 before going on.

1. ______ Two of the most common causes of failure are laziness and lack of self-discipline.
2. ______ Only one thing was needed: a boat.
3. ______ He tried three different tactics: phone calls, flowers, and flattery.
4. ______ On the list we must include: chips, mix, ice, and peanuts.
5. ______ The instructor's first words were not encouraging: "Half of you are going to fail, and the other half won't get jobs."
6. ______ Three qualities of a good quarterback are: leadership, intelligence, and physical strength.
7. ______ There are two things that every ambitious person strives for: money and power.
8. ______ The pond is: deep and cold.
9. ______ Dogs have many qualities that make them superior to cats; loyalty, intelligence, working ability, and friendliness.
10. ______ Let me give you an example, Abraham Lincoln.

## Exercise 2

Put a check next to the sentences that are correctly punctuated. Check your answers before going on to exercise 3.

1. _______ I'd like to help: but I can't.
2. _______ I'll take the following volunteers, John, Susan, David, and Colin.
3. _______ We'll have to go back to get: tent poles, matches, and paddles.
4. _______ Two very good card games are bridge and canasta.
5. _______ The debate will be lively if they choose a certain topic: religion.
6. _______ No one wants to go with him, for two very good reasons money and time.
7. _______ He's involved in all types of athletics: skiing, hiking, hockey, and football, to name a few.
8. _______ My boss is so mean she must be: bitter or crazy.
9. _______ She won more medals at the Games than we expected: two gold and a bronze.
10. _______ They were unlucky twice: when they bought that car and when they sold it.

## Exercise 3

Insert colons in the following sentences where necessary, and then check your answers. If you find you've made any mistakes, review the explanation, and be sure you understand why your answers were wrong.

1. You'll succeed only if you win the lottery or marry money.
2. They finally realized there was only one course open to them obedience.
3. Gary had trouble with his canoe it tipped over and then sank.
4. There is someone who can save us, though, Captain America!
5. He tossed and turned all night and found the same images recurring in his dreams a river and a wolf.
6. His body was beyond the point of exhaustion, but he tried to force himself on by thinking of one thing victory.
7. They tried to make ends meet by making their own candles, soap, and butter.
8. I have a very large garden, but it grows only two things tomatoes and weeds.

9. She has one goal that she is determined to achieve the world record.
10. Two issues remained to be settled wages and benefits.

---

## Exercise 4

Correct the incorrectly punctuated sentences in exercise 1.

---

## Exercise 5

Correct the incorrectly punctuated sentences in exercise 2.

---

# Chapter 17

# The Comma

The comma is the most frequently used and the most frequently misused punctuation mark. The omission of a necessary comma can distort the meaning of a sentence. Unnecessary commas can distract the reader and give your sentences a jerky quality. Perhaps nothing is so sure a sign of a competent writer as the correct use of commas, so it is very important that you master them. This chapter presents four rules that will give you a good indication of when you should use commas. If a sentence you are writing is not covered by one of the four rules, and if you aren't sure whether a comma is needed, remember this:

| When in doubt, leave it out! |
|---|

## Four Comma Rules

Here's the first rule:

| Use commas to separate items in a series of three or more. |
|---|

Required subjects are math, English, bookkeeping, and business law.

Walk up the hill, turn left, go two blocks, and you'll be there.

Henry went to the show, Joan went home in tears, Norah and Phil talked until dawn, and I went upstairs to bed.

## EXERCISES

---

### Exercise 1

Insert commas where necessary in the following sentences. Check your answers on p. 285.

1. Careful investment of money and time can lead to wealth fame and happiness.
2. Cats and dogs make the best pets.
3. Does anyone fail to remember John Paul George and Ringo?
4. Country-music fans and rock fans sat side by side and enjoyed the music.
5. Cutting the lawn washing the dishes and doing the shopping are my least favorite activities.
6. Cleopatra Casanova Rasputin and Brigitte Bardot are four dissimilar people who have at least one thing in common.
7. He is an all-around athlete who enjoys many sports: skating skiing cycling riding and hunting.
8. She has strong ambition a cool head good health and an inquiring mind; everyone hates her.
9. He really wants to get married, but he can't decide between Cheryl and Farrah.
10. Many Americans see Canada as a land where only French is spoken ice and snow are year-round hazards and violent hockey is the only pastime.

---

Here is the second rule:

> Use comma(s) to separate from the rest of the sentence any word or expression that is not *essential* to the sentence's meaning or that means the same as something else in the sentence.

Writing business letters isn't difficult, if you're careful.

The phrase "if you're careful" is not essential to the meaning of the sentence, so it's separated from the rest of the sentence by a comma.

> Harry Houdini, one of the world's greatest escape artists, died on Halloween, 1926, and promised on his deathbed to free himself from the grave.

The phrase "one of the world's greatest escape artists" means the same as "Harry Houdini." The two expressions refer to the same person, so the second is set off by commas. When a nonessential word or phrase occurs in the middle of a sentence, rather than at the beginning or the end, be sure to put commas *both* before and after it.

> If it were up to me, Judy, I'd hire you right now.

The word "Judy," the name of the person spoken to, is unnecessary to the meaning of the sentence, so it's set off by commas.

## EXERCISE

---

### Exercise 2

Insert commas where necessary in the following sentences. Check your answers before going on.

1. He is you know one of our best teachers.
2. If my favorite team wins football is the sport I like best.
3. You'll have to do better than that Steve if you want to join us.
4. Despite her reputation, she is we have found out fairly bright.
5. Listening to music is a perfect way to relax after a tough day at school.
6. Where will you go now Heather?
7. Baseball games despite the huge increases in seat prices are still always sold out in my hometown.
8. The bride in a departure from tradition wore a yellow pants suit.
9. We tried all of us to be of some help.
10. One of my favorite writers is Tom Wolfe the man who wrote the book *The Electric Kool Aid Acid Test.*

---

The third rule is as follows:

> Place a comma between independent clauses when they are joined by these transition words: **and, or, so, nor, but, for,** and **yet.**

It was a good party, but last year's was better.
I'm not speaking to her, so you'll have to tell her.
I can't make it to class, yet I feel I should go.
Ross is a good student, for he studies hard.

When applying this rule, be sure your sentence contains *complete independent clauses*, not just a single subject with a multiple verb. (See pages 50–51 for discussion of multiple subjects and verbs.)

*independent clauses:* We ate very well in Paris, and both of us gained five pounds.

*single subject with multiple verb:* We ate very well in Paris and gained five pounds.

## EXERCISE

### Exercise 3

Insert commas where necessary in the following sentences. Then check your answers.

1. He and I are good friends yet we sometimes argue.
2. Now we'll have to try bribery or we can resort to force.
3. We can't win this game nor can we afford to lose it.
4. The car swerved wildly but it narrowly missed the crossing guard.
5. She tried and tried and soon her efforts paid off.
6. I'd like to buy a house as an investment but I can't afford the down payment right now.
7. My part-time job isn't very rewarding so I'm coming back to school next fall.
8. There are not many dangers so we must conquer our fear of failure.
9. This is her last semester so she's concentrating on school for a change.
10. Clutching his wounded shoulder he fell through the air but he managed to land on his feet.

---

Finally, here is the fourth comma rule:

> Put a comma after any word or group of words that comes before an independent clause.

Charley, you aren't paying attention. (The second rule applies here, too.)
Though tattered and torn, the book was worth a fortune.
Wherever you go, remember me.
If that's all there is, we'd better buy more.
Until he got his promotion, he was quite friendly.

## EXERCISE

Write out the four comma rules below. Then do the exercise.

1. ______________________________

2. ______________________________

______________________________

______________________________

______________________________

______________________________

3. ______________________________

______________________________

______________________________

______________________________

______________________________

4. ______________________________

______________________________

______________________________

---

## Exercise 4

Insert commas where necessary in the following sentences. Check your answers when you're done.

1. In the end quality will win.
2. John if you don't quiet down you'll have to leave.

3. If there were any justice I'd have been rewarded for what I did.
4. Well I don't believe it!
5. When the sun came up in a clear blue sky we all sighed with relief.
6. Adorned with blue bows her shoes clashed with her green outfit.
7. Moved beyond words he was able only to gesture his thanks.
8. Carefully placing one foot in front of the other she managed to walk along the white line for several feet.
9. Falling staggering to his feet then falling again he stumbled painfully toward the finish line.
10. Where a huge hardwood forest had stood now there was only blackened ground.

---

One final note about the comma before you try your hand at the review exercises: never place a *single* comma between a subject and its verb:

*right:* Homer and Liz are going into business.
*never:* Homer and Liz, are going into business.

*Two* commas between a subject and its verb are all right, however, *if* they are setting off nonessential material:

Homer and Liz, both recent graduates, are going into business.

## EXERCISES

Insert commas where necessary in the following exercises. Check your answers to each set of ten and make sure you understand any mistakes before you go on to the next exercise.

---

### Exercise 5

1. The job interview isn't so bad if you're prepared relaxed and confident.
2. With a shout of glee the boys ran to the heavily laden Christmas tree.
3. There is something wrong here but I haven't yet determined what it is.
4. In the end they'll be caught so all we have to do is wait.
5. George Washington the first President of the United States was an officer in the British army before the American Revolution.
6. Clam chowder baked beans and Indian Pudding are typical New England recipes found in my *Fannie Farmer Cookbook*.
7. Well Mrs. O'Hara if that's the best you can do it's out of my hands.
8. The Great Lakes form an inland passageway by which the great seagoing ships reach the heart of the North American continent.

9. A good dictionary used properly can be an important tool for developing a mature vocabulary.
10. If there were any point in complaining I would have protested long ago but I don't think anything can change their course of action now.

---

## Exercise 6

1. My world is made up of handsome men fast cars loud music expensive clothes and other dreams.
2. The movie despite some excellent action sequences was a failure because of the terrible script.
3. If starvation and lack of recognition made great artists many of my friends would be Picassos.
4. The letter of application is the most important document you will ever write yet you have spent only an hour composing it.
5. Wrapping the watch in a handkerchief he produced a mallet and smashed the expensive timepiece to smithereens or so it appeared.
6. The retirement of Bobby Orr from hockey was the end of an era for the game but those who saw him play will never forget it.
7. In the 1960s blue jeans became a uniform for the young but today jeans are popular only as very casual attire and a much more fashionable look has emerged.
8. Despite some early problems the Golden Gate Bridge has become one of the most interesting and exciting sights in North America don't you think?
9. There you've gone and broken it again!
10. Doing punctuation exercises is tedious work but is cleaner than tuning the car.

---

## Exercise 7

1. Your fall order which we received last week has been filled.
2. An excellent pool is available for those who like to swim and for those who play golf there is a beautiful eighteen-hole course.
3. John realizing his position resigned.
4. Inside the piano was going at full blast.
5. What you hear what you read and what you think all help to form your intellectual background.
6. Quickly girls or we'll be late.
7. Ever since I have been a regular theater goer.
8. A few days after they sailed the boat sprang a leak.

9. A fine fellow a member of the yacht club was drowned.
10. Antonio's grandmother was very short black-haired and extremely thin.

---

## Exercise 8

1. When you enter the store go to the counter on your left ask for Ms. Bertrand and tell her that you want to see the latest prints.
2. These cold wet gray days are not good for the crops.
3. The thick syrup boiled over and spilled on the stove on the table and on the floor.
4. Alice was neither wife nor mother.
5. Conflicts have occurred between students and faculty students and administration and faculty and administration.
6. However capable he was he failed miserably in this case.
7. Oh excuse me. I didn't hear you come in.
8. Nearby an old oak lifted its gaunt limbs to the sky.
9. Mr. Smith the head of the department despite his vast knowledge of his subject couldn't change a light bulb if his life depended on it.
10. I dressed you will be amazed to learn in two minutes flat and was out the door before his knock had stopped echoing.

---

## Exercise 9

1. For the last ten years oil-consuming nations have been struggling with the "energy crisis" or more specifically the "oil crisis."
2. Everyone is familiar with the problems the crisis has created: ever-increasing prices higher taxes and political conflict to name only a few.
3. Many solutions ranging from the practical to the fantastic have been proposed. Almost every magazine or newspaper we read contains at least one article on the exciting possibilities of solar power tidal power biomass or wind power.
4. Despite the optimism of the writers however most readers do not find such articles very reassuring. All the solutions proposed are realizable only in the future; the problem confronts us now today.
5. What is needed immediately is not new sources of electric power; we have time to develop those. What is needed immediately is a new source of *fuel.*
6. The ideal fuel would be first one that could be manufactured from an inexhaustible American resource.
7. Second the ideal fuel would be one that could be used to power

existing cars trucks buses planes and other transit vehicles without major mechanical alterations.

8. Third the ideal fuel must be safe powerful and nonpolluting.
9. One possible fuel that meets these requirements is hydrogen the most abundant element in the universe.
10. According to Roger Billings of Independence Missouri who is the leading expert in hydrogen-powered automobiles almost any internal combustion engine that runs on gasoline can be converted inexpensively to run on hydrogen.

---

## Exercise 10

1. "The world is changing" my friends in data processing told me. They warned me that I a naive English teacher would not be able to keep up with my students unless I learned some basic computer skills.
2. They assured me that machines with nonthreatening names like PET and Apple would do a better job than I could in teaching students about commas colons semicolons and spelling.
3. Then I would be free my friends maintained to teach the things that *really* mattered. In the cybernetic world of the future computers would take care of the details of grammar spelling and punctuation and I had better prepare myself for the revolution.
4. Furthermore they told me silicon chips would soon be doing my cooking balancing my checkbook and even going shopping for me. If a computer could do all that I thought dreamily perhaps it could even be programmed to sort socks.
5. Curiosity finally outweighed my lifelong distrust of machines and I enrolled in a course called "Your Friendly Computer."
6. I must admit the little demon seemed friendly at first. It quickly established itself on a first-name basis with me but the mass of information about inputs outputs modems disks bits and bytes soon left me dazed and bewildered.
7. Recognizing a rank amateur when it saw one my friendly computer attempted to win my trust and inspire my confidence by allowing me to pick off PacMans blast Rasters and incinerate Invaders. Dots gobblers and rocketships appeared and disappeared on the screen with dazzling speed.
8. Ever cheerful the computer tried to console me for my pitiful scores. "Not bad" it blinked but my hand-eye coordination was obviously unequal to the demands of video games.
9. Thinking I would feel more comfortable in the slower world of punctuation exercises I tried a program on exclamation marks

question marks and periods. Nothing I thought could possibly go wrong now.

10. To my surprise the machine no longer friendly flashed "GIGO—GIGO—GIGO" at me. Even I ignorant and inexperienced as I was knew what GIGO meant: "Garbage In Garbage Out." So I left the blinking computer behind me and went home to sort socks.

---

# Chapter 18

# The Semicolon

The colon and semicolon are often confused and used as if they were interchangeable. They serve very different functions, however, and their correct use can dramatically improve a reader's understanding of your writing. Here is one function of the semicolon:

> The semicolon can replace the period; in other words, it can appear between two independent clauses.

You should use the semicolon when the two clauses (sentences) you are joining are closely connected in meaning or when there is a cause-and-effect relationship between them.

> I'm too tired; I can't stay awake any longer.
>
> There's a good movie on tonight; it's a science fiction film called *Close Encounters of the Third Kind.*

A period could have been used instead of the semicolon in either of these sentences, but the close connection between the clauses prompted the writer to use a semicolon.

Certain connecting or transition words are sometimes put between independent clauses to show cause and effect or continuation of an idea. Words used in this way must be preceded by a semicolon and followed by a comma.[1]

> Put a semicolon in front of these words and a comma after:
>
> | | | |
> |---|---|---|
> | ; consequently, | ; besides, | ; furthermore, |
> | ; however, | ; for example, | ; in fact, |
> | ; therefore, | ; nevertheless, | ; thus, |
> | ; moreover, | | |

We had hiked for two hours; consequently, we were glad for the rest.
There are only two of us; however, we're both pretty big.
The sun was very hot; therefore, we stopped at an ice-cream store.

Note that the semicolon and transition word are used *together* to connect the two independent clauses.

Sometimes semicolons should be used in a list instead of commas:

> To make a lengthy, complex list easier to read and understand, put semicolons between the items instead of commas.

Here's an example:

A few items are necessary: matches to start a fire; an ax or hatchet to cut wood; cooking utensils and eating implements; and, of course, the food itself.

## EXERCISES

---

### Exercise 1

Put a check next to the sentences that are correctly punctuated. Check your answers on p. 290 before continuing.

1. ______ He sat down in a convenient bar; he was very thirsty.
2. ______ He sat down near a refreshing stream; for he was very tired.

[1]Sometimes the words listed in the box are used in sentences as nonessential expressions rather than as connecting words. They are then separated from the rest of the sentence by commas. See chapter 17, p. 153.

3. ______ My cats get along fine with the dog; it's each other that they hate.
4. ______ It's a beautiful day; just right for a long walk.
5. ______ Six of the Indian nations joined together in a loose union, they were called Iroquois.
6. ______ The lawn needs to be cut, the hedge needs to be trimmed, the flowers need to be watered, and, not least of all, the gardener needs to be paid.
7. ______ I'd like to help, however, I'm supposed to rest all day.
8. ______ We reached Canoe Lake in time to meet the others; in fact, we arrived a little ahead of schedule.
9. ______ New Orleans is a fascinating city; I hope to go back this summer.
10. ______ Ice cream is something Americans really understand; ice-cream cones, sundaes, and sodas are practically necessary for our survival.

---

## Exercise 2

Put a check next to the sentences that are correctly punctuated. Then check your answers.

1. ______ It's far too expensive; besides, we don't really need one.
2. ______ There are only a few who could catch him; and I'm sure she isn't one of them.
3. ______ Coffee prices are ridiculous, yet I still must have my morning cup or two.
4. ______ She wants to be an Olympic gymnast; consequently, she spends six hours a day in training.
5. ______ We'll have to go soon; for it's getting late.
6. ______ The weather is bad; I have a cold; the electricity is out; and, to top it all off, my in-laws are coming for dinner.
7. ______ If ever there were a time to act; it is now.
8. ______ Some people are skilled in many fields; Gary, for example, is both a good plumber and a great cook.
9. ______ She disobeyed the rules; so she will have to be punished.
10. ______ She is always late, however she's worth waiting for.

---

## Exercise 3

Correct the faulty punctuation in exercises 1 and 2.

---

## Exercise 4

Insert commas and semicolons where necessary in these sentences. Then check your answers carefully.

1. There seems to be no end to the work that must be done furthermore there isn't enough time in which to do it.
2. There must be a way or we're finished before we've begun.
3. I can't afford a Porsche therefore I drive a Volkswagen.
4. Shirley is one of my favorite people she can always cheer me up.
5. There will be ample opportunity to finish your homework but right now I need your help.
6. The flooring was all knotty pine yellowed with age the walls and furniture were of such design and color as to blend with it.
7. Mark Twain made a fortune as a writer but he lost it as an unsuccessful inventor.
8. Killer whales at Marineland look very dangerous however their high intelligence makes them relatively tame and easy to train.
9. John has gone away to become a teacher Martha now has twin baby girls Kevin is unemployed Julie is a lawyer or stockbroker (I forget which) and Paul is as usual drifting from job to job.
10. When the rain started they were trapped in the open nevertheless they stayed where they were until it let up and then watched the game with enjoyment despite being a little wet.

## Exercise 5

Correct the punctuation in these sentences[2] by changing commas to semicolons or colons where necessary.

1. I have grown fond of semicolons in recent years. The semicolon tells you that there is still some question about the preceding full sentence, something needs to be added.
2. It is almost always a greater pleasure to come across a semicolon than a period. The period tells you that that is that, if you didn't get all the meaning you wanted or expected, anyway you got all the writer intended to parcel out and now you have to move along.
3. But with a semicolon there, you get a pleasant little feeling of expectancy, there is more to come, read on, it will get clearer.

[2]Adapted from Lewis Thomas, "Notes on Punctuation," in *The Medusa and the Snail: More Notes of a Biology Watcher* (New York: Viking Press, 1979), pp. 126–127. 

4. Colons are a lot less attractive, for several reasons, firstly, they give you the feeling of being rather ordered around, or at least having your nose pointed in a direction you might not be inclined to take if left to yourself, and, secondly, you suspect you're in for one of those sentences that will be labeling the points to be made, firstly, secondly, and so forth, with the implication that you haven't enough sense to keep track of a sequence of notions without having them numbered.
5. Also, many writers use this system loosely and incompletely, starting out with number one and number two as though counting off on their fingers but then going on and on without the succession of labels you've been led to expect, leaving you floundering about searching for the ninthly or seventeenthly that ought to be there but isn't.

---

# Chapter 19

# Capital Letters

Capital letters should be used in a few specific places and nowhere else. Some people seem to have "capitalitis": they put capital letters on words randomly, regardless of whether the words are nouns, adjectives, or verbs. Like "exclamatosis," "capitalitis" is a disease communicated by comic books, which capitalize every word.

Not very many people have this problem. If you are in the majority who generally use capitals properly, skip this chapter and go on to something else. If you are puzzled about capital letters, though, or have readers who are puzzled by your use of them, read on.

Capitalize the first letters of the following words:

1. the first word of a sentence:

   Put out the garbage.

2. the names of specific persons:

   Sam Snead　　Billie Jean King

   the names of specific places:

   Kansas　　Elm St.
   Mars　　Morocco
   Oz　　Seattle

and the names of specific things:

Cape Canaveral
American Revolution
Hilltop Towers

3. the days of the week and the months of the year (but not the seasons):

| | |
|---|---|
| Monday | July |
| Friday | summer |
| October | winter |

4. the titles of specific people (but not the names of their positions), books, films, and courses (but not subject names, unless they're languages):

General Patton *but* the rank of general
Secretary of State George Schultz *but* the position of secretary of state
Mr. and Ms. O'Connor
*The Bare Essentials*
*Star Wars*
Mathematics 101 *but* the subject of mathematics
English 101; the English language

5. the names of specific companies, businesses, organizations, and departments:

Ford Motor Company
Bethlehem Steel Corporation
Watertown Rotary Club
Republican Party
Personnel Department

## EXERCISES

### Exercise 1

Correct the capitalization in these sentences. Answers are on p. 292.

1. henry smith wants to be a prince when he grows up.
2. the queen of england visited australia last winter.
3. Confident of Victory, we marched on Paris, led by our Heroic Captain.
4. The Lotta Crabtree Foundation sponsors a scholarship to the University of Massachusetts.
5. Laurie tries hard, but she'll never be as good at Typing as Frank.
6. *Santa claus Conquers the Martians* was a film that featured a cute little martian named dropo.

7. Do you think fords are better than chevies in the middle price range?
8. We study English and mathematics as well as our major subjects.
9. High School is a time of growing and Development for Young People, a time for them to find a Direction for the rest of their Lives.
10. Office Supplies are in great demand, so if you need pens or paper, you'd better see ms. Carlo in supplies right away.

---

## Exercise 2

Correct the capitalization.

1. Sue ellen rode down Grant avenue every day in the Fall to look at the leaves.
2. I went with my English Professor to the Newport jazz festival.
3. Alan goes to the city on Weekends to see french films.
4. He told his parents he was at college and then went off to spend the winter in Mexico.
5. I want to grow up to be a movie Star, or at least a Company President.
6. Jane studied Cooking, Art History, and French in Europe last Summer.
7. The Committee we had elected deprived us of our Human Rights.
8. He considers himself Liberal on matters such as the Dress Code.
9. Jim works for the Phone Company, which has an office on a Street near his home.
10. Are the doctor's rates too high?

---

## Exercise 3

Write a "process paper" of about two pages explaining how to do or make something or giving directions on how to get somewhere. Don't forget to check your spelling, sentence structure, and grammar. Pay particular attention to correct punctuation, and try to use an exclamation mark, a semicolon, and a colon at least once in the paper. Here are some topics you might choose from:

1. how to hitchhike
2. how to buy a used car
3. how to pick up girls/boys at a singles bar
4. how to win at Monopoly (poker, backgammon, bridge . . .)
5. how to prepare for a camping trip

6. how to choose a career (boss, husband/wife, college, apartment . . .)
7. how to cheat on a test
8. how to pour wine (stop a sneeze, throw a ball, pot a plant, go blonde . . .)
9. how to make someone happy
10. how to become unpopular

---

# UNIT FIVE

# Organizing Your Writing

# Chapter 20

# Finding Something to Write About

Everybody knows that "content" is important in writing. Not so many seem to know that organization is just as important. In fact, you can't really separate the two: *what you say is how you say it.* Writing a paper (or an essay, or a report, or a letter, or anything else) is like doing a chemistry experiment: you need the right amount of the right ingredients, put together in the right proportions and in the right order. There are five steps to follow:[1]

1. Choose a satisfactory subject.
2. Choose the main points of your subject.
3. Write a thesis statement,

   *or*

   Write an outline.
4. Write the paragraphs.
5. Revise the paper.

If you follow these steps faithfully, in order, we guarantee that you will write clear, organized papers.

[1]Some of the ideas presented in this unit are adapted from the method developed by Sidney P. Moss in *Composition by Logic* (Belmont, Calif.: Wadsworth, 1966).

Notice that when you get to step 3, you have a choice. You can choose to organize your paper either by means of a thesis statement or by means of an outline. The thesis-statement approach works well for very short papers—those no longer than about 400 words. An outline is necessary for longer papers and is often useful for organizing shorter papers as well. (Ideally, you should learn to use both methods of organizing your writing; in fact, your teacher may insist that you do.)

Steps 1, 2, and 3 make up the preparation stage of the writing process. Be warned: these three steps will take you as long as, if not longer than, steps 4 and 5, which involve the actual writing. *The longer you spend on the preliminary steps, the less time your writing will take, and the better your paper will be.*

## Step 1: Choose a Subject

Unless you are assigned a specific subject by a teacher or by a superior at work, choosing your subject can be the most difficult part of writing a paper. Apply the following guidelines carefully, because no amount of instruction can make you write a good paper on something you don't know anything about or on something that is inappropriate for your purpose.

> A satisfactory subject is significant, single, specific, and supportable.

1. Your subject should be **significant.** As we have been suggesting all the way through this book, it is essential that you *keep your reader in mind.* Here, this means that you should write about something that someone would like to read about. Consider your audience and choose a subject that will be significant to that audience. This doesn't mean that you can't ever be humorous, but, unless you're another Erma Bombeck, an essay on "how I deposit money in my bank" will probably be of little significance to your reader. The subject you choose must be worthy of the time and attention you expect the reader to give to your paper.

2. Your subject should be **single.** Don't try to do too much in your paper. A thorough discussion of one topic is much more satisfying to read than a skimpy, superficial treatment of several topics. A subject like "the problems of league expansion in football and other sports" includes too much to be dealt with well in one paper. Limit yourself to a single topic, such as "the problems of league expansion in the NFL."

3. Your subject should be **specific.** This requirement is very closely tied to the "single" requirement. Given a choice between a broad, general topic

and a narrow, specific one, you should choose the latter. In a short paper, you can't hope to say anything new or significant about a very large topic—"employment opportunities in the United States." But you could write an interesting, detailed discussion on a more specific topic, such as "summer employment opportunities at the Sun Valley Lodge." You can narrow a broad subject by applying one or more "limiting factors" to it. Try thinking of your subject in terms of a specific *kind*, or *time*, or *place*, or *number*, or *person* associated with it. To come up with the Sun Valley Lodge topic, for example, we limited the subject of employment opportunities in the United States in terms of both place and kind.

4. Your subject must be **supportable.** You must know something about the subject (preferably more than your reader knows about it), or you must be able to find out about it. Your discussion of your subject will be clear and convincing only if you can include examples, facts, quotations, descriptions, anecdotes, and other supporting details. Supporting evidence can be taken from your own experience or from the experience of other people. That is, your topic may or may not require you to do some research.

## EXERCISES

---

### Exercise 1

Test the following subjects against the guidelines we've given. Can you tell what's wrong with them? Check your answers on p. 293.

1. war
2. space travel in the twenty-first century
3. the five senses
4. Shakespeare's guilt complex
5. the abuse of alcohol and other drugs
6. why I like ink
7. the importance of mankind
8. attitudes of men and children
9. the world's major religions
10. my new Adidas

---

### Exercise 2

List five subjects that you might choose to write about. Be sure each subject is significant, single, specific, and supportable.

---

## Step 2: Choose the Main Points of Your Subject

Now that you have an appropriate subject for your paper, give some thought to the approach you're going to take to it. There are many possible ways of thinking and writing about a subject. In a short paper, you can deal effectively with only a few aspects of your topic. How do you decide what is the best approach to take? How do you decide which aspects of your subject to discuss, what **main points** to make and explain? One way is to make a list of everything you can think of that you might want to say about the subject. Some preliminary research may help too; you may turn up some points about the subject that you hadn't thought of.

Another way—especially useful if you find you're stuck for ideas—is to ask yourself questions about your subject. Run your subject through this list of questions and see which one "fits" it best. (The symbol S stand for your subject.)

1. How is S made or done?
2. How does S work?
3. What are the main parts of S?
4. What are the main functions of S?
5. What are the important features or characteristics of S?
6. What are the causes of S?
7. What are the effects or consequences of S?
8. What are the main kinds or types of S?
9. What are the main points of comparison (or contrast) between S and ____?
10. What are the main advantages (or disadvantages) of S?
11. What are the reasons for (or against) S?

These questions suggest some of the various ways of looking at, or thinking about, a subject. Most subjects will yield answers to more than one of these questions, but the question that produces the answers closest to what you want to say about your subject is the one that you should focus on. The answers to that question are the main points that you will discuss in your paper.

Here's how the procedure works. Assume you've been forced to accept as your subject "writing good business letters." Don't despair. Run down the list of questions until you find the one you can answer best. The process might go something like this:

1. How is a business letter written?
   No answer comes to mind. Scratch that question.

2. How does a business letter work?
   Silly question; it doesn't make sense.
3. What are the main parts of a business letter?
   Well, there are the inside address, the body, the salutation, and the complimentary close, but you don't know enough about these to write on them.
4. What are the main functions of the business letter?
   You can think of three: to request information, to place an order, and to complain about some product or service. This has possibilities, but you're not wildly enthusiastic about these aspects of your subject, so you go on.
5. What are the important characteristics of a good business letter?
   At last! Here's one you can answer satisfactorily. You know that a business letter should be clear, brief and to the point, and courteous. Assuming that you know (or can find out) a fair amount about these characteristics, you don't need to look any further. *Clarity, conciseness,* and *courtesy* are the main points of your subject that you will discuss in your paper. (Before you go any further, though, it's a good idea to apply the remaining questions in the box to your subject, just to be sure there isn't another question that yields answers you like even better.)

Selecting the main points to write about isn't really a difficult process, but it can be time-consuming. Don't rush. Take the necessary time; this is a crucial stage in the writing process.

Here are a few sample subjects, together with some main points that were discovered through this questioning procedure. Study this chart until you're sure you understand how to find suitable main points for any subject.

| Subject | Selected Question | Main Points |
|---|---|---|
| a part-time job | 10. What are some advantages of having a part-time job? | improved decision-making skills<br>increased sense of responsibility<br>increased self-confidence<br>increased independence |
| the correctional worker | 4. What are the main functions of a correctional worker? | to maintain security<br>to control inmates |

| Subject | Selected Question | Main Points |
|---|---|---|
| public speaking | 8. What are the main kinds of speeches? | demonstrative<br>informative<br>persuasive |
| teenage suicides | 6. What are some causes of teenage suicides? | lack of strong religious faith<br>lack of strict moral codes |
| making the hospital patient comfortable | 1. How can nurses make a hospital patient comfortable? | by providing a quiet environment<br>by providing clean linen<br>by providing adequate privacy |
| my opinion of college | 11. What are my reasons for liking college? | the courses interest me<br>the courses challenge me<br>the social life is great |
| television for children | 11. What are my reasons for disapproving of television for children? | it gives a distorted picture of life<br>it teaches false values<br>it inhibits creativity |

As a general rule, you should try to identify *between two and five main ideas* for your subject. If you have only one main idea, you have a subject suitable for a paragraph, not an essay. If you have more than five, you have too much material for a short paper. Choose only the most important aspects of the subject, or else take another look at your subject to see whether it can be narrowed down somewhat.

## EXERCISE

### Exercise 3

For each of the five subjects you chose in exercise 2, list two to five main points. If suitable main points do not immediately leap to mind, apply the eleven questions in the box on p. 175 one at a time to your subject, until you find the one that fits best. The answers to that question are your main points.

---

Now, take a close look at the main points you've chosen in exercise 3. It may be necessary to revise some of these before going any further. Are some points really too minor to bother with? Do any of the points overlap in meaning? Are there any points that are not really related to the subject?

To be completely satisfactory, the main points you have chosen must all be **significant**—worth writing a paragraph or more on. You shouldn't have any trivial ideas mixed in with the important ones.

Second, each of the main points you've chosen must be **different** from all the others: there must be no overlap in meaning. Check to be sure you haven't given two different labels to what is really only one aspect of the subject.

Third, the main points you have chosen must all be clearly **related** to the subject. They must all be aspects of *that* subject, not some other subject. For example, if you're writing about the advantages of a subject, cross out any disadvantages that may have appeared on your list.

## EXERCISES

---

### Exercise 4

Here is a list of subjects, each followed by some possible main points. Circle the unsatisfactory point(s) in each group.

| | |
|---|---|
| 1. problems of adolescence | parental pressure<br>school pressure<br>acne<br>acceptance by peers |
| 2. benefits of regular exercise | improved appearance<br>more dates<br>improved health |
| 3. some essentials of a good business letter | neat appearance<br>appropriate structure<br>good visual impact<br>neat signature |

4. major causes of divorce
   - in-laws
   - economic difficulties
   - sexual incompatibility
   - unemployment
   - adultery

5. reasons for legalizing euthanasia
   - the family would benefit
   - the patient would benefit
   - the spouse would benefit

6. uses of color in industry
   - safety
   - identification
   - warning
   - fluorescent paint

7. advantages of solar heating
   - economy
   - requires southern exposure
   - efficiency
   - ease of maintenance
   - availability
   - three main kinds

8. reasons for legalizing prostitution
   - to save taxpayers money
   - to control spread of venereal disease
   - to eliminate juvenile prostitution
   - to ensure regular health checkups for prostitutes
   - to decriminalize prostitution

---

## Exercise 5

Study the main points you chose in exercise 3 (p. 177). Cross out any that aren't significant, different from all the others, or related to the subject. If necessary, add new main points, so that you end up with at least two main points for each subject.

---

Now that you've decided on a few good main points to discuss, put them in the **order** in which you want them to appear in your paper. There are four main ways to arrange your points; choose the way that is most appropriate for your particular subject.

1. **Chronological order** means in order of time, from first to last. Here's an example:

| *Subject* | *Main Points* |
|---|---|
| the process of dating | attraction<br>meeting<br>discovery<br>intimacy<br>disillusionment |

2. **Climactic order** means saving your strongest or most important point for last. Generally you would present your strongest point last, your second-strongest point first, and the others in between, like this:

| *Subject* | *Main Points* |
|---|---|
| disadvantages of cigarette smoking | danger to those around you<br>disapproval of others<br>expense<br>danger to yourself |

3. **Logically linked order** means that the main points are connected in such a way that one point must be explained before the next can be understood. Look at this example:

| *Subject* | *Main Points* |
|---|---|
| main causes of juvenile delinquency | lack of opportunity for work<br>lack of recreational facilities<br>boredom |

The logical link here is this: it's because of unemployment that recreational facilities are needed, and it's because of both unemployment and inadequate recreational facilities that boredom becomes a problem. The first two points must be explained before the reader can fully understand the third.

4. **Random order** means the points can be explained in any order. A random arrangement of points is possible only if the main points are all equal in significance and not logically linked, as in this case:

| *Subject* | *Main Points* |
|---|---|
| the garbage-disposal crisis | disposal sites are hard to find<br>costs are high<br>new technologies are not yet fully developed |

## EXERCISE

---

### Exercise 6

Using the revised list of subjects and main points that you came up with in exercise 5, arrange the main points for each subject in the most appropriate order.

---

In this chapter you've learned how to choose a satisfactory subject and how to select (and order) the main points of that subject—the first two steps in the five-step process we outlined at the beginning of the chapter. Now it's time to decide whether you'll organize your paper by the thesis-statement method or by the outline method. Although we think the former generally works better for short papers and the latter for longer papers, this distinction isn't hard and fast. So, depending on your teacher's instructions, turn now to either chapter 21, "Writing the Thesis Statement," or chapter 22, "Writing the Outline."

# Chapter 21

# Writing the Thesis Statement

Now that you've chosen your topic and selected some main points to discuss (see chapter 20), you're ready for the third step in organizing your writing.

## Step 3: Write a Thesis Statement

The key to clear organization of a very short paper is the **thesis statement**—a statement near the beginning of your paper that announces its subject and scope. The thesis statement is a tremendous help both to you and to your reader. It plans your paper for you, and it tells your reader exactly what he or she is going to read about. In fiction, letting readers know in advance what they're going to find would never do. But, for practical, everyday kinds of writing, this "advance notice" works very well. Term papers, technical reports, research papers, office memoranda, and business letters are no place for suspense or surprises. In these kinds of writing, you're more likely to get and keep your readers' interest if you indicate the subject and scope of your paper at the outset. The thesis statement acts like a table of contents, giving a clear indication of what is to follow. It's a kind of map of the territory covered in your paper; it keeps your reader (and you) on the right track.

Specifically, *a thesis statement is a sentence that clearly and concisely indicates the subject of your paper, the main points you will discuss, and the order in which you will discuss them.*

To write a thesis statement, you join the **subject** to the **main points,** which you have already chosen and arranged in order. To join the two parts of a thesis statement, you use a **link.** Your link can be a word or phrase, such as *are, include, consist of, because, since,* or it can be a colon.[1] Here is the simple formula for constructing a thesis statement:

| S (subject) | consists of (link) | I, II (III, IV, V) (main points) |
|---|---|---|

Here's an example:

S I II III
Three characteristics of a good business letter (are) conciseness, clarity, and courtesy.

## EXERCISE

### Exercise 1

In each of the following thesis statements, underline the subject with a wavy line, circle the link, and underline the main points with a straight line. Answers are on p. 294.

1. There are four kinds of patients whom doctors hate to treat: clingers, demanders, help rejecters, and deniers.
2. The most prolific producers of unnecessary jargon are politicians, sportswriters, advertising copywriters, and educators.
3. The principles of good child care include understanding the development of the child, accepting his need to regress as well as progress, and encouraging him to become independent.
4. Seventy-five per cent of Americans over twenty suffer from cardiovascular disease because we eat too much, we eat the wrong kinds of food, and we exercise too little.
5. According to Aaron Copland, people listen to music on three planes simultaneously: the sensuous plane, the expressive plane, and the "sheerly musical" plane.
6. Standardized examinations should be introduced in all college courses in order to force students to learn the work and to ensure a fair assessment of each student's ability.
7. Since children are expensive, time-consuming, and often ungrate-

[1]Remember that a colon can be used only after an independent clause. See chapter 16 if you need a review.

ful, young couples should think carefully before deciding to become parents.

8. Three passions, simple but overwhelmingly strong, have governed my life: the longing for love, the search for knowledge, and unbearable pity for the suffering of mankind. (Bertrand Russell, "What I Have Lived For")
9. Supermarket people take us for fools, presuming that we know nothing about food, that we shop impulsively and irrationally, and that we can be cheated with impunity. (John Keats, "Rip-Off at the Supermarket")
10. Several subtle aspects of the relationship between population growth and environmental degradation operate to make man's predicament even more perilous than superficial analyses indicate. Four to be considered here are synergisms, threshold effects, trigger effects, and time-lag effects. (Paul R. Ehrlich and John P. Holdren, "Hidden Effects of Overpopulation")

---

When you combine your subject with the main points into a thesis statement, there is one rule to remember:

| The main points should be grammatically parallel. |
|---|

This rule means that if main point I is a word, then main points II and III and so on must be words, too. If point I is a phrase, then the rest must be phrases. If I is a dependent clause, then the rest must be dependent clauses. Study the model thesis statements you analyzed in exercise 1, noting that in each case the main points are in grammatically parallel form. For each of those thesis statements, decide whether words, phrases, or dependent clauses were used. If you feel your understanding of parallelism is a bit wobbly, review chapter 9 before doing the following exercises.

## EXERCISES

---

### Exercise 2

Correct the faulty parallelism in the following thesis statements.

1. The chief characteristics of good writing are clarity, brevity, and you should be simple and accurate as well.
2. Two features of the semester system are flexibility and it's economical.

3. The elderly deserve more attention: they have valuable knowledge to offer, extra time, and the desire to be useful.
4. To win, a team needs discipline, determination, and its members should be able to work well together.
5. The cost of eating out has increased enormously because we're paying for more than food: we're paying for décor, we're paying for service, and we want to be entertained as well.
6. There are three ways to find a job: by reading the want ads, you can consult an employment agency, and letters to company personnel managers.
7. Basic principles to be observed in caring for the premature infant include maintaining body temperature, maintaining adequate oxygen intake, you must protect the infant from infection, and maintenance of adequate fluid and calorie intake.
8. Individual communities can no longer cope with our state's garbage-disposal crisis because disposal sites are so hard to find, high costs, and new technologies are not yet fully developed.
9. A high level of motivation, experience in dealing with all sorts of problems, and not worrying about your decisions are necessary if you hope to run a successful business.
10. Two questions about battery-operated vehicles need answering: how soon are practical models likely to become available and the role the government might play in their production?

---

## Exercise 3

Find the subjects and main points you produced for exercise 6 in chapter 20. Combine each subject with its main points to make a thesis statement. Be sure the main points are in parallel form.

---

We said at the beginning of this chapter that the thesis statement plans your whole paper for you. Before we turn to the actual writing of the paper, it will be useful for you to have a general idea of what the finished product will look like. In a very short paper, each main point can be explained in a single paragraph. The main points of your subject become the **topics** of the paragraphs, as is shown in this model format for a paper with three main points:

Title ____________________

Paragraph 1: contains the introduction and the thesis statement { ____________________<br>____________________<br>____________________<br>S consists of I, II, and III.

Topic sentence introducing main point I.

Paragraph 2: contains your explanation of I

Topic sentence introducing main point II.

Paragraph 3: contains your explanation of II

Topic sentence introducing main point III.

Paragraph 4: contains your explanation of III

Paragraph 5: conclusion

Chapter 23 will tell you how to fill in the blanks. But, before you go on to that chapter, notice the proportions of the paragraphs in the model format. Since the main points are approximately equal in significance, the paragraphs of the body of the paper are approximately equal in length. (If your last main point is more important than the other points, however, the paragraph that explains it may be longer than the other paragraphs.)

Notice too, that the beginning and ending paragraphs are much shorter than the ones that explain the main points. Your introduction should not ramble on, and your conclusions should not trail off. Get to your main points as quickly as you can, and end with a bang, not a whimper.

Two papers that follow the model format are Brian Green's "Writing a Good Business Letter" and Bertrand Russell's "What I Have Lived For," which appear in appendix A. Read them now; then turn to chapter 23.

# Chapter 22

# Writing the Outline

For longer compositions, business and technical reports, research papers, and the like, the outline method often proves more successful than the thesis-statement approach. A good outline maps out your paper from beginning to end. It shows you—*before* you begin to write—what you have to say about each of your main points. Outlining spares you the agony of discovering too late that you have too much information about one point and little or nothing to say about another.

## Step 3: Write an Outline

Once you've chosen a satisfactory subject and the main points you wish to discuss, the next step is to expand what you have into a point-form plan for your finished paper. To do this, you may need to do some further thinking or reading, gathering additional information and supporting facts. For ideas about what kinds of information you might use, see "Developing Your Paragraphs," pp. 193–196. After you've assembled all the information you think you'll need, prepare the outline.

First, write down your main points in the order you've decided to discuss them. Leave lots of space under each main point. Using Roman numerals, number your main points I, II, III, etc. Now, under each point, indent and list the examples, facts, ideas, or other information you're going to use to explain it. Again, leave lots of space. Check to be sure these items are arranged in an order that will be clear to your reader.[1] Now label these A, B, C, etc.

If any of these pieces of information needs to be explained or developed, indent again and list the supporting materials, numbering them 1, 2, 3, etc. Minor details, if there are any, are indented under the supporting materials to which they relate and are labeled a, b, c. Add the introduction and conclusion, and you're done. Your outline might look something like this:

Introduction[2]
    Attention-getter
    Thesis statement or statement of subject
I. First main point
    A. Item that develops first main point
    B. Item that develops first main point
        1. Supporting material that develops subheading B
        2. Supporting material that develops subheading B
II. Second main point
    A. Item that develops second main point
    B. Item that develops second main point
    C. Item that develops second main point
III. Third main point
    A. Item that develops third main point
        1. Supporting material that develops A
            a. Detail
            b. Detail
        2. Supporting material that develops A
    B. Item that develops third main point
Conclusion
    Summary
    Memorable statement

You'll probably find that before you can assign a number or a letter to a piece of information, you need to think carefully about where the item belongs in your paper. Questions about how to arrange your information under each main point and how much time to spend on any one point should be cleared up at the outline stage. If, for example, you find you have nine subheadings under main point I and only one under main point II, you need to do some rethinking to balance your paper. Main points should contain approximately equal amounts of information.

Preparing a satisfactory outline takes time. Be prepared to spend time adding, deleting, and rearranging your ideas and supporting material until

[1]The four kinds of order explained in chapter 20 can apply to the arrangement of ideas within a paragraph as well as to the arrangement of main points in a paper.

[2]Chapter 23 explains how to construct an introduction and a conclusion.

you're completely satisfied both with the arrangement and with the proportion of your outline.

## EXERCISE

---

### Exercise 1

Below are the main points for a paper on writing good business letters. Beneath these are nine statements that might be used to support and develop these points. Read through the list and complete the outline by arranging the supporting items logically below the appropriate points. Discard any items that are not relevant to the main points. Turn to p. 296 to check your outline against ours.

A good business letter is concise, clear, and courteous.

I. Conciseness

II. Clarity

III. Courteousness

Avoid sarcasm and insults.
Don't waste time with irrelevant personal details.
Use an accepted business-letter format.
Include all information your reader might need.
Include specific information such as names, dates, product numbers.
Always type your letter.
Cut out all unnecessary words.
Include file number or other reference number, if possible.
Politely request what action you want the reader to take.

---

With your outline in hand, all you have to do to write your paper is to make the supporting points into sentences and the main points (and the introduction and conclusion) into paragraph divisions. Chapter 23 explains how.

To show you the relationship between an outline and the final product, we've re-created the outline that Martin Luther King might have used in writing "The Dimensions of a Complete Life" (in Appendix A).

The Dimensions of a Complete Life

Introduction

*Attention-getter*: John's vision of the new Jerusalem and its meaning
*Statement of subject*: The three dimensions of a complete life: length, breadth, and height

I. The length of life
   A. Definition: the dimension of life in which one is concerned with self
   B. The need to love oneself properly
      1. Joshua Liebman's explanation in *Peace of Mind*
      2. Responsibility of each person to discover his or her "calling"
         a. Example of street-sweeper
         b. Douglas Mallock's verse
   C. The danger of getting bogged down in the length of life

II. The breadth of life
   A. Definition: the dimension of life in which one is concerned about others
   B. The need to be concerned about all humanity
      1. Parable of the Good Samaritan
      2. Significance of the parable in our time
         a. Racial groups often interested only in their own status
         b. Nations often concerned only about their own well-being
      3. Interdependence of all individuals and nations
         a. Poverty affects all
         b. Disease affects all
         c. John Donne, "No man is an island . . ."

III. The height of life
   A. Danger of neglecting this dimension
   B. Difficulty of maintaining religious belief in today's world
   C. Need to remember that many great things are invisible:
      1. Law of gravitation
      2. The mind of an architect
      3. Human personality
      4. God
   D. Power of belief in God

Conclusion

*Summary:* Relationship between the three dimensions of life and the Commandments
*Memorable statement*: Prayer that all people may share in John's vision

Once you've mapped out your plan of attack in an outline, writing the paper becomes perhaps not an easy task, but certainly not the terrifying, impossible task it often seems to be if you have no plan to follow. Remember, *the more time you spend planning, the less time you spend writing—and the better your writing will be.*

## EXERCISES

### Exercise 2

Read "The Dimensions of a Complete Life" in appendix A. Find the paragraphs that correspond to the various headings and subheadings in our outline of the piece. Label King's paragraphs to show where you think they fit in the outline: I, A, B, 1, 2, etc. Then turn to the answer section to check your labeling.

### Exercise 3

Read John Keats' "Rip-off at the Supermarket" in appendix A. In the space below, write the outline for his second main point (paragraphs 14 to 17). We've filled in the main point to get you started.

II. Supermarket managers view us as impulsive and unthinking shoppers.

A. ______________________________

1. ______________________________

2. ______________________________

3. ______________________________

4. ______________________________

B. ______________________________

1. ______________________________

2. ______________________________

### Exercise 4

Turn to the subjects and main points you developed for exercise 6 in chapter 20, and create an outline for a paper on one of those subjects.

# Chapter 23

# Writing the Paragraphs

You are now at step **4** in the writing process. Armed with either your thesis statement or your outline, you are ready to turn your main points into paragraphs. Sounds like a magician's trick? It isn't. The "sleight-of-pen" involved requires only that you know what a paragraph looks like and how to put one together.

A paragraph looks like this:

A sentence that introduces the **topic** (or main idea) of the paragraph goes here.

Three or more sentences that specifically support or explain the topic go in here.

______________________________
______________________________
______________________________
______________________________
______________________________
__________________.

Sometimes a main point can be explained satisfactorily in a single paragraph. Sometimes, if it's a complicated main point requiring lots of support, several paragraphs are needed. Nevertheless, whether it is explaining a main point of a paper or an item supporting a main point, every paragraph contains two things: a statement of the topic (usually the first sentence in the paragraph) and development of the topic.

## EXERCISE

### Exercise 1

Turn to appendix A and read Bertrand Russell's "What I Have Lived For." Find and underline the statement of topic in the second, third, and fourth paragraphs. Check your answer on p. 297.

## Developing Your Paragraphs

How do you put a paragraph together? First, write your **topic sentence,** telling your reader what point or idea you're going to discuss in the paragraph. Next, develop your point. An adequately developed paragraph gives enough supporting information to make the topic completely clear to the reader. An average paragraph runs between 75 and 150 words (except for introductions and conclusions, which are shorter), so you can see you will need lots of supporting information for each point.

Now, unless you are writing from a very detailed outline and have all the supporting material you need listed in front of you, you should do a little more thinking at this point. Put yourself in your reader's place. What does the reader need to know in order to understand your point clearly? If you ask yourself questions like the ones listed below, you'll be able to decide what **kinds of development** to use to support a particular topic sentence.

1. Is a *definition* necessary? If you're using a term that may be unfamiliar to your reader, you should define it. Below, Brian Green defines what he means by "concise":

> The business letter must be concise: don't waste words. Little introduction or preliminary chat is necessary. Get to the point, make the point, and leave it. It is safe to assume that your letter is being read by a very busy person with all kinds of paper to deal with. Such a person does not want to spend very much time with a newsy letter about your ski trip or medical problem. Reread and revise your message until the words and sentences you have used are precise. This takes time, but is a necessary part of writing a good letter. A short business letter that makes its point quickly has much more impact on a reader than a long-winded, rambling exercise in creative writing.

You should include a definition, too, if you're using a familiar term in an unusual way. Here, Martin Luther King defines what he means by "the length of life":

> Now let us notice first the length of life. I have said that this is the dimension of life in which the individual is concerned with developing his inner powers. It is that dimension of life in which the individual pursues personal ends and ambitions. This is perhaps the selfish dimension of life, and there is such a thing as moral and rational self-interest. If one is not concerned about himself he cannot be totally concerned about other selves.

2. Would *examples* help clarify the point? Listing a number of examples is probably the most common method of developing an idea. In this paragraph, John Keats offers two examples to prove his point:

> Presuming the public is unobservant, or unthinking, or both, a store will advertise a "Special! Three cans for 60¢!" when each can of that item regularly sells for 20¢. Similarly, a supermarket may advertise a sale on one brand of salad oil. In the store will be a large placard announcing this sale. Beneath the placard, however, will be a huge display of some other brand of much more expensive salad oil. The brand to which the advertising and placard refer may be found in a distant aisle on a shelf display two bottles wide among the Harvard beets.

In his paragraph on courtesy in writing, Brian Green first gives the reader examples of what courtesy is *not*, then of what it *is*:

> The business letter must be courteous. Sarcasm and insults are ineffective and can often work against you. If you are sure you are right, point that out as politely as possible, explain why you are right, and outline what the reader is expected to do about it. Always put yourself in the place of the person to whom you are writing. What sort of letter would you respond to? How effective would sarcasm and threats be in making you fulfil a request? Another form of courtesy is taking care in your writing and typing of the business letter. Grammatical and spelling errors (even if you call them typing errors) tell a reader that you don't think enough of him or her to be careful. Such mistakes can lower the reader's opinion of you faster than anything you say, no matter how idiotic. There are excuses for ignorance; there are no excuses for sloppiness.

Sometimes a single, detailed example is enough to allow your reader to see clearly what you mean. In this paragraph, King uses a famous story from the Bible as an example of showing proper concern for others:

> You remember one day a man came to Jesus and he raised some significant questions. Finally he got around to the question, "Who is my neighbor?" This could easily have been a very abstract question left in mid-air. But Jesus immediately pulled that question out of mid-air and placed it on a dangerous curve between Jerusalem and Jericho. He talked about a certain man who fell among thieves. Three men passed, two of them on the other side. And finally another man came and helped the injured man on the ground. He is known to us as the good Samaritan. Jesus says in substance that this is a great man. He was great because he could project the "I" into the "thou."

3. Is a *series of steps* or *stages* involved? Here's an example of a paragraph organized according to the series principle:

> First and most important, we must define our goal. Precisely what do we wish to achieve? Second, we must discover, through research, how others have attained the same or a similar goal. We may then apply their experiences to our own situation. Next, we must break the process down into stages or steps so that eventually we may proceed in a logical, ordered, and precise manner. Finally comes the most difficult part of the entire operation: we must cease all this procrastination and begin!

4. Would *specific details* be useful? Keats uses concrete, descriptive details effectively in this paragraph:

> As Krell told his stories, I considered other reasons for the price of supermarket food. He had mentioned his membership in a country club near his home. He was a man in his middle fifties who wore his hair youthfully long and dressed in close-fitting double-knit slacks, colorful sports jackets, and Florentine shoes with square gold buckles on them. His wife, too, was fashionably turned out. Every year they took a winter vacation at Acapulco and a summer holiday in Europe. On every working day they arrived at their store at seven in the morning. At seven in the evening, they turned out the lights, locked the store, and drove home in their Cadillac, which was new each year and always white. They worked long and hard for their money, but they seemed to live rather well on what they earned.

Sometimes numerical facts or statistics are the kinds of details you need to include, as Keats does in paragraphs 9, 28, and 33 of "Rip-off at the Supermarket."

5. Would a *comparison* clarify your point? If you have a difficult, abstract topic to explain, try comparing it to something with which your reader is familiar, as King does in this paragraph:

> These are the three dimensions of life, and without the three being correlated, working harmoniously together, life is incomplete. Life is something of a great triangle. At one angle stands the individual person, at the other angle stand other persons, and at the top stands the Supreme, Infinite Person, God. These three must meet in every individual life if that life is to be complete.

6. Would a *quotation* or *paraphrase* be appropriate? Occasionally, you will find that someone else—an expert in a particular field, a well-known author, or a respected public figure—has said what you want to say better than you could ever hope to say it. In these cases, quotations—as long as they are kept short and not used too frequently—are useful in developing your topic. Notice how King uses a famous quotation to sum up the point of this paragraph:

> As long as there is poverty in the world I can never be rich, even if I have a billion dollars. As long as diseases are rampant and millions of people in this world cannot expect to live more than twenty-eight or thirty years, I can never be totally healthy even if I just

> got a good check-up at Mayo Clinic. I can never be what I ought to be until you are what you ought to be. This is the way our world is made. No individual or nation can stand out boasting of being independent. We are interdependent. So John Donne placed it in graphic terms when he affirmed, "No man is an island entire of itself. Every man is a piece of the continent, a part of the main." Then he goes on to say, "Any man's death diminishes me because I am involved in mankind, and therefore never send to know for whom the bell tolls; it tolls for thee." When we discover this, we master the second dimension of life.

A paraphrase is a summary—in your own words—of someone else's idea. Don't forget to indicate whose idea it is you are paraphrasing, the way King does below:

> Some years ago a learned rabbi, the late Joshua Liebman, wrote a book entitled *Peace of Mind.* He has a chapter in the book entitled "Love Thyself Properly." In this chapter he says in substance that it is impossible to love other selves adequately unless you love your own self properly. Many people have been plunged into the abyss of emotional fatalism because they did not love themselves properly. So every individual has a responsibility to be concerned about himself enough to discover what he is made for. After he discovers his calling he should set out to do it with all of the strength and power in his being.

In writing your own paragraphs, you will often find that you need to use more than one method of development to explain your point. The six methods can be used in any combination you choose.

## EXERCISES

---

### Exercise 2

Name the kinds of development used in the following paragraphs. Then turn to p. 298 to check your answers.

1. "What I Have Lived For," paragraph 4
2. "Writing a Good Business Letter," paragraph 3
3. "The Dimensions of a Complete Life," paragraph 3
4. "The Dimensions of a Complete Life," paragraph 7
5. "The Dimensions of a Complete Life," paragraph 16
6. "Rip-off at the Supermarket," paragraph 9
7. "Rip-off at the Supermarket," paragraph 12
8. "Rip-off at the Supermarket," paragraph 14
9. "Rip-off at the Supermarket," paragraph 16
10. "Rip-off at the Supermarket," paragraph 33

---

## Exercise 3

Choose one of the following topic sentences or make up one of your own. Write a paragraph of about 100 words, using at least two different methods of development.

1. True education takes place outside the classroom.
2. Money can't buy happiness.
3. The Hollywood movie industry is in deep trouble.
4. I am convinced I made the right career choice.
5. I am the most interesting person I know.

## Writing Introductions and Conclusions

Two paragraphs in your paper are *not* developed in the way we've just outlined: the introduction and conclusion. All too often, these are dull or clumsy paragraphs that detract from a paper's effectiveness. But they needn't be: here's how to write good ones.

The introduction is worth special attention because that's where your reader either sits up and takes notice of your paper or sighs and pitches it into the wastebasket. Occasionally, for a very short paper, you can begin simply with your thesis statement or statement of subject. This is what Bertrand Russell does in "What I Have Lived For." More usually, though, an **attention-getter** comes before the statement of subject. An attention-getter is a sentence or two designed to get the reader interested in what you have to say.

There are several kinds of attention-getters to choose from:

1. interesting incident or anecdote related to your subject (see "The Dimensions of a Complete Life," paragraphs 1 & 2)
2. statement of opinion that you intend to shoot down (see "Rip-off at the Supermarket," paragraphs 1 & 2)
3. definition (see "Writing Better Business Letters," paragraph 1)
4. quotation
5. little-known or striking fact

Add your thesis statement to the attention-getter, and your introduction is complete.

The closing paragraph, too, usually has two parts: a summary of the main points of your paper (phrased differently, please—not a word-for-word repetition of your thesis statement or your topic sentences) and a **memorable statement.** Your memorable statement may take several forms:

1. value or significance of your subject ("Writing Better Business Letters," paragraph 5, and "Rip-off at the Supermarket," paragraphs 47, 48)
2. reference to the content of your opening paragraph ("Dimensions of a Complete Life," paragraph 20)
3. relevant or thought-provoking quotation
4. relevant or thought-provoking question
5. suggestion for change
6. challenge
7. solution to the problem discussed in the paper

## Keeping Your Reader with You

As you are writing your paragraphs, keep in mind that you want to make it as easy as possible for your reader to follow you through your paper. Clear **transitions** and an appropriate **tone** can make the difference between a paper that confuses or annoys readers and one that enlightens and pleases them.

Transitions are those words or phrases that show the relationship between one point and the next, causing a paragraph or a paper to hang together and read smoothly. They are like turn signals on a car: they tell the person following you where you're going. Here are some common transitions that you can use to keep your reader on track:

1. *to show a time relation*: first, second, third, next, before, during, after, now, then, finally, last
2. *to add an idea or example*: in addition, also, another, furthermore, similarly, for example, for instance
3. *to show contrast*: although, but, however, instead, nevertheless, on the other hand, in contrast, on the contrary
4. *to show a cause-effect relation*: as a result, consequently, because, since, therefore, thus

Here is a paragraph that has adequate development but no transitions:

> There are many reasons why you should not smoke. Smoking is harmful to your lungs and heart. It is annoying and dangerous to those around you who do not smoke. It is an unattractive and dirty habit. It is difficult to quit smoking. Most worthwhile things in life are hard to achieve.

Not very easy to read, is it? Readers are jerked abruptly from point to point until, battered and bruised, they reach the end. This kind of writing is unfair to the readers. It makes them do too much of the work. The ideas may all be there, but the readers have to figure out for themselves how everything fits together. After a couple of paragraphs like this one, even patient readers can become annoyed.

Now read the same paragraph with the transitions added:

> There are many reasons why you should not smoke; among them, three stand out as the most persuasive. First, smoking is harmful to your lungs and heart. Second, it is both annoying and dangerous to those around you who do not smoke. In addition to those compelling facts, smoking is an unattractive and dirty habit. On the other hand, once you begin, it's awfully difficult to quit; but then, most worthwhile things in life are hard to achieve.

Here the readers are gently guided from one point to the next. By the time they reach the conclusion, they know not only what ideas the writer had in mind but also how they fit together. The transitions make a reader's job easy and rewarding.

One final point. As you write the paragraphs of your paper, try to be conscious of your **tone.** *Tone* is a word used to describe a writer's attitude toward the subject and the reader. The words you use, the examples, quotations, and other supporting materials you choose to help explain your main points, all contribute to your tone. When you are trying to explain something to someone—particularly if it's something you feel strongly about—you may be tempted to be highly emotional in your discussion. If you allow yourself to get carried away, chances are you won't be convincing. What will be communicated is the strength of your feelings not the depth of your understanding or the validity of your opinion. To be clear and credible, you need to restrain your enthusiasm (or your anger) and present your points in a calm, reasonable way.

We have two suggestions that may help you find and maintain the right tone. First, never insult your readers, even unintentionally. Avoid phrases like "any idiot can see," "no sane person could believe," and "it is obvious that . . ." Remember that what is obvious to you isn't necessarily obvious to someone who has a limited understanding of your subject or who disagrees with your opinion. Don't "talk down" to your readers, as though they were children or simpletons. Don't use sarcasm. And avoid profanity.

Second, don't apologize for your interpretation of your subject. Have confidence in yourself: you've thought long and hard about your subject, you've found good supporting material to help explain it, and you believe in its significance. Present your subject in a *positive* manner. If you hang back, using phrases like "I may be wrong, but . . ." or "I tend to feel that . . .," your readers won't be inclined to give your points the consideration they deserve. Keep your readers in mind as you write, and your writing will be both clear and convincing.

## EXERCISES

### Exercise 4

Rewrite the following paragraph, adding transitions where necessary and correcting any lapses in tone. Turn to p. 298 for our suggested revision.

I'm no expert—in fact, I really don't know anything about it—but it seems to me that anyone who enjoys baseball is a masochist. I may be wrong (I usually am), but it's a very dull game, don't you think? About every third pitch, the batter swings. The fielders do nothing. There are about fifteen hits in a three-hour game. The players actually do something for approximately seven and one half minutes of an entire afternoon. Home runs are dull. One man trots around the bases. The others stand and watch. An awful lot of people seem to like baseball, so I guess there's something wrong with me. People who like baseball are probably boring people.

### Exercise 5

Write a reply to this attack on baseball. Remember to keep your tone consistent, and don't forget transitions.

### Exercise 6

Choose either A or B:

A. Using one of the thesis statements you prepared in chapter 21, exercise 3, write a paper of approximately 300 words.
B. Using the outline you prepared in chapter 22, exercise 4, write a paper of approximately 500 words.

# Chapter 24

# Revising the Paper

At last you've reached the final step in the writing process. By now you're probably tired, fed up, and wishing you'd never even heard of your subject. Revising the paper is a step you'll be strongly tempted to skip. Don't! Until you've looked back (which is what *revised* means), your paper is not ready to be sent out into the world. Ideally, you should revise *several days after writing the paper.* After this "cooling off" period, you'll be able to see your paper more accurately than you could right after you finished writing it. The danger in rereading too soon is that you're likely to "read" what you *think* you've written—what's in your head rather than what you've really got on the paper.

A thorough revision requires at least two "looks back." The first time, read the paper aloud from beginning to end. Check for the overall effectiveness of your paper. Does it do what you hoped it would? Are your points all clearly explained? Has anything been left out? Now is the time to check carefully for transitions and tone.

The second time you read through your paper, do it with the Revision Guide (which is on the inside of the back cover) in front of you for easy reference. As you follow the guide, pay particular attention to the points that tend to give you trouble. (The more of these points there are, of course, the more rereadings will be required.) The last time you reread, do so from end to beginning to check your spelling. Reading from back to front, you're forced to look at each word in isolation, so you're more likely to spot your spelling mistakes. If you find this step too much to bear, ask someone else to read over your paper for you, while you check his or hers.

## EXERCISE

---

Using the Revision Guide, reread and revise the paper you wrote for exercise 6 in chapter 23.

---

# UNIT SIX

# Beyond the Bare Essentials

# Introduction

We have now covered all the essentials for clear, correct, well-organized, and easily understood writing. In this short unit, we will go beyond those essentials to some of the pitfalls you may encounter when applying all you've learned up to now. We'll discuss levels of usage; how to avoid clichés, jargon, and slang; the problem of wordiness; and what we've termed *abusages*—misused phrases and words that creep into writing and reveal ignorance of the language.

Many of the errors we will describe in this unit are not grammatical errors; however, they do interfere with your ability to communicate with your reader. A reader may simply not understand what you're talking about if you use jargon or slang; he or she may think very poorly of you (and your message) if your level of usage is inappropriate or if you use clichés or abusages. Your message will be communicated if your writing is clear and correct (the bare essentials); your message will be more easily and favorably received if your writing is appropriate to the message and to the reader (beyond the bare essentials).

Although these chapters go beyond the essentials of writing, they do contain information that may improve your writing as much as anything else you've learned in this book. Now that you're writing longer papers and having less trouble with the essentials, you are ready to consider the points in this unit in your rereading and revision. The result will be writing that is not only technically correct but also stylistically appropriate.

# Chapter 25

# Levels of Usage

All communication involves three factors: a sender, a message, and a receiver. This book is designed to help the sender—the person who has something to say—to communicate clearly and correctly. What the sender has to say is, of course, the message. Messages should always be adjusted to suit the receiver. This adjustment is the responsibility of the sender. There is no point in sending a message, whether it's a love letter or a spoken instruction, in Spanish if the receiver understands only English. Likewise, there is little to be gained from sending a message in colloquial English (such as you would use when speaking with your close friends) when the receiver is a prospective employer whom you have just met.

There are many **levels of usage** in spoken English. They range from almost unintelligible mutters and groans, through colloquial slang and professional jargon, right up to the formal, correct English used in law courts, in the State of the Union Address, and on other formal occasions. The same range is possible in written English: from graffiti up to the formal essay. The subject matter often helps determine the level.

The key to finding the proper level for your message is to consider not only the subject but also the receiver. Sometimes compromises must be made, as when you send one message to a wide variety of receivers. In general, you aim at the higher level of receiver and trust that the others will understand. Thus, wedding invitations, even those to the bridegroom's buddies, are usually stylized and formal.

No one has to tell you what level of language to use when you communicate with your friends at lunch or after school; that level has been clearly established over many years. Sometimes, however, it's not clear what level you should be using, and at such times, a careful consideration of the needs and preferences of your receiver is necessary. If your sociology teacher wants you to write papers in a formal style, and you want to get good marks, you will have to write formally. Likewise, because employers in general favor formal letters of application over casual ones, if you want to get a job, you will have to write your letter in a formal style. A more relaxed and personal style may be appropriate for a talk given to your class. Letters to friends and conversations with parents are still less formal, although they probably retain a degree of correctness not found in your conversations with your friends (or enemies).

There are no hard-and-fast divisions of language into levels; nevertheless, to help you choose the style most appropriate to the message and the receiver you are considering, we have outlined the basic characteristics of colloquial, general, and formal language.

| | Colloquial | General | Formal |
|---|---|---|---|
| Vocabulary | casual, everyday speech; many short words; some slang; many contractions | the language of educated persons; nonspecialized; short and long words; almost no slang; some contractions | many long words; often technical or specialized; no slang; no contractions |
| Sentence and Paragraph Structure | sentences short, simple; some sentence fragments; paragraphs short | complete sentences of varying length; paragraphs vary, but often short | all sentences complete; sentences usually long, complex; paragraphs fully developed, often at length |
| Tone | conversational, casual; sounds like ordinary speech | varies to suit message and purpose of writer | impersonal, serious, often instructional |

| | Colloquial | General | Formal |
|---|---|---|---|
| Typical Uses | personal letters, some fiction, some newspapers, much advertising | most of what we read: newspapers, magazines, novels, business correspondence | legal documents, some textbooks, academic writing, scientific reports |

No level is "better" than another. Each has its place and function. Your message, your receiver, and your purpose in writing are the factors that determine which level of usage is appropriate.

## EXERCISES

### Exercise 1

Write three paragraphs explaining why you were late for an important meeting—one for an employment interviewer, one for your father, and one for your teammates.

### Exercise 2

In the books, magazines, notes, and so on that you have with you now, try to find a piece of writing that is clearly colloquial, one that is general, and one that is formal. Then list briefly the characteristics of the typical person for whom each piece of writing is intended. Include physical features in your description, as well as education, hobbies, and anything else that you can speculate on.

# Chapter 26

# Clichés, Jargon, and Slang

## Clichés

A **cliché** is a group of words that was put together, quite creatively, long ago and that has been used and overused ever since. To write in clichés all the time is to write boringly or, even worse, to have your serious meaning sound funny.

He was sick as a dog, but we got him to the hospital in the nick of time.

"Sick as a dog" and "nick of time" are clichés. They do have meaning for your reader, but they're tired, worn-out ways of expressing that meaning. It is difficult, if not impossible, to eliminate clichés from your writing, but you can be aware of them and try to use them infrequently. Don't write automatically. Spend some time thinking about what you want to say; then say it in your own words, not someone else's.

### EXERCISE

### Exercise 1

Rewrite these sentences, expressing the ideas in your own, original words.

1. Tom stared at his plate and went white as a sheet.

______________________________________________

2. From staying in the shade she was as cool as a cucumber but as pale as a ghost. ______________________________

______________________________

3. My little niece is as cute as a button and as neat as a pin.

______________________________

4. He was green with envy until he learned that my new car was a lemon. ______________________________

______________________________

5. Slowly but surely the money rolled in.

______________________________

6. She was pretty as a picture for once in her life.

______________________________

7. After the game, they were happy as larks.

______________________________

8. His ace in the hole was his mother, who was loaded with dough.

______________________________

9. She tried to convince him that crying in his beer would only lead to rack and ruin. ______________________________

______________________________

10. He flipped his wig when he saw that she had stood him up.

______________________________

______________________________

Broadcasting is one of the chief refuges of the cliché. It's a rare newscast that doesn't include the expression "informed sources" or "claimed the life" or "skyrocketing inflation." Listening carefully for such overworked phrases on the radio and TV will make you more aware of them in your own writing and perhaps less likely to use them.

## EXERCISES

### Exercise 2

Write a postcard from wherever you wish. Use as many clichés as you can.

### Exercise 3

List ten clichés that you might hear on tonight's news and sports broadcast.

## Jargon

**Jargon** is a special breed of cliché. It is made up of the technical words or phrases used in connection with a particular trade or profession. Often such "trade language" enters the everyday language we use outside our jobs. Like other types of cliché, jargon is a poor substitute for original expression. The sports world has a highly developed jargon: "Third and six," "at the post," "slapshot," "uppercut," "on deck." Many of these expressions find their way into everyday conversation. Other professions have their own jargon. Although jargon may be useful or even necessary in the context of the job, it is clumsy and inappropriate in most writing.

The chief fault in using jargon is that it limits your audience to those who have the same vocabulary as you. To the rest of the world, your writing becomes difficult to understand or even meaningless. You can't expect to communicate in your English papers with sentences like this: "The professor replied with a logical uppercut that caught George right between the eyes and laid him out for the count." This may be a colorful way to describe the winning of an argument, but it will be effective only with readers who are boxing fans.

At its worst, jargon is the imitation of a specialized vocabulary. With its abstract words and long, complicated sentences, such jargon becomes sound without meaning, as the following sentence illustrates.

> Thus the meaningful verbalization of conceptual improvisation at the interpersonal interface is contra-indicated by frustrations arising from idiosyncratic linguistic actualization, vocabulary-wise, so that the verbalized formulations of the initiating consciousness actuate the latent rejection mechanisms.

The cure for this kind of jargon is consideration for your reader. If you really want your reader to understand you, write in a simple, straightforward style.

## EXERCISE

### Exercise 4

Write as many examples of jargon as you can for each of the following. If you treat this as a class exercise, you'll quickly see just how many examples there are.

1. card games: hit, cut, stay, run

2. film-making: pan, wipe, tracking shot

3. business: bottom line, arm's length, FOB, return

4. politics: stonewall, pork barrel, supply-side economics

5. computing: glitch, debugging, peek, on-line

### Exercise 5

Write a memo to someone in your field of study, directing his or her attention to a recent development. Use as much jargon as you can.

## Slang

**Slang** is street talk, inappropriate for the written language. There are innumerable examples of slang, from *A-OK* to *zowie,* and even dictionaries don't attempt to keep all the terms straight. Unless you're quoting someone who uses slang, avoid it and find words or expressions appropriate to written English. If you're in doubt, check your dictionary. The notation *sl.* or *slang* will appear after the word if it is slang, or after the meaning of the word that is a slang meaning. (Some words, such as *chick* and *neat*, have both a general meaning and a slang meaning.)

Like jargon, slang can limit or even block your communication with a reader. Slang is the most quickly dated type of language: what is appropriate now may well be laughed at in a few months. ("Right on, man. What a groovy scene! Far out!") Also, like jargon, slang is understood only by a limited group of people. You may exclude many readers if you use slang familiar only to a small group.

## EXERCISES

### Exercise 6

For one day, keep a list of the slang expressions you hear or read.

### Exercise 7

Pretend you are a basketball player/cheerleader whose team has just won the championship. Describe the winning game, using as much slang as you can.

# Chapter 27

# Wordiness

**Wordiness** is a problem that may develop if you try too hard to impress a reader with your use of words. Keep in mind that no reader wants to read "fill" or "padding." All writing should be as concise as it can be and still convey the message clearly. Even authors like Dickens and Michener, who have written huge quantities, choose their language carefully and don't waste their readers' time with unnecessary words.

Here's an example of what can happen when, in trying to impress, you lose sight of the need to communicate. Do you recognize any of your writing in this?

> In my own opinion, I feel very strongly indeed that the government of these United States of America is basically in need of an additional amount of meaningful input from its electors, the people of this great country of ours, at this point in time, frankly speaking. For too long a period of time, the leaders of this nation in Washington, D.C., have, rightly or wrongly, gone heedlessly off on their own particular course of action without the benefit of consultation or dialogue with the people, who, it stands to reason, are most willing and able to provide, clearly and without doubt, a distinct and clear path to follow into the future world of tomorrow.

By eliminating wordiness, make this into a clear statement.

The following are some of the worst offenders we have discovered in student writing. In some cases, many words are used when one or two would do. In other cases, the wording is redundant (says the same thing twice).

| *Wordy* | *Acceptable* |
| --- | --- |
| absolutely complete | complete |
| absolutely nothing | nothing |
| at that point in time | then |
| at this point in time | now |
| basic fundamentals | fundamentals |
| circled around | circled |
| collect together | collect |
| completely free | free |
| continue on | continue |
| dead bodies | corpses *or* bodies |
| disappear from view | disappear |
| entirely eliminated | eliminated |
| equally as good | as good |
| exactly identical | identical |
| final conclusion | conclusion |
| green in color | green |
| having the same thing in common | having in common |
| I personally feel | I feel |
| in my opinion, I think | I think |
| in this day and age | now |
| new innovation | innovation |
| personal friend | friend |
| proceed ahead | proceed |
| real, genuine leather | genuine leather |
| repeat again | repeat |
| repeat the same | repeat |
| seven A.M. in the morning | seven A.M. |
| small in size | small |
| such as, for example | such as |
| surround on all sides | surround |
| total disaster | disaster |
| totally wrecked | wrecked |
| true fact | fact |
| very (most, quite, rather) unique | unique |

## EXERCISES

### Exercise 1

Revise these sentences, making them more concise and understandable. Answers are on p. 298.

1. Basically, I myself prefer the real, genuine article to a phony imitation. ______________________________

______________________________

2. Although small in size and an ugly yellow in color, the car was, in point of fact, exactly identical to his last one. ______________

______________________________

3. The final conclusion wasn't known until he was completely free to announce himself successfully elected. ______________

______________________________

4. I will repeat again, for those of you who disappeared from view, that at this point in time we are completely free. ______________

______________________________

5. They circled around behind the enemy and, at four A.M. in the morning on July twelfth, surrounded them on all sides and entirely eliminated the threat of an invasion. ______________

______________________________

______________________________

6. There was absolutely nothing they could do except keep on repeating the true facts. ______________________________

______________________________

7. In my opinion, it is my belief that this particular new innovation will never live to see the light of day. ______________

______________________________

8. There comes a certain point in time when the last final reckoning is done, and you reach a final conclusion. ______________________

______________________________________________

9. Although his ideas seem to be fairly unique, we must be absolutely and completely positive that we don't repeat the same mistake again. ______________________________________

______________________________________________

10. I personally think she is faking her illness and pretending to be sick so she can stay home and not have to go to work. ______________

______________________________________________

## Exercise 2

Tell a well-known fairy tale or story in one paragraph, using as much padding and wordiness as you can. Exchange paragraphs with another student and simplify his or her horrible prose.

# Chapter 28

# Abusages

Some words and terms that appear in writing are simply incorrect or used incorrectly. We've named these misspelled, misused, or made-up words **abusages.** The presence of abusages in writing makes the writer appear ignorant in the eyes of anyone who knows anything about the English language. The list of abusages that follows is a partial one but does include some of the worst offenders. You should add to it the abusages that your teacher hates most.

| | |
|---|---|
| **alot** | This is actually two words: *a lot.* |
| **anyways** | Also, "anywheres" and "a long ways." There is no *s* on these words. |
| **could of** | Also, "would of," "might of," "should of," and so on. The helping verb is *have:* "could have." |
| **didn't do nothing** | This, along with all other double negatives ("couldn't get nowhere," "wouldn't talk to nobody," and so on), is wrong. Write "didn't do anything" or "did nothing." |

**irregardless** — There is no such word. Use *regardless.*

**irrevelant** — This is a misspelling. Spell the word *irrelevant.*

**media** used as a singular word — The word *media* is plural. The singular is *medium.* Write "TV is a mass medium. Print and radio are also examples of mass media." Reserve the word *mediums* for spiritualists.

**off of** — Use *off* alone: "I fell off the wagon."

**prejudice** used as an adjective — It is wrong to write "She is prejudice against men." Use *prejudiced.*

**prejudism** — There is no such word. Use *prejudice:* "He should show no prejudice to either side."

**real** used as an adverb — "Real sad," "real swell," and "real nice" are wrong. Use *really* or *very.*

**reason is because** — Use "the reason is that": "The reason is that I don't use a deodorant."

**suppose to** — Also, "use to." Use "supposed to" and "used to."

**themself** — Also "theirself," "ourselfs," "yourselfs," and "themselfs." The plural of *self* is *selves: themselves, ourselves,* and so on. Don't use "theirselves," though; there's no such word.

**youse** — There is no such word. "You" is used for both singular and plural. When waiting on tables, don't say "May I help youse?" to a group of English instructors, if you want a tip.

## EXERCISE

---

### Exercise 1

Correct the following sentences where necessary. Answers are on p. 299.

1. I could of done alot of things, but I chose to become rich and powerful real quickly.
2. Irregardless of what you say, I think the media is generally reliable.
3. The reason Dennis came home was because he couldn't do nothing more to help at the hospital.

4. They teach us alot of irrevelant things at this school.
5. Debbie's father is not prejudiced; he hates all her boyfriends, regardless of their background.
6. Mark was suppose to be in the race, but he fell off of his bike during practice.
7. I should of stayed home, but I went anyways.
8. The reason youse are failing is because you don't do no homework.
9. The police department was accused of prejudism against minority groups.
10. Steve did nothing to keep her from doing what she was supposed to do.

---

A whole category of abusages is created by misuse of pronouns.

Him and I had a fight.
Bob and her are the best spellers.
It came down to a choice between she and me.

There are two groups of pronouns: those used for subjects and those not used for subjects. In chapter 4 you reviewed how to find the subject of a sentence. When that subject is, or is referred to by, a pronoun, the pronoun should be one of these:

| | |
|---|---|
| I | we |
| you | |
| he, she | they |

When the pronoun is *not* the subject of the sentence, you should use one of these

| | |
|---|---|
| me | us |
| you | |
| him, her | them |

*He* and *I* had a fight. (The pronouns are the subject of the sentence.)

Bob and *she* are the best spellers. (The pronoun is part of the multiple subject "Bob and she.")

It came down to a choice between *her* and *me.* (The pronouns are not the subject of the sentence.)

The girls in the blue uniforms are *they.* (The pronoun stands for the subject of the sentence, *girls.*)

*He* is more honest than *she.* (The verb *is* is understood at the end of the sentence, and *she* is the subject of that verb.)

## Exercise

## Exercise 2

Correct the pronouns in these sentences as necessary.

1. Her and me did a really stupid thing.
2. He is a better cook than her, although she plays snooker better than him.
3. If I were you, I'd avoid them until they apologize.
4. We and them are not the best of friends anymore.
5. In fact, them and us are now enemies as you and he used to be.
6. No one is happier than me that this is the last exercise in this book.
7. Her and me are so glad to see the end that we are going to celebrate with them and their friends.
8. I can't believe that you and her got higher marks than me!
9. Can anything be done for them if they appeal to us for help?
10. She and I approve of Ralph and her joining them and we.

# Appendices

Appendix A Readings

Appendix B Progress Chart

Appendix C Answers

# Appendix A

# Readings

## Writing a Good Business Letter

*Brian Green*

1 A good business letter is one that gets results. The best way to get results is to develop a letter that, in its appearance, style, and content, conveys information efficiently. To perform this function, a business letter should be concise, clear, and courteous.

2 The business letter must be concise: don't waste words. Little introduction or preliminary chat is necessary. Get to the point, make the point, and leave it. It is safe to assume that your letter is being read by a very busy person with all kinds of paper to deal with. Such a person does not want to spend very much time with a newsy letter about your ski trip or medical problem. Reread and revise your message until the words and sentences you have used are precise. This takes time, but is a necessary part of writing a good letter. A short business letter that makes its point quickly has much more impact on a reader than a long-winded, rambling exercise in creative writing. This does not mean that there is no place for style and even, on occasion, humor in the business letter. While it conveys a message in its contents, the letter also provides the reader with an impression of you, its author: the medium is part of the message.

3 The business letter must be clear. You should have a very firm idea of what you want to say, and you should let the reader know it. Use the structure of the letter—the paragraphs, topic sentences, introduction, and conclusion—to guide the reader point by point from your thesis, through your reasoning, to your conclusion. Paragraph often, to break up the page and to lend an air of organization to the letter. Use an accepted business-letter format: there are several, and they can be found in any book of business English. Reread what you have written from the point of view of someone who is seeing it for the first time, and be sure that all explanations are adequate, all information provided (including reference numbers, dates, and other identification). A clear message, clearly delivered, is the essence of business communication.

4 The business letter must be courteous. Sarcasm and insults are ineffective and can often work against you. If you are sure you are right, point that out as politely as possible, explain why you are right, and outline what the reader is expected to do about it. Always put yourself in the place of the person to whom you are writing. What sort of letter would you respond to? How effective would sarcasm and threats be in making you fulfil a request? Another form of courtesy is taking care in your writing and typing of the business letter. Grammatical and spelling errors (even if you call them typing errors) tell a reader that you don't think enough of him or her to be careful. Such mistakes can lower the reader's opinion of you faster than anything you say, no matter how idiotic. There are excuses for ignorance; there are no excuses for sloppiness.

5 The business letter is your custom-made representative. It speaks for you and is a permanent record of your message. It can pay big dividends on the time you invest in giving it a concise message, a clear structure, and a courteous tone.

## What I Have Lived For

*Bertrand Russell*

1 Three passions, simple but overwhelmingly strong, have governed my life: the longing for love, the search for knowledge, and unbearable pity for the suffering of mankind. These passions, like great winds, have blown me hither and thither, in a wayward course, over a deep ocean of anguish, reaching to the very verge of despair.

2 I have sought love, first, because it brings ecstasy—ecstasy so great that I would often have sacrificed all the rest of life for a few

hours of this joy. I have sought it, next, because it relieves loneliness—that terrible loneliness in which one shivering consciousness looks over the rim of the world into the cold unfathomable lifeless abyss. I have sought it, finally, because in the union of love I have seen, in a mystic miniature, the prefiguring vision of the heaven that saints and poets have imagined. This is what I sought, and though it might seem too good for human life, this is what—at last—I have found.

3 With equal passion I have sought knowledge. I have wished to understand the hearts of men. I have wished to know why the stars shine. And I have tried to apprehend the Pythagorean power by which number holds sway above the flux. A little of this, but not much, I have achieved.

4 Love and knowledge, so far as they were possible, led upward toward the heavens. But always pity brought me back to earth. Echoes of cries of pain reverberate in my heart. Children in famine, victims tortured by oppressors, helpless old people a hated burden to their sons, and the whole world of loneliness, poverty, and pain make a mockery of what human life should be. I long to alleviate the evil, but I cannot, and I too suffer.

5 This has been my life. I have found it worth living, and would gladly live it again if the chance were offered me.

## The Dimensions of a Complete Life[1]

*Martin Luther King, Jr.*

1 Many, many centuries ago, out on a lonely, obscure island called Patmos, a man by the name of John caught a vision of the new Jerusalem descending out of heaven from God. One of the greatest glories of this new city of God that John saw was its completeness. It was not partial and one-sided, but it was complete in all three of its dimensions. And so, in describing the city in the twenty-first chapter of the book of Revelation, John says this: "The length and the breadth and the height of it are equal." In other words, this new city of God, this city of ideal humanity, is not an unbalanced entity but it is complete on all sides.

From *The Measure of a Man*, by Martin Luther King, Jr. (Philadelphia: Christian Education Press, 1959). Reprinted by permission.

[1]King originally wrote "Dimensions" as a speech and later published it as part of a book. As King's piece demonstrates, the principles of organization we have explained in unit V can be applied to oral presentations just as successfully as they can to writing.

"Dimensions" is a fairly challenging piece of reading, because King uses a very wide range of vocabulary. Don't let the unfamiliar words discourage you or throw you off the track, however. If you read carefully, you'll notice that King frequently defines or explains difficult words as he uses them.

2 Now John is saying something quite significant here. For so many of us the book of Revelation is a very difficult book, puzzling to decode. We look upon it as something of a great enigma wrapped in mystery. And certainly if we accept the book of Revelation as a record of actual historical occurrences it is a difficult book, shrouded with impenetrable mysteries. But if we will look beneath the peculiar jargon of its author and the prevailing apocalyptic symbolism, we will find in this book many eternal truths which continue to challenge us. One such truth is that of this text. What John is really saying is this: that life as it should be and life at its best is the life that is complete on all sides.

3 There are three dimensions of any complete life to which we can fitly give the words of this text: length, breadth, and height. The length of life as we shall think of it here is not its duration or its longevity, but it is the push of a life forward to achieve its personal ends and ambitions. It is the inward concern for one's own welfare. The breadth of life is the outward concern for the welfare of others. The height of life is the upward reach for God.

4 These are the three dimensions of life, and without the three being correlated, working harmoniously together, life is incomplete. Life is something of a great triangle. At one angle stands the individual person, at the other angle stand other persons, and at the top stands the Supreme, Infinite Person, God. These three must meet in every individual life if that life is to be complete.

5 Now let us notice first the length of life. I have said that this is the dimension of life in which the individual is concerned with developing his inner powers. It is that dimension of life in which the individual pursues personal ends and ambitions. This is perhaps the selfish dimension of life, and there is such a thing as moral and rational self-interest. If one is not concerned about himself he cannot be totally concerned about other selves.

6 Some years ago a learned rabbi, the late Joshua Liebman, wrote a book entitled *Peace of Mind.* He has a chapter in the book entitled "Love Thyself Properly." In this chapter he says in substance that it is impossible to love other selves adequately unless you love your own self properly. Many people have been plunged into the abyss of emotional fatalism because they did not love themselves properly. So every individual has a responsibility to be concerned about himself enough to discover what he is made for. After he discovers his calling he should set out to do it with all of the strength and power in his being. He should do it as if God Almighty called him at this particular moment in history to do it. He should seek to do his job so well that the living, the dead, or the unborn could not do it better. No matter how small one thinks his life's work is in terms of the norms of the world and the so-called big jobs, he must realize that it has cosmic significance if he is serving humanity and doing the will of God.

7 To carry this to one extreme, if it falls your lot to be a street-sweeper, sweep streets as Raphael painted pictures, sweep streets as Michelangelo carved marble, sweep streets as Beethoven composed music, sweep streets as Shakespeare wrote poetry. Sweep streets so well that all the hosts of heaven and earth will have to pause and say, "Here lived a great street-sweeper who swept his job well." In the words of Douglas Mallock:

> If you can't be a highway, just be a trail;
> If you can't be the sun, be a star,
> For it isn't by size that you win or you fail—
> Be the best of whatever you are.

When you do this, you have mastered the first dimension of life—the length of life.

8 But don't stop here; it is dangerous to stop here. There are some people who never get beyond this first dimension. They are brilliant people; often they do an excellent job in developing their inner powers; but they live as if nobody else lived in the world but themselves. There is nothing more tragic than to find an individual bogged down in the length of life, devoid of the breadth.

9 The breadth of life is that dimension of life in which we are concerned about others. An individual has not started living until he can rise above the narrow confines of his individualistic concerns to the broader concerns of all humanity.

10 You remember one day a man came to Jesus and he raised some significant questions. Finally he got around to the question, "Who is my neighbor?" This could easily have been a very abstract question left in mid-air. But Jesus immediately pulled that question out of mid-air and placed it on a dangerous curve between Jerusalem and Jericho. He talked about a certain man who fell among thieves. Three men passed; two of them on the other side. And finally another man came and helped the injured man on the ground. He is known to us as the good Samaritan. Jesus says in substance that this is a great man. He was great because he could project the "I" into the "thou."

11 So often we say that the priest and the Levite were in a big hurry to get to some ecclesiastical meeting and so they did not have time. They were concerned about that. I would rather think of it another way. I can well imagine that they were quite afraid. You see, the Jericho road is a dangerous road, and the same thing that happened to the man who was robbed and beaten could have happened to them. So I imagine the first question that the priest and the Levite asked was this: "If I stop to help this man, what will happen to me?" Then the good Samaritan came by, and by the very nature of his concern reversed the question: "If I do not stop to help this man, what will happen to him?" And so this man was great because he had the mental equipment for a danger-

ous altruism. He was great because he could surround the length of his life with the breadth of life. He was great not only because he had ascended to certain heights of economic security, but because he could condescend to the depths of human need.

12 All this has a great deal of bearing in our situation in the world today. So often racial groups are concerned about the length of life, their economic privileged position, their social status. So often nations of the world are concerned about the length of life, perpetuating their nationalistic concerns, and their economic ends. May it not be that the problem in the world today is that individuals as well as nations have been overly concerned with the length of life, devoid of the breadth? But there is still something to remind us that we are interdependent, that we are all involved in a single process, that we are all somehow caught in an inescapable network of mutuality. Therefore whatever affects one directly affects all indirectly.

13 As long as there is poverty in the world I can never be rich, even if I have a billion dollars. As long as diseases are rampant and millions of people in this world cannot expect to live more than twenty-eight or thirty years, I can never be totally healthy even if I just got a good check-up at Mayo Clinic. I can never be what I ought to be until you are what you ought to be. This is the way our world is made. No individual or nation can stand out boasting of being independent. We are interdependent. So John Donne placed it in graphic terms when he affirmed, "No man is an island entire of itself. Every man is a piece of the continent, a part of the main." Then he goes on to say, "Any man's death diminishes me because I am involved in mankind, and therefore never send to know for whom the bell tolls; it tolls for thee." When we discover this, we master the second dimension of life.

14 Finally, there is a third dimension. Some people never get beyond the first two dimensions of life. They master the first two. They develop their inner powers; they love humanity, but they stop right here. They end up with the feeling that man is the end of all things and that humanity is God. Philosophically or theologically, many of them would call themselves humanists. They seek to live life without a sky. They find themselves bogged down on the horizontal plane without being integrated on the vertical plane. But if we are to live the complete life we must reach up and discover God. H. G. Wells was right: "The man who is not religious begins at nowhere and ends at nothing." Religion is like a mighty wind that breaks down doors and makes that possible and even easy which seems difficult and impossible.

15 In our modern world it is easy for us to forget this. We so often find ourselves unconsciously neglecting this third dimension of life. Not that we go up and say, "Good-by, God, we are going to leave you now." But we become so involved in the things of this world that we are unconsciously carried away by the rushing tide of materialism which

leaves us treading in the confused waters of secularism. We find ourselves living in what Professor Sorokin of Harvard called a sensate civilization, believing that only those things which we can see and touch and to which we can apply our five senses have existence.

16 Something should remind us once more that the great things in this universe are things that we never see. You walk out at night and look up at the beautiful stars as they bedeck the heavens like swinging lanterns of eternity, and you think you can see all. Oh, no. You can never see the law of gravitation that holds them there. You walk around this vast campus and you probably have a great esthetic experience as I have had walking about and looking at the beautiful buildings, and you think you see all. Oh, no. You can never see the mind of the architect who drew the blueprint. You can never see the love and the faith and the hope of the individuals who made it so. You look at me and you think you see Martin Luther King. You don't see Martin Luther King; you see my body, but, you must understand, my body can't think, my body can't reason. You don't see the me that makes me me. You can never see my personality.

17 In a real sense everything that we see is a shadow cast by that which we do not see. Plato was right: "The visible is a shadow cast by the invisible." And so God is still around. All of our new knowledge, all of our new developments, cannot diminish his being one iota. These new advances have banished God neither from the microcosmic compass of the atom nor from the vast, unfathomable ranges of interstellar space. The more we learn about this universe, the more mysterious and awesome it becomes. God is still here.

18 So I say to you, seek God and discover him and make him a power in your life. Without him all of our efforts turn to ashes and our sunrises into darkest nights. Without him, life is a meaningless drama with the decisive scenes missing. But with him we are able to rise from the fatigue of despair to the buoyancy of hope. With him we are able to rise from the midnight of desperation to the daybreak of joy. St. Augustine was right—we were made for God and we will be restless until we find rest in him.

19 Love yourself, if that means rational, healthy, and moral self-interest. You are commanded to do that. That is the length of life. Love your neighbor as you love yourself. You are commanded to do that. That is the breadth of life. But never forget that there is a first and even greater commandment, "Love the Lord thy God with all thy heart and all thy soul and all thy mind." This is the height of life. And when you do this you live the complete life.

20 Thank God for John who, centuries ago, caught a vision of the new Jerusalem. God grant that those of us who still walk the road of life will catch this vision and decide to move forward to that city of complete life in which the length and the breadth and the height are equal.

## Rip-off at the Supermarket

*John Keats*

1 It is the glory and triumph of the American supermarket to have made more food of more kinds available to more people at lower cost than any marketing system heretofore seen on the face of the earth. Such, at least, is the opinion of our supermarket executives, who add that their margins of profit are so paper-thin as to be virtually nonexistent. Their margin is less than a penny on the dollar, they say, and even though food prices are high, they are nonetheless giving us food practically at cost.

2 Another view is provided by Federal Trade Commission figures, which suggest that in addition to their enormous profits, supermarkets steal no less than $2.6 billion from us every year—through overcharges alone. The FTC estimate refers to false weights and measures and other deceitful business practices, and does not include whatever mistakes cash register operators may make by hitting the wrong keys.

3 My view of our supermarkets is that I don't care half so much about what they earn or steal as I care about the moral swamp in which they operate. Supermarket people take us for fools, presuming that we know nothing about food; that we shop impulsively and irrationally; that we can be cheated with impunity and misled into wasting our money on trash. That is their attitude; that is their view of you and me; and if you step over here to the meat counter, I will show you what I mean.

4 Chuck Roast, 87¢; California Roast, blade in, $1.03; Cross Rib Pot Roast, $1.39; Under Blade Pot Roast, 99¢; Arm Pot Roast, bone in, $1.29; Chuck Roast, boneless, $1.27; Arm Steak, $1.18; London Broil, $1.53; Cube Steak, $1.49; Stewing Cubes, $1.59; Chuck Steak, 87¢.

5 You will notice that all of these meats are marked SPECIAL! Now, this store advertises its employment of "Master Butchers."

6 "The quality of every cut of meat is backed by the signature of a Master Butcher," their advertising says. "Behind every great cut of meat there's one of our 108 Master Butchers. He puts his signature on each cut he's responsible for. Proudly. Because he knows there isn't a meat case in town that holds better value than his. In quality. In trim. He has seen to that—personally. Get to know the name of your Master Butcher. Better yet, get to know him."

7 Better still, try to find him. If you do, you will learn that his mastery lies as much in creative writing as it does in butchery. All of the meats we see in this case, all of these apparently different cuts at their different prices, happen to be chuck cut in slightly different ways. By

The *Atlantic*, May 31, 1976, pp. 27–34 (abridged).

masterful butchery and inventive naming, five dollars' worth of chuck has become worth twelve dollars.

8 Here is another meat counter, full of packages of grayish-pink hamburger. A sign over this display says the hamburger has been "extended" by the addition of textured vegetable protein. This means that protein taken from soybeans has been added to the meat. But the sign fails to say what percentage of the hamburger is soybean. You will notice that the individually wrapped packages fail to say there is any at all. Instead, their labels say "MEAT: Beef, 50%; Pork, 25%; Poultry, 25%."

9 Here is a third meat counter, where the Master Butcher is offering us top round steak at $1.69, and a steak called "Bracciole" at $1.83. "Bracciole" is a top round steak cut thin. Look at the "Quick Fry Pork Chops!" They cost 20¢ more per pound than the other pork chops, the difference being that, as in the case of the "Bracciole," they have been cut thin. Oh, now here they have porterhouse steak at $2.29, tenderloin at $3.99, and sirloin at $2.99. The tenderloin and the sirloin come from the same porterhouse. So we can buy the porterhouse at $2.29—and remove the bone at home if we want the tenderloin one night and the sirloin another—or we can pay the Master Butcher roughly $2.40 to cut out the T-bone for us. Since it would take the Master Butcher just as long to remove the T-bone from a three-pound porterhouse as it would for him to remove the T-bone from a two-pound porterhouse—namely, about ten seconds—the rate the store is charging for this boning service is higher than the hourly rate charged by a Park Avenue psychiatrist.

10 What the store thinks of us is now very clear. It believes that we cannot tell the difference between a chuck steak and an off hind hoof, and that we cannot reason. It also believes we cannot do arithmetic. For example, you may have seen those bags of onions piled up near the turnstiles as we entered the store. The three-pound bags marked 79¢? Today's SPECIAL! on onions? Well, now, over here, in the produce counters, there is a bin of loose onions. They are identical to the ones in the bags. But they are priced at 25¢ a pound.

11 Down the street is another supermarket. This chain advertises that it is honest. "We Don't Play Games!" their advertisement says. In this store, we find a special sale of mushrooms at 49¢, but when we take the mushrooms to the check-out counter, the girl rings up 98¢. When we protest, she shows us the chart of prices posted beside her machine. Sure enough, on the chart mushrooms are 98¢. But when we tell her that the sign on the produce bin said 49¢, she gives us the mushrooms for 49¢, saying, "They never tell us about specials." If someone is not playing games, then someone is making mistakes that happen to be profitable ones.

12 Sometimes mistakes in meaning are made. One seafood supply house advises its client stores that turbot looks like a cross between a halibut and a fluke, and that turbot fillets can therefore "be used as you

would fluke or sole." One store's interpretation of this advice was to sell halibut fillets as "lemon sole" and "Dover sole"—at sole prices. Likewise, rounds punched from skate wings became "scallops" and crayfish became "baby lobster tails."

13 Another store cuts wheels of cheddar into wedges, wraps the wedges in differently tinted plastic, and sells them at different prices under the names "sharp," "old sharp," and "aged sharp." The large crumbs caused by the cutting are put into small plastic bags and sold at an even higher price as "cheese bits."

14 Supermarket managers presumably view us as captive easy marks, impulsive and irrational in our buying habits. To capitalize on this notion they have designed store floor plans and displays to serve as psychological traps. For example, knowing children to be what they are (which is bored, restless, and wishing they were somewhere other than in the store), clever store managers put candy and other juvenile junk food on bottom shelves in easy view of little eyes and within the reach of tiny hands. The children will reach for it and, the manager believes, parents will let them keep the junk for fear of starting a row if they are told to put it back.

15 The store is laid out so as to bring the shoppers first to the high-profit items, because research suggests that shoppers begin filling their carts when they come to the first displays of foods. Thus large displays of the higher-profit foods will be located at adult arm and eye levels at the ends of the aisles. The lower-profit ones will be found in smaller displays in the middle of the aisles, and/or on shelves above and below normal arm and eye levels.

16 To satisfy the shoppers' penchant for impulse buying (meaning the selection of something the shopper had not intended to buy but will put into his shopping cart now that he sees it), the impulse items such as soft drinks, snacks, and "gourmet foods" will be placed across the ends of the aisles and close to the check-out counters. Another impulse purchase is the "go-together." If a store puts on a loss leader sale of broccoli, and if the manager has his wits about him, next to the broccoli will be extremely high-profit bottles of hollandaise sauce.

17 Presuming the public is unobservant, or unthinking, or both, a store will advertise a "Special! Three cans for 60¢!" when each can of that item regularly sells for 20¢. Similarly, a supermarket may advertise a sale on one brand of salad oil. In the store will be a large placard announcing this sale. Beneath the placard, however, will be a huge display of some other brand of much more expensive salad oil. The brand to which the advertising and placard refer may be found in a distant aisle on a shelf display two bottles wide among the Harvard beets.

18 What these practices have in common with out-and-out cheating is that both are based on psychological manipulation. The general public, as studies of consumer shopping habits suggest, may very well be

ignorant, unobservant, easily misled, impulsive, and irrational. But what kind of people use this knowledge deliberately to take vicious commercial advantage; to build a store that is a trap; to create situations scientifically designed to lead people to act irrationally; to wring the most money out of the least thoughtful and the least informed (who, by the way, are also likely to be the least able to pay the price)? One wonders what these store managers really think of what they are doing, and what they think of themselves.

19 A man I shall call Oswald Krell was most helpful in answering these questions. Together with his wife, Krell owns and operates a somewhat less than super market that competes with three gigantic chain outlets. He has been in the marketplace ever since he started as a stock boy thirty-five years ago. Krell laughed when I told him about the SPECIAL! on the three-pound bag of onions that cost 4¢ more than three pounds of loose onions.

20 "Ah, that's merchandising," he said, and chuckled. "It's that 4¢, that's what's so special about them."

21 "Look," he said seriously, "you show me where in the law it says that if you mark something 'special' it has to mean it's specially *low*. Maybe it means it's specially *high*. 'Special' doesn't have to mean any price, high or low. All it means is, it's special, there's something special about it. All the store was saying is that those onions were special, and that's what they were: special."

22 Krell saw nothing wrong with the idea of selling the same part of a steer at several different prices under several different names. "Ah, that's merchandising," he said again. It was not really overcharging, because it was a service to the customer.

23 "You take a bone out for a customer, and you do him a service, so you charge for the service."

24 Krell readily agreed that any customer who wanted to cut up his own chickens and roasts at home could save perhaps a thousand dollars a year by doing so, but instead of seeing the store's fees as unreasonable, if not grotesque, he said that it just went to show how valuable the store's services were.

25 Because I was one of his customers, and because I evinced a serious interest in marketing and was eager to learn, Krell was glad to tell me what he knew. A series of conversations ensued over a period of weeks, and at the first of these, I wondered how he and his wife could operate a small, independent supermarket in direct competition with three gigantic chain stores in the same section of the city, particularly when his fixed costs are relatively higher than theirs, and when he has to charge more than they do for many items. Part of the answer, he said, lies in personal service. Unlike the giant stores, Oswald Krell's store will take telephoned orders and make deliveries. Krell will cash checks for regular customers. At Christmastime he sets out liquor and cheeses, cookies and meats for his customers. He allows charge

accounts. He keeps an excellent line of meats, and his butchers will cut, trim, and bone to order. There is seldom a long line at either of his two check-out counters. Krell makes a point of remembering names, and because of his courtesy and service, his clientele is willing to pay his often-higher-than-giant-supermarket prices. The rest of the answer, however, lies in certain "supermarket" prices, which seem high enough to permit anyone to stay in business.

26 Each morning Krell receives from his supplier a printed statement showing what every store in the city has paid for its supplies that day, together with the prices they are charging their customers. He showed me such a statement. Generally speaking, the figures were sufficiently identical to suggest telepathy, if not collusion. Different prices on some of the same brands and items did obtain in different sections of the city, however, and often within the same chain of stores. When asked about this, Krell explained that every store charges all it can get.

27 "Like take produce," Krell said. "My markup on produce averages 34 percent. I know, that's low, but the kind of stuff they send me, it's terrible, and anyway, that's not where the money is. But if I had the store in Crestwood Hills, I could mark it up 100 percent, because those people have so much money they don't care, and anyway, they'd never know the difference. Your markup depends on the neighborhood."

28 Krell showed me his books. His markup on meat was 25 percent; on canned goods and staples, 14 percent; frozen foods, 25 percent. The overall average markup on all items in the store was only 18 percent. This figure seemed in line with the general average, according to what could be deduced from the daily reports of supermarket wholesale prices and retail markups. As Krell explained, he could not afford to get too far out of line.

29 He turned next to a daily report from New York City, which, he said, comes out "like on a stock ticker." The report gives the daily changes in wholesale prices.

30 "Now you know you're not supposed to change the price once you put the item on the shelf," he said. "So what you do is put two cans of it on the shelf, and you keep the other 500 cans of it in the basement. So you look at the ticker, and it says fruit cocktail is 51¢ a can today, up 3¢ from yesterday, and you remember that you paid 40¢ last week for all those cans in the basement. So as soon as you sell the two cans off the shelf, or throw them away, you go down in the basement. Today's wholesale price is 51¢, so you add your 14 percent markup for canned goods, and you put the can on the shelf for 58¢, and now you're selling a 40¢ can for 58¢. There's no law that says you can't buy when it's cheap and not display it till the price goes up. People do it all the time. It's what business is all about, you make a little money." . . .

31 "Of course there's money in it," Krell [said.] "I've been in this business thirty-five years. You asked me who's primarily responsible for the high price of food today, and out of my experience, I'll tell you

this: it's the stores. And particularly it's the big food processors who also own the chain stores, and smart guys like that one who set up Tremendous Kitchens as an outfit in the middle between the processor and the Giant Plastic stores that Tremendous Kitchens owns."

32 I asked him to explain.

33 "Well, okay," he said. "So your wife buys Junkies. Those corn things? Say the wholesale price of Junkies is 20¢. So this guy orders Junkies by the ton for Tremendous Kitchens. So the Junkie people give him 5 percent off—if you're a big guy, you call it a discount and you're a businessman; if you're a little guy they call it a kickback and you're a crook, right? Anyway, he sells those Junkies to his Giant Plastic stores at the wholesale price, 20¢ a bag, so he's made 5 percent, selling to himself. But then Giant Plastic marks up the bags, 36¢ apiece; they make 16¢ a bag. The Giant Plastic stores got to make money or they wouldn't be in business. But Giant Plastic is making money for Tremendous Kitchens as well as making money for Giant Plastic, right? And this guy owns *both.* Plus he's getting his 5 percent when he buys from Junkies and sells to Plastic. If you think he's going to give that 5 percent to the customer, you're out of your mind. What the hell, it's a business."

34 We discussed, briefly, an article that had appeared in the morning newspaper. The president of a supermarket chain had told a meeting of stockholders that food retailers were being subjected to "unwarranted and unjustified" criticism on profits. He was quoted as saying that retail food profits "are too low to provide a proper return on the capital investment necessary to operate in today's competitive climate," and that "if we eliminated all the retail food profits," the customer would benefit only to the extent of 8¢ per person per week.

35 Krell burst into a roar of laughter.

36 "That's the guy!" he said, and laughed. "That's the guy I was telling you! He's the one who owns Tremendous Kitchens and Giant Plastic! Listen, I know the guy, he's a member of our country club. Look what else the article says. Tremendous Kitchens' earnings were $8.9 million last year, which is up $2.7 million over the year before—and while he's telling the stockholders this, he's talking about 8¢ a week per customer is all that Giant Plastic is making. But Plastic is making money for Tremendous, as well as for Plastic. Eight cents a week; he's got to be kidding." . . .

37 As Krell told his stories, I considered other reasons for the price of supermarket food. He had mentioned his membership in a country club near his home. He was a man in his middle fifties who wore his hair youthfully long and dressed in close-fitting double-knit slacks, colorful sports jackets, and Florentine shoes with square gold buckles on them. His wife, too, was fashionably turned out. Every year they took a winter vacation at Acapulco and a summer holiday in Europe. On every working day they arrived at their store at seven in the morning. At seven

in the evening, they turned out the lights, locked the store, and drove home in their Cadillac, which was new each year and always white. They worked long and hard for their money, but they seemed to live rather well on what they earned.

38 One day a salesman entered the store. He represented a bakery specializing in French bread, and after a few minutes he left without having made a sale.

39 "You know, those people are very naïve," Krell mused as we watched the salesman depart. "They have a good product, but, you know, they didn't give me one loaf of bread, not even one roll. How do they expect to do business like that? When the Humble Pie Farms guy comes in, he says 'I want you to have these 500 loaves you can give away to your customers so they'll try them.' You know what I mean?"

40 "Yes. It means he gives you 500 free loaves that you can sell for 55¢ apiece."

41 "That's right," Krell said. "I mean you're not naïve, Humble Pie isn't naïve, I'm not naïve, but those French bread people—how naïve can you get?"

42 He paused to wonder about this.

43 "I'll be honest with you," he said. "You know how much I make on milk? I make enough on milk alone to pay the mortgage on the house and buy a new car every year. You know how it works? You say to the dairy, okay, I'll sell only your products, right? Then you sell so many quarts over a certain number, and a guy comes around and hands you 5 percent in cash. If they don't show that cash on their books, which they don't, you don't have to show it on yours, right? The customer comes in and he thinks milk costs so much a bottle; all over town that's the price of milk. *He* thinks. The customer doesn't know what milk costs. The farmer might not be getting any money, but the dairies are making money so fast they give you 5 percent. I was very naïve about milk till I was talking with some guys and they said, 'Ossie, are you stupid or something, you don't ask for 5 percent?' That's how I learned. You have to ask for it. So I asked, and the guy comes around with the 5 percent in cash."

44 "It's like with cigarettes," Krell said. "For every carton you order, they give you two free packs. At 50¢ a pack, they give you a dollar, right? So you order 20 cartons, and what the customer doesn't know, and naturally what the IRS doesn't know, is you get 24 cartons, a gift of $20. I ask you, are the cigarette people making money? Are the dairies and the bread people making money? They're making so much money they can give it away."

45 If milk paid the mortgage and bought the car, then it was likely that cigarettes paid for Acapulco and bread paid for Europe; or maybe it was just that all those cans in the basement paid for everything and Oswald Krell was actually more of a saint than he wished to appear at

the country club. In any case, someone was paying for the gifts that Krell received, and it is not difficult to imagine who is ultimately picking up the bill. Nor is it difficult to imagine what gifts might be given to entrepreneurs much more powerful than an operator as small as Oswald Krell. . . .

46 While the conversations with Krell touched upon a man's life and work, it seemed to me that they revealed a man making what way he could while contending with circumstances over which he had no control and which were certainly none of his devising. He was different from other supermarket store managers in that he and his wife owned their business, and therefore had a more direct interest in it than the salaried managers of corporate chains. This direct interest they expressed in the personal services they offered their customers, services that were largely responsible for their ability to remain in business in competition with huge stores that sold many foodstuffs at prices lower than their own. But otherwise, Krell, like the larger supermarketeers, accepted the terms of a system that told him he was a businessman dealing with the public, rather than a grocer dealing with neighbors. Granted that the neighborhood grocer is a businessman, too. Yet there is a difference between a big business dealing with an anonymous public and a small business dealing with recognizable individuals.

47 Krell had accepted the outlook of big business; he shared the view that he was free to do anything the law did not expressly prohibit. If the law was silent with respect to the meaning of the word "special," then he was free to give the word his own meaning. His store, too, was laid out as a psychological trap for the customers to whom he otherwise provided courtesies and services—and he thought this was clever. He almost, but not quite, equated sharp practice with dishonesty. His view was rather like that of a great university that hires ringers for its football team and pretends that they are scholars, in that it is a view that lacks a moral base. It embraces the notions *If the other guys can get away with it, so can I* and *You're stupid if you don't do it.* Whatever is advantageous is seen as intelligent, and whatever is disadvantageous is seen as stupid, and advantage is measured in terms of dollars and cents.

48 At bottom, if a moral swamp can be said to have a bottom, is the notion that business is a game, and that the point of playing a game is to win it. Since this is a prevalent American point of view, it is scarcely surprising that Krell should share it. Few, in any case, question who the losers are.

# Appendix B

# Progress Chart

On the next two pages is a chart for you to fill in as your marked assignments are returned to you. If you keep it up to date, you'll have a complete and easy-to-read record of your progress, and, more important, you'll be able to spot any recurring errors. You should deal with these by carefully reviewing the relevant chapter (or chapters) in this book.

If you make a spelling or apostrophe error, write down your mistake and then either use your dictionary or turn back to unit 1 to find the correct form. Write the correction in the next column, beside the mistake. For the other columns in the chart, identify each error (your teacher's notations will help), and then look up the error in the book. Reread the rule and study the examples given. Then enter the page number of that information in the space provided. (We've written in sample entries for a paper titled "My Summer Vacation.")

The main purpose of this chart is to keep you from making the same error over and over. After you've entered the results of two or three assignments on your chart, you will begin to see exactly where you need to do more work. If a careful review of the point in this book doesn't cure the problem, ask your instructor for additional help.

## Progress Chart

| Assignment | Spelling and Apostrophe | | Sentence Structure *(Enter number of errors and page reference)* | | | Grammar *(Enter number of errors and page reference)* | | | Punctuation | | | Mark/Grade Received |
|---|---|---|---|---|---|---|---|---|---|---|---|---|
| | Error | Correction | Type of Error | number | page | Type of Error | number | page | Error | number | page | |
| "My Summer Vacation" | its | it's | sentence fragment | 2 | 68 | tense agreement | 2 | 131 | semi-colon | 1 | 162 | C+ |
| | neccessary | necessary | parallelism | 1 | 102 | subject-verb agreement | 4 | 110 | comma | 2 | 152 | |
| | procede | proceed | | | | | | | | | | |

# Appendix C

# Answers

## Chapter 1: Three Suggestions for Quick Improvement

### Exercise 1

1. surely
2. liking
3. believable
4. arrangement
5. moving
6. barely
7. radiator
8. experiencing
9. absolutely
10. using

### Exercise 2

1. safely
2. arguing
3. sizable
4. accelerator
5. extremely
6. improvement
7. reducing
8. usable
9. immediately
10. requiring

## Exercise 3

1. sincerely
2. coherence
3. valuable
4. guidance
5. settling
6. icy
7. completely
8. purchasing
9. collapsible
10. dispensing

## Exercise 4

1. boring
2. movement
3. scarcely
4. unusable
5. careful
6. advertisement
7. excusable
8. providing
9. sensible
10. improvement

## Exercise 5

1. safety
2. ranging
3. reducible
4. balancing
5. entirely
6. insurance
7. definitely
8. careless
9. collapsible
10. distancing

## Exercise 7

1. banning
2. stopping
3. admitted
4. nailing
5. stirred
6. jumper
7. equipping
8. writing
9. mapping
10. interrupted

## Exercise 8

1. swimmer
2. beginning
3. dropped
4. training
5. redder
6. appearance
7. planned
8. happening
9. stopper
10. insisted

## Exercise 9

1. suffering
2. quizzed
3. permitting
4. shipped
5. meeting
6. compelling
7. cropped
8. tipping
9. programer
10. quartered

## Exercise 10

1. preferring
2. omitted
3. transferring
4. developing
5. controller
6. occurred
7. putting
8. forgettable
9. biting
10. preferred

## Exercise 11

1. biddable
2. comforting
3. forgetful
4. accepted
5. available
6. regretting
7. mentioned
8. controllable
9. disappearance
10. deferred

## Exercise 12

1. overlapped
2. expelling
3. bidder
4. acquitted
5. appearing
6. planning
7. developed
8. transferred
9. paralleled
10. commissioner

## Exercise 13

1. occurrence
2. existence
3. coherence
4. deterrence
5. interference
6. subsistence
7. difference
8. dependence
9. recurrence
10. insistence

## Exercise 15

1. brief
2. cashier
3. receive
4. pierce
5. relief
6. retrieve
7. ceiling
8. believe
9. deceitful
10. hygiene

## Exercise 16

1. thief
2. piece
3. grief
4. conceive
5. priest
6. frontier
7. chandelier
8. conceit
9. perceive
10. Fahrenheit

## Exercise 17

1. wiener, weighed
2. freight, surveillance
3. receipt, eight
4. relief, conceit
5. reigns, heir

## Exercise 18

1. chow mein, stein
2. Neither, Geiger counter
3. neighbor, niece
4. reins, sleigh
5. conceivable, either

## Exercise 19

1. grieved, vein
2. their, belief, protein
3. species, height
4. seized, receivers, foreign

## Exercise 20

1. heroes
2. histories
3. buses (busses)
4. ghettos
5. lives
6. crises
7. sheep
8. phenomena
9. nuclei (or nucleuses)
10. appendixes (or appendices)

### Exercise 21

1. loneliness
2. copied
3. craziness
4. easier
5. prettiest
6. replies
7. replying
8. thirtieth
9. unnecessarily
10. trafficking

### Exercise 22

1. let–ter
2. con–sists
3. pa–tients
4. man–age–ment
5. pro–cess
6. ship–ping
7. naph–tha
8. through *(Words of one syllable cannot be divided.)*
9. dis–tri–bu–tion
10. suc–cess

## Chapter 2: Sound-Alikes, Look-Alikes, and Spoilers

### Exercise 1

1. effect, courses
2. Our, accepted
3. dessert, than
4. you're, losing
5. quiet, hear
6. whose, conscience
7. fourth, than
8. it's, its
9. advise, choose
10. Does, dining

### Exercise 2

1. principle, principal
2. fourth, chose
3. except, dessert
4. You're, conscience
5. quiet, hear
6. except, minor
7. lose, too, morale
8. conscience, your
9. stationary, its
10. Does, woman

### Exercise 3

1. hear, here
2. stationery, two
3. lose, it's
4. your, minors
5. piece, dessert
6. accept, Council

7. coarse, effect
8. peace, quiet
9. Who's, women's
10. piece, forth

## Exercise 4

1. deserted, then
2. Where, quiet
3. two, latter
4. consul, principle
5. Many, lose
6. You're, your, dose
7. principle, then
8. It's, later
9. later, except
10. quite, woman

## Exercise 5

1. allot, dining
2. peace, our
3. women, desert
4. Where, we're
5. stationary, forth
6. hear, you're, chose, course
7. are, conscious, their
8. affected, morale
9. whose, advice
10. principal, peace, minor

## Exercise 6

1. affects, morale
2. compliment, than
3. advice, personal
4. miner, does
5. their, moral
6. hear, you're
7. Who's, personal, stationery
8. choose, latter, course
9. dessert, quite
10. Too, where

## Exercise 7

1. dessert, course
2. You're, conscience
3. it's, principle
4. advise, personal
5. accepted, compliments
6. minors, they're
7. chose, dining
8. hear, your
9. than, our
10. too, coarse, to

## Exercise 8

1. its, too, to
2. chose, council
3. Personnel, then, counsel
4. choose, course
5. does, affect
6. Council, its, later

7. personal, women
8. compliment, conscious
9. council, advice
10. complements, effectively

---

### Exercise 9

1. quite, you're
2. choose, whose
3. Here, its
4. Many, personnel, morale
5. too, we're
6. then, your
7. coarse, desert
8. conscious, effect
9. its, does
10. conscious, effects

---

### Exercise 10

1. then, excepted
2. loose, accept
3. Whose, complement
4. too, dessert
5. advice, counsel
6. There, lose
7. stationery, where
8. minor, effect
9. than, morals
10. council, whose, advise

---

## Chapter 3: The Apostrophe

---

### Exercise 1

1. there's
2. didn't
3. they'll
4. it's
5. don't
6. it'll
7. it's
8. we're
9. you're
10. he's

---

### Exercise 2

1. she'll
2. we've
3. I'm
4. won't
5. who's
6. shouldn't
7. they're
8. who's
9. you'll
10. hasn't

---

## Exercise 3

1. can't
2. you're
3. they'll
4. wouldn't
5. who's
6. won't
7. it'll
8. they're
9. we've
10. you've

## Exercise 4

1. They'll have to stay home because they're still sick.
2. It's been a long time since they've had a good holiday.
3. We're many miles from where we were then.
4. You're not going to try your luck again, are you?
5. It's been a long time since someone who'll stand up for what is right has run for office.
6. You're going to class because it's good for you; you'll never get far unless you've got your education.
7. Let's see if they're up to the standards we've set.
8. We'll have to do better if we're to succeed.
9. They've finally done what she's suggested.
10. Since you've been to Europe, we've adopted two more children.

## Exercise 5

1. Who's, I've
2. There's, we've
3. It's, you've
4. I've, they're, there's
5. you'll, isn't
6. couldn't, I'm
7. won't, he's
8. I've, you're
9. You'll, he's
10. We're, we'll, he's, haven't, doesn't

## Exercise 6

1. wagon's
2. sea's
3. everybody's
4. love's
5. Alice's
6. horse's
7. men's
8. Ross'
9. class'
10. agents'

## Exercise 7

1. saleswoman's
2. nurses'
3. its
4. candy's
5. someone's
6. Jones'
7. Niagara Falls'
8. women's
9. stewardess'
10. lady's

## Exercise 8

1. your
2. Bess'
3. their
4. children's
5. babies'
6. history's
7. one's
8. actress'
9. chairmen's
10. ladies'

## Exercise 9

1. month's, their
2. children's, yours
3. dog's, its
4. George's, wife's
5. its, jeweler's
6. Phyllis', Moses'
7. Fishermen's, their
8. spray's, trees'
9. Indians', government's
10. moment's, week's

## Exercise 10

1. Hikers' equipment is on special during the week's sale at Brown's Sporting Goods.
2. Women's liberation is a touchy topic for Gail's sister, who's lost a job to a man.
3. The waitress' tip ended up in the busboy's pocket.
4. correct
5. The men's room is down the hall, but its door isn't marked.
6. Gordie Howe's records may eventually fall, but his career's achievements will never be surpassed.
7. Thousands of mourners who visit Elvis Presley's grave annually prove that they take literally his song "Love Me Tender."
8. Its coat shone like gold in the sun's dying rays.

9. Pornographers' books are not chosen by our school's curriculum planners.
10. Men's and women's traditional roles are being questioned as this generation's leaders refuse to take any of yesterday's values for granted.

---

## Exercise 11

1. It's, its, it's, week's
2. They're, it's
3. You're, police's, your
4. Betty's, Children's
5. Who's, anybody's
6. Their, their, they're
7. It's, your, son's
8. Today's, melodies, its
9. you're, it's, their
10. boys, cheater's, Gord's, father's

---

## Exercise 12

1. I don't think we're as far from the fire station as your calculations indicate.
2. Can't you admit you're wrong and apologize for all their trouble?
3. There were six of them there, but Mike's friend wasn't afraid, because he knew Mike's reputation for getting out of tight spots.
4. You shouldn't cheat, even if they're not looking at your paper.
5. A turtle's life can exceed 100 years, while a mayfly's life is only one day.
6. Food is so expensive it's hard to provide for your family.
7. Marty's brother went to work for the CBS at their New York studios.
8. Summer's heat gradually fades into autumn's cool, which then becomes winter's biting cold.
9. We're lucky that you're able to control their quarrels; otherwise, we'd have nothing but fighting all night long.
10. Amos' first rule was to treat others the way you'd want them to treat you.

---

## Exercise 13

1. boys'
2. knife's
3. audience's
4. its
5. secretaries'
6. they're

7. who's
8. you're
9. it's
10. couldn't

## Exercise 14

1. gentlemen's
2. typist's
3. anyone's
4. enemy's
5. enemies'
6. won't
7. it's
8. there's
9. hasn't
10. shouldn't

## Exercise 15

1. A Hollywood star, famous for his capacity for overdrinking, told his new lady love: "I've put your picture in the one spot I'm sure to see it every night: under the table."
2. A regular patron at Shnop's bar reports that he and his girl can't seem to agree on wedding plans. "She wants a big church wedding with ushers and bridesmaids and I just don't want to get married."
3. Winston Churchill once was asked if he knew any professional women. He answered promptly, "I've never met any amateur ones."
4. Discouragement: watching your secretary yawn while typing one of your most amusing letters.
5. A Carolina genius has perfected a new baby food that's half orange juice and half garlic. Its secret is it not only makes the baby healthier, but easier to find in the dark.
6. There's one bus driver on the Madison Avenue route who's hung one of those shrunken heads over his coin box. He explains to curious passengers, "He wouldn't move to the rear of the bus."
7. A frugal Vermonter complains that his grandfather displayed the first dollar he earned in a frame that cost ten cents. Now the frame's worth a dollar and the dollar's worth a dime.
8. Short-haired girl to long-haired boy: "Of course Daddy doesn't mind our being alone together every night. He thinks you're a girl."
9. "I'm in real trouble," a man confessed to an analyst. "I can't rid myself of the conviction that I'm a dog." "Jiminy!" exclaimed the analyst. "How long has this been going on?" The man answered, "Since I was a puppy."
10. In Las Vegas, the owners of the famous Caesar's Palace are very annoyed with the kid who's opened an orange juice stand nearby. He's calling it Squeezer's Palace.

## Chapter 4: Cracking the Sentence Code

### Exercise 1.

1. Alan met
2. bear met
3. bear was
4. bulge was
5. Grizzlies are
6. Meeting is
7. bears run
8. (you) believe. They do
9. Females are known
10. How to defend oneself presents

### Exercise 2

1. Donald Duck appeared.
2. language has
3. Mark Twain is
4. Are you
5. drivers are
6. exceptions are
7. Crime is
8. is San Diego Zoo
9. jogging is
10. crouched cat

### Exercise 3

1. Money does
2. are steps
3. Coca-Cola was created
4. idea was
5. (you) drive
6. Study makes
7. (you) turn
8. lives mayor
9. love comes
10. is Volkswagen Beetle

### Exercise 4

1. Doing is
2. friend is
3. Were they
4. were children
5. are files
6. Are you

7. Boston Marathon is held
8. Replacing is
9. (you) stop
10. boardwalk extends

## Exercise 5

1. He has tried
2. You should have been paying
3. Should we write
4. Desert View Watchtower overlooks
5. is gas station
6. We do want
7. do you want
8. men will think
9. baby has fallen
10. swam shark

## Exercise 6

1. country is covered
2. would anyone want
3. Alex Haley was becoming
4. will I agree
5. person may forgive
6. have been notices
7. You can become
8. did you stay
9. Have you been
10. have women been interested

## Exercise 7

1. gasoline will be
2. I will have been working
3. are teeth displayed
4. man will take
5. Dodge City, Kansas, was termed
6. Joe Hall is being discovered
7. Could anyone have done
8. Have you been caught
9. little is known
10. Are you

## Exercise 8

1. A bird ~~in the hand~~ is worth two ~~in the bush~~.
2. Most ~~of us~~ plan to go ~~on Saturday~~.
3. Many ~~of your answers~~ are unreadable.

4. Do you want either ~~of them~~?
5. Meet me ~~at twelve in the cafeteria~~. (The subject is you.)
6. A couple ~~of hamburgers~~ should be enough.
7. A dozen brands ~~of video recorder~~ are now ~~on the market~~.
8. There is a movie ~~about cloning on television~~ tonight.
9. ~~After eight hours of classes~~, the thought ~~of collapsing in front of the TV set~~ is very appealing.
10. One episode ~~of "The Gong Show"~~ is more than enough.

---

## Exercise 9

1. A stitch ~~in time~~ saves nine.
2. ~~For many students,~~ lack ~~of money~~ is probably the most serious problem.
3. ~~In the middle of May, after the end of term,~~ the Intercollegiate Arm-Wrestling Championships will be held.
4. One strand ~~of fiber optics~~ can carry both telephone and television signals.
5. ~~During the second week of term,~~ the class will be taken ~~on a tour of the resource center.~~
6. ~~Contrary to your expectations,~~ and ~~despite the rumors,~~ your instructor does not bite.
7. ~~On Callisto,~~ one ~~of Jupiter's thirteen moons,~~ snow may "fall" up, not down.
8. ~~At Millhaven Penitentiary,~~ a prisoner blinded himself last week ~~in an effort~~ to escape.
9. One ~~of the most expensive movies~~ made ~~in the 1930s~~ was *King Kong.*
10. ~~In similar circumstances,~~ most ~~of us~~ would probably have accepted his help.

---

## Exercise 10

1. ~~By this time,~~ you may be tired ~~of the notion of Superman.~~
2. The happiness ~~of every country~~ depends ~~upon the character of its people.~~
3. ~~Above my desk~~ hangs someone else's diploma.
4. ~~During the course of the discussion,~~ several ~~of us~~ went to sleep.

5. ~~In the summer~~ and ~~on weekends,~~ he works ~~on his log cabin with his wife.~~
6. The "short side" ~~of a goalie~~ is the side closer ~~to the post.~~
7. New steps should be taken to encourage the flow ~~of capital into small businesses.~~
8. ~~After waiting for more than an hour,~~ we finally left ~~without you.~~
9. So far only two ~~of your answers to the questions~~ have been incorrect.
10. One ~~of the country's most distinguished reporters~~ will speak ~~on the responsibilities of the press.~~

---

## Exercise 11

1. ~~On the average~~, people ~~on the west coast~~, especially ~~in California~~, are taller than those ~~in the East~~.
2. ~~By waiting on tables, (by) babysitting~~, and ~~(by) doing other odd jobs,~~ I manage to make ends meet.
3. The pile ~~of books and papers on your desk~~ is about as neat as a tossed salad.
4. Almost no one ~~in television news~~ bothers to analyze the issues.
5. ~~But for you,~~ we would be finished ~~with this meeting by now.~~
6. No book ~~about famous smokers~~ would be complete ~~without a mention of Winston Churchill, Sigmund Freud, and Mark Twain.~~
7. ~~Despite Chou En-lai's wishes to the contrary,~~ the Chinese plan to build a memorial ~~to him.~~
8. A daily intake ~~of more than 600 mg. of caffeine~~ can result ~~in headaches, (in) insomnia,~~ and ~~(in) heart palpitations.~~
9. Six to ten cups ~~of coffee~~ will contain 600 mg. ~~of caffeine.~~
10. ~~Despite its strong taste,~~ espresso contains no more caffeine than regular coffee.

---

## Exercise 12

1. ~~On the floor next to the computer~~ sat the frazzled technician ~~with his head in his hands.~~
2. ~~In the dog world~~, poodles ~~on an average~~ bite more people than do Doberman pinschers.
3. ~~Within a week,~~ please give me your report ~~on the pyrazine anion project.~~ (The subject is you.)

4. ~~In the spring~~, parked ~~in front of his TV set,~~ Barry trains ~~for the Stanley Cup playoffs.~~
5. Government programs to encourage investment ~~in small business ventures~~ have failed ~~in the past few years.~~
6. ~~In the Arctic wastes of Ungava,~~ there is a mysterious stone structure ~~in the shape of a giant hammer~~ standing ~~on end.~~
7. There is no obvious explanation ~~for its presence in this isolated place.~~
8. ~~According to archeologist Thomas E. Lee,~~ it may be a monument left ~~by Vikings in their travels west from Greenland.~~
9. Here, ~~on an island called Pamiok,~~ are the ruins ~~of what may have been a Viking long house~~.
10. If so, then, centuries ~~before Columbus' "discovery" of America,~~ the Vikings were ~~in what is now northern Quebec.~~

---

## Exercise 14

1. Jack, Jill went
2. Georgie Porgie kissed, made
3. Jack, Jill went, fetched
4. cotton, soybeans are
5. I tried, tried, did succeed
6. Jim, Brian will go
7. canoeists, dog were missing
8. Alan Alda writes, directs, acts
9. (you) wait, phone
10. Reading, singing are

---

## Exercise 15

1. Misspellings can create, (can) cause
2. *Durham County Register* printed
3. soldier was praised, was described
4. soldier called, demanded
5. writer, editor soothed, promised
6. paper apologized, explained
7. (you) drive, see; (you) drive, see
8. drivers obey, lose
9. (you) do, be
10. Come-by-Chance, Blow-me-Down, Run-by-Guess, Jerry's Nose are

---

### Exercise 16

1. (you) take, (you) leave
2. Jan, I studied, failed
3. were goldfish, ball, couple
4. He worked, saved, died
5. Everybody went, spent
6. are cheddar, Swiss, Muenster
7. companies, publishers, manufacturers are profiting
8. we drove, went
9. politicians attempt, try
10. government will create, (will) train, (will) support, (will) push

### Exercise 17

1. heat . . . scarcity . . . made
2. was . . . thing . . . anything
3. Families must be fed . . . dishes (must be) washed
4. Babies must be fed . . . (must be) washed . . . (must be) dressed . . . (must be) "changed" . . . (must be) rocked . . . (must be) watched . . . (must be) kept
5. Fires must be lighted . . . (must be) kept going
6. Cows must be milked . . . cream (must be) skimmed . . . butter (must be) churned
7. Hens must be fed . . . eggs (must be) gathered . . . filth (must be) shoveled
8. Diapers must be washed . . . drawers . . . rompers . . . overalls . . . work-shirts . . . dresses . . . aprons . . . towels . . . socks . . . articles
9. Floors must be swept . . . (must be) scrubbed . . . stoves (must be) cleaned . . . war (must be) waged
10. activities . . . made up

## Chapter 5: Still More about Verbs

### Exercise 1

1. became
2. brought
3. had
4. sang

5. flung
6. froze
7. got (gotten)
8. lent
9. swung
10. laid

---

## Exercise 2

1. led
2. lost
3. said
4. slept
5. swum
6. told
7. threw
8. stolen
9. rode
10. written

---

## Exercise 3

1. wore, worn
2. built, built
3. slid, slid
4. blew, blown
5. bore, borne
6. hit, hit
7. ridden, rode
8. spent, spent
9. won, won
10. told, told

---

## Exercise 4

1. wound, wound
2. tore, torn
3. lay, lain
4. bit, bitten
5. grew, grown
6. had, had
7. burst, burst
8. ran, run
9. made, made
10. brought, brought

---

## Exercise 5

1. bid, bid
2. rung, rang
3. saw, seen
4. broken, broke
5. fought, fought
6. kept, kept
7. put, put
8. wrote, written
9. threw, thrown
10. taken, took

---

## Exercise 6

1. thought, thought
2. begun, began
3. felt, felt
4. bought, bought
5. done, did
6. gave, given

7. paid, paid
8. lent, lent
9. gone, went
10. hurt, hurt

---

## Exercise 7

1. came, come
2. rose, risen
3. left, left
4. sped, sped
5. taught, taught
6. fell, fallen
7. chose, chosen
8. heard, heard
9. flew, flown
10. struck, struck

---

## Exercise 8

1. held, held
2. stole, stolen
3. swung, swung
4. hid, hidden
5. said, said
6. drew, drawn
7. met, met
8. swore, sworn
9. forgave, forgiven
10. laid, laid

---

## Exercise 9

1. driven, drove
2. meant, meant
3. hung, hung
4. dealt, dealt
5. found, found
6. led, led
7. known, knew
8. forgot, forgotten (forgot)
9. sold, sold
10. spoke, spoken

---

## Exercise 10

1. hanged, hanged
2. stood, stood
3. lost, lost
4. got, got (gotten)
5. slept, slept
6. froze, frozen
7. shaken, shook
8. set, set
9. swum, dived; swam, dived (dove)
10. ate, drank; eaten, drunk

---

## Chapter 6: Solving Sentence-Fragment Problems

We have made the sentence fragments into complete sentences only for the first set and only to give you an idea of how the sentences might be formed.

Many different sentences can be made out of the fragments given; just be sure each of your sentences has a subject and a verb.

## Exercise 1

1. F This chapter is about sentence fragments.
2. F I was sorry to hear about your decision to quit school.
3. F I'll be glad to do it for you.
4. F She keeps falling asleep in class, after working all night.
5. F The poker players are meeting in the cafeteria.
6. S
7. F Concert attendance is down because of high ticket prices.
8. F We have just learned of the proposed increase in bus fares.
9. F I have saved for just such an emergency.
10. S

## Exercise 2

1. F
2. F
3. F
4. F
5. F
6. F
7. S
8. F
9. F
10. S

## Exercise 3

1. S
2. S
3. F
4. F
5. F
6. F
7. F
8. F
9. F
10. F

## Exercise 4

1. F
2. S
3. F
4. F
5. F
6. F
7. S
8. S
9. F
10. S

## Exercise 5

1. F
2. F
3. S
4. F
5. F
6. F
7. F
8. F
9. F
10. F

## Exercise 6

1. F Although
2. F Before
3. F Since
4. F Whichever
5. F Where
6. F As
7. F If
8. S
9. F What
10. S

## Exercise 7

1. F After
2. F Whatever
3. F Even if
4. F Because
5. F Who
6. F Unless
7. F who
8. S
9. F When
10. S

## Exercise 8

1. F when
2. S
3. F Since
4. F If
5. F Provided that
6. F Even though
7. S
8. F While
9. F that
10. F so that

## Exercise 9

1. F who
2. S
3. F So that
4. S
5. F Where
6. F since
7. S
8. F whichever
9. F until
10. F that

### Exercise 10

1. S
2. F Though
3. F that
4. S
5. S
6. S
7. F If
8. F Since, what
9. F Until, as long as, whichever
10. F When, where

## Chapter 7: Solving Run-on Problems

### Exercise 1

1. Kevin is lazy; Allan is no better. *Or:* Kevin is lazy. Allan is no better.
2. Stop me if you've heard this one. There was this bus driver on his first day at work.
3. correct
4. Ronnie says he likes hiking, but he never goes very far. Maybe that's because he has asthma.
5. correct
6. It bothers me to see her playing cards all the time; she could easily fail her classes.
7. Denise was transformed; overnight she had turned from a plain-looking student into a sex symbol.
8. Fall is my favorite time of year; the colors are beautiful.
9. A fine mess this is. I'll never forgive you for getting me into this situation.
10. correct

### Exercise 2

1. Last Saturday we had a great idea; we went to see Dracula and then went out for a bite.
2. Two silkworms were once having a race; however, they ended up in a tie.
3. Some of the convicted Watergate defendants are writing their memoirs. They will be able to use their pen names.
4. The rematch race between the tortoise and the rabbit was extremely close; it was won by a hare.
5. Jobs in a garbage-collecting service are usually fairly secure, for business is always picking up.

6. Garbage collectors have a tendency to be depressed most of their working careers; they're often down in the dumps.
7. Jewelers who repair watches for a living put in extremely long hours; they're always working over time.
8. Under a display of stuffed animals in a gift shop in Florida is a sign that reads, "Please do not feed the animals. They are already stuffed." (*or* ;)
9. The elephants at the circus in town are planning to go on strike; supposedly, they are tired of working for peanuts.
10. A man called a veterinarian to look at his son's pony because it sounded sick. The vet found the pony to be all right; it was just a little hoarse.

---

## Exercise 3

1. Mark Twain once said that giving up smoking was no problem at all; he had done it himself, dozens of times.
2. I picked up my new car on Wednesday. One week later, it was recalled for a safety check.
3. Cats are too independent for my taste. I much prefer dogs, who can be counted on to be there when you need them.
4. Very few movies are rated G anymore, and many parents are unhappy with this trend. (*or* ;)
5. Americans are fascinated by science; they regard it with both wonder and fear.
6. Correct.
7. San Francisco's new symphony hall is shaped like a horseshoe, the international symbol for good luck. Perhaps its shape will prove to be a good omen.
8. Frankly, I don't think very highly of Joan. Since she is bad-tempered and lazy, I doubt she'll make a good gym teacher.
9. Correct.
10. On the banks of the Mississippi River, in the city of St. Louis, stands a monumental arch designed by Eero Saarinen. More than 600 feet high, sheathed in gleaming plates of steel, it is called the Gateway Arch.

---

## Exercise 4

1. *Ordinary People* is one of my favorite films because it seems so true to life. I'm thinking of reading the book.
2. People tend to forget that a complete education involves the body as well as the mind. In most high schools, physical education isn't

taken seriously, while at college there is even less emphasis on athletics except for support of a few varsity teams. All this might change, however, if the Department of Education changed its policy.

3. When The Band split up, my favorite group became The Eagles. I don't listen to music much anymore, though, because my stereo's broken. I haven't got a summer job, so I can't afford to have it fixed.
4. Bruce hates alarm clocks and refuses to keep one in his apartment. He's the guy who used to go out with my sister.
5. It's always best to tell the truth, because one lie leads to another, and eventually you'll get caught.
6. They took up sailing last year; we haven't seen them since.
7. I'm tired, and I guess you must be, too. Let's just finish this last one and then turn in. We can get an early start tomorrow and polish off the rest before noon so we can have the rest of the day to ourselves.
8. Foolish people are those who, through ignorance or stupidity, refuse to believe there's anything they don't know. When a situation comes along they aren't familiar with, and they don't know how to act, they just plow ahead without a care. Usually they end up making the situation worse and adding to their richly deserved reputation as fools.
9. I think there are many components of a sense of humor; one is the ability to see the absurd in normal situations, and another is the very rare gift of being able to see oneself as an object of fun or ridicule. Almost no one has the latter ability to any degree.
10. The American political system is really very straightforward and simple, if you think about it. We have several levels of government, each with its own powers and jurisdictions and each responsible to its constituents. Difficulties arise, though, when jurisdictions overlap or aren't clearly defined.

---

## Exercise 5

1. Why did he do it? He knew he couldn't get away with it.
2. Jasmine isn't going with them, though she wants to. As far as I know, she wasn't even asked.
3. You asked me for my opinion of that group, so here it is. The lead vocalist can barely carry a tune, and her voice is so thin she can scarcely be heard even with a microphone. The drummer seems always to be about half a beat behind and looks as though he's half asleep. The keyboard man isn't bad, though.
4. Anything else wouldn't have worked. We were sure we had done the right thing, even though the outcome wasn't quite what we had expected.

5. Correct.
6. It's a good thing he likes you, for he could be a very dangerous enemy. You know that as well as I do.
7. No one else was up, so I walked out of the house and down to the beach. The shore was empty and silent, except for the soft sounds of the waves.
8. Several students I know have no interest in school; they play cards or watch TV most of the time rather than study. They would prefer to be out working and feel that they are accomplishing something worthwhile.
9. In many cities, there is an acute shortage of rental housing, and landlords are under little competitive pressure to hold rents down, so rents are likely to be high. The ever-increasing cost of renting compounds the problems facing those on welfare, or on fixed incomes, or with low-paying jobs. These are the people who have no choice but to rent; they can never hope to own their own homes.
10. We have little choice but to depend on science and technology to find solutions to the energy crisis, perhaps through the utilization of new energy sources such as fusion, solar power, and geothermal energy. We must depend on science, too, for solutions to the problems of nuclear and chemical pollution as well as to the new problems that are being caused by advances in genetic engineering.

---

## Exercise 6

1. Considering my background in the field, my high level of achievement since the completion of my education, and the fact that my uncle is the sales manager of the company, I ought to be able to get a job.
2. correct
3. Writing true comedy is not easy; in fact, few disciplines are more demanding.
4. I was shown the evidence that was being presented against him and realized the hopelessness of his case.
5. It concerns me to see him on trial with such a lawyer; he could easily lose a case he should win.
6. The thought was there; just the same, that doesn't help if no action was taken.
7. correct
8. Isaac Asimov, the well-known science fiction writer, has published a new novel.
9. correct
10. Fishing for perch on a bright spring day from the dock near his summer cottage, he hooked a record-breaking pike.

---

## Exercise 7

1. Although he was a wonderful dancer, he wasn't popular.
2. He had very large feet; these enormous growths did not permit him to be as graceful as he wished.
3. One day, as he sat dreaming in the park, he decided to take a trip.
4. We must try to understand the emotional suffering of a man who was doomed to have the largest feet in America. If we cannot at least be sympathetic, the burden may well be too much for him to bear; he will be spiritually, not to mention physically, alone forever.
5. On his journey to Europe he encountered severe difficulties. He persevered, however, and, after many embarrassing experiences, arrived in France.
6. He claimed that his feet would be an asset to the wine industry.
7. The people cheered as he approached; he was a genuine marvel.
8. On his ninth day of work in the wine vats he met with trouble. A jealous coworker had put a banana skin among the grapes; he had hidden it just where the ambitious grape masher would be sure to slip on it.
9. correct
10. A kindly passerby rushed him to the hospital. There he was attended by an efficient nurse who won his heart, and he married her as soon as he was released from the hospital. They were very happy, and not one of their children had large feet.

## Exercise 8

It is loosely estimated that some 3,000,000 Americans belong to about 1,000 religious cults, the largest of which bear names like the Unification Church, the Divine Light Mission, the Hare Krishna, and the Way, each of which has temples or branches in most major cities. . . . Just why is it that such groups can command almost total dedication and obedience from their members? Their secret is simple. They understand the need for community, structure, and meaning, for these are what all cults peddle.

For lonely people, cults offer, in the beginning, indiscriminate friendship. Says an official of the Unification Church, "If someone's lonely, we talk to him or her. There are a lot of lonely people walking around." The newcomer is surrounded by people offering friendship and beaming approval. Many of the cults require communal living. So powerfully rewarding is this sudden warmth and attention that cult members are often willing to give up contact with their families and former friends, to donate their life's earnings to the cult, to forego drugs and even sex in return.

But the cult sells more than community. It also offers much-needed structure. Cults impose tight constraints on behavior. They demand and create enormous discipline, some apparently going so far as to impose that discipline through beatings, forced labor, and their own forms of ostracism or imprisonment. Psychiatrist H. A. S. Sukhdeo . . . concludes,

"Our society is so free and permissive, and people have so many options to choose from that they cannot make their own decisions effectively. They want others to make the decisions and they will follow."

## Chapter 8: Solving Modifier Problems

### Exercise 1

1. Some people never go to movies unless they're French or Italian.
2. Tony bought plants that cost $6.50 for his aquarium.
3. They decided to pay me nearly $245 a week.
4. correct
5. We laughed at the antics of the clown wearing two left shoes and a funny little flowered hat.
6. I hate parties where food is served on little paper plates to the guests.
7. The shawl was exactly what Valerie had been looking for.
8. Bonita came back in a rage before I could escape.
9. There is just enough time left.
10. On Tuesday, Mr. Harrison told us there would be a test.
    Or: Mr. Harrison told us there would be a test on Tuesday.

### Exercise 2

1. With difficulty, Barbara Walters convinced John Dean he should talk.
2. Only two suitable jobs were advertised.
3. This course can be completed in six weeks by anyone who has learned English grammar.
4. For a small fee, the obituary column lists the names of people who haved died recently.
5. The lead guitarist played professionally in Europe before coming to Chicago.
6. The shawl in the window was exactly what Valerie had been looking for.
7. They told me to come back every week and check the notice board.
   Or: They told me to come back and check the notice board every week.
8. For their own satisfaction, parents want to know what their children are doing in school.
9. The cause of the accident was a little guy with a big mouth in a small car.

10. Anyone who has spent a night in the woods can easily identify with the frightening picture Thoreau has painted.

---

## Exercise 3

1. Some games, such as hockey, depend very much on the decisions of officials.
2. He watched television almost all night.
3. Clint Eastwood eagerly tried to persuade the other actors to follow his proposal.
4. With the wooden spoon, stir the flour into the butter in the saucepan.
5. correct
6. On tonight's show, Raymond Giles, the well-known interior designer, will be discussing with Julia Child how to design an efficient kitchen.
7. With only an old black powder rifle, he took a stand against a tree while waiting for the bear.
8. Walking to class, I passed the security guard and two workmen.
9. Correct
10. Government subsidies, properly administered, would act as an incentive to the student who is preparing for a career.

---

## Exercise 5

1. As a college English teacher, I am upset by dangling modifiers.
2. Having finished the bedroom, we planned to paint the kitchen next.
3. Turning to the Appendix, you will find in the third paragraph the example I quoted.
4. Before applying the varnish, sand the surface smooth.
5. Upon entering, I saw the store was completely empty.
6. Even as a very small boy, Louis wanted to be a Harlem Globetrotter.
7. Raging uncontrolled for two days, a fire set by an arsonist ravaged the Napa Valley grape crop.
8. Correct
9. Looking over his shoulder, the man slowly backed up the car.
10. In very cold weather, you should warm up the engine thoroughly before attempting to drive.

---

## Exercise 6

1. After changing the tire, you should release the jack.
2. Having decided on pizza, we should decide next whether to order beer or wine.

3. After waiting for you for an hour, I knew the evening was ruined.
4. correct
5. After spending $9 on them, I have lost most of the spare keys.
6. When comparing their personalities and interests, I find Julie and Jessie completely different.
7. Having completed the beginning, we will turn to the ending, the next most important part of the essay.
8. correct
9. After having been isolated for so long, the paroled man found the world to be spinning at a hectic pace.
10. After shoveling the walks, the driveway, and the sidewalk, I was annoyed when it snowed another four inches.

---

## Exercise 7

1. Since I am a college English teacher, dangling modifiers upset me.
2. Since I had finished the bedroom, the kitchen was next to be painted.
3. If you turn to the Appendix, the example I quoted is in the third paragraph.
4. The surface must be sanded smooth before you apply the varnish.
5. When I entered, the store was completely empty.
6. Even when he was a very small boy, being a Harlem Globetrotter was Louis' ambition.
7. After a fire set by an arsonist had raged uncontrolled for two days, the Napa Valley grape crop was ravaged.
8. correct
9. As the driver looked over his shoulder, he slowly backed up the car.
10. In very cold weather, the engine should be thoroughly warmed up before you attempt to drive.

---

## Exercise 8

1. After you change the tire, release the jack.
2. The next question is whether to order beer or wine, now that we have decided on pizza.
3. After I had waited for you for an hour, the evening was ruined.
4. correct
5. Most of the spare keys, after I spent $9 on them, have been lost.
6. Julie and Jessie are completely different, if you compare their personalities and interests.
7. After you have completed the beginning, the ending is the next most important part of the essay.

8. correct
9. After the paroled man had been isolated for so long, the world seemed to be spinning at a hectic pace.
10. After I had shoveled the walks, the driveway, and the sidewalk, it snowed another four inches.

---

## Exercise 9

1. Because the glasses are made of very thin crystal, the dishwasher breaks them as fast as I can buy them.
2. The menu featured deep-fried artichoke hearts in mayonnaise.
3. As a college student constantly faced with stress, I find the pressure intolerable.
4. His socks, which were long and red, were full of holes.
5. Although I am not a churchgoer, respect for others is an important part of my philosophy.
6. After deciding whether the wine should be blended, add the sugar.
7. From coast to coast, environmental groups protested the damage done by oil slicks.
8. The sign in the restaurant window read, "Our Establishment Serves Tea in a Bag Just as Mother Did" (or, "Just Like Mother, Our Establishment Serves Tea in a Bag").
9. Animals, especially small ones, are loved by many people.
10. Having broken its wings, the seagull was taken to the S.P.C.A.

---

## Exercise 10

1. Although he lives fifty miles away, he manages to come to nearly every class.
2. We went on a motorcycle to the party that Sandie gave for Lucille's promotion.
3. The lion was recaptured by the trainer before anyone was mauled or bitten.
4. After reading the assigned material, we had an emotional discussion.
5. Through a plate-glass window, I saw the Queen and her entourage arrive.
6. Having ruled out the other two engines, we'll choose the Wankel.
7. Swimming isn't a good idea if the water is cold or polluted.
8. Pet-lover Doris Day will interview William Shatner, who is also a pet owner, and his dog Spock.
9. In last week's letter, I learned about Joan's having a baby.
10. In most cases, the person who is successful has a large vocabulary.

---

## Exercise 11

1. After completing the study of staffing requirements, we will hire an assistant to the personnel manager.
2. The Historical Society that was studying the matter submitted its report last week.
3. On Monday, our English teacher explained how to skim and scan.
4. Our guests didn't find the meal, which was left over from last week's party, very appetizing.
5. Employees who are frequently late are dismissed without notice. *Or:* Employees who are late are frequently dismissed without notice.
6. Since Jim forgot twice this week to pick me up, I'm quitting his car pool.
7. Just like the wall plate, the switch is attached to the wall with screws.
8. Before they could dispose of much of the loot, the thieves were caught by the police.
9. After it started coughing, sputtering, and leaking all over the road, we helped Sonny push the old Ford into the nearest service station.
10. When Jamie was five, the barber first cut his hair which curled nearly to his shoulders.

# Chapter 9: The Parallelism Principle

## Exercise 1

1. The three main kinds of speech are demonstrative, informative, and persuasive.
2. . . . Two of the most difficult are supporting her household and being sole parent to her child.
3. He advised me to take two aspirins and call him in the morning.
4. Books provide us with information, education, and entertainment.
5. To make your court appearance as painless as possible, prepare your case thoroughly, and maintain a pleasant, positive attitude.
6. The apostrophe is used for two purposes: contraction and possession.
7. Swiftly and skillfully the woman gutted and scaled the fish.
8. I am overworked and underpaid.
9. You need to develop skill, strategy, and agility to be a good tennis player.

10. The two main responsibilities of a corrections officer are security and control.

---

## Exercise 2

1. A part-time job can develop your decision-making skills, your sense of responsibility, your self-confidence, and your independence.
2. The three keys to improving your marks are study, hard work, and bribery.
3. I couldn't decide whether I should become a chef or a data processor.
4. . . . : the widespread lack of strong religious beliefs and the absence of strict moral codes.
5. A course in logical reasoning will help him to evaluate what he reads and to make sound decisions.
6. When you're buying a new car, you should look at more than just the size, style, and cost. The warranty, operating cost, and trade-in value should also be taken into consideration.
7. Mrs. Hunter assigns two hours of homework every night and an essay each week.
8. The two most important characteristics of a personal work space are how neat and well organized it looks and how private it is.
9. Playing with small construction toys is beneficial to young children because it develops their fine motor skills, encourages concentration and patience, and stimulates their creative imagination.
10. My supervisor told me that my performance was generally satisfactory but that my writing must improve.

---

## Exercise 3

1. The role of the health instructor is to teach preventive medicine, care of the sick, and rehabilitation of the injured.
2. The most common causes of snowmobile accidents are mechanical failure, poor weather conditions, and driver carelessness.
3. The portable classrooms are ill-equipped, poorly lighted, and inadequately heated.
4. The advantages of a thesis statement are that it limits your topic, clarifies the contents of your paper, and shows how your paper will be organized.
5. Unemployment deprives the individual of purchasing power and reduces the country's national output.
6. A good nurse is energetic, tolerant, sympathetic, and reliable.

7. The money spent on space exploration should be used to provide aid to underdeveloped countries and funding for medical research.
8. The best house cats are quiet, clean, affectionate, and elsewhere.
9. . . . : a new appreciation for the beauty of nature and a new admiration for members of the opposite sex.
10. You can conclude a paper with a summary of main points, a question, or a quotation.

---

### Exercise 4

1. mechanically manually
2. being a nurse being a pilot
3. achieve her goals find true happiness
4. sense of humor wealth intelligence
5. daily exercise wholesome food regular checkups
6. a good cigar a glass of brandy conversation with friends
7. speed comfort good cornering
8. look for bargains choose quality shop for value
9. security value safety
10. tanned golden brown clothed in a skimpy bathing suit accompanied by a big boyfriend

---

## Chapter 10: Subject-Verb Agreement

---

### Exercise 1

1. an ostrich and a penguin
2. numbers
3. World Disco Dancing Championships
4. invoices
5. volcanoes
6. print media
7. cockroach
8. advantages
9. anything
10. pressures

---

### Exercise 2

1. They tell me they are unwilling to work overtime.
2. Those policy changes affect the entire program.
3. Their papers are late because they've been ill.
4. The union leaders complain that their lot is not a happy one.
5. He does his best work when he is unsupervised.

6. She insists on having her way.
7. Both of Cinderella's sisters were horrid in their own way.
8. Those men's wives aren't doing them any good.
9. The peanut farmers stand to lose money unless they diversify their crops.
10. All those who deposit $50 have their names entered in the draw.

## Exercise 3

1. Motorcycles are Laurie's only interest.
2. Clothes are what he spends most of his money on.
3. The one luxury I allow myself is cigarettes.
4. The reason for our success was long hours of practice.
5. Strong leadership and more jobs are what America needs now.
6. Too many absences from class were the reason for his failure.
7. The cause of strikes is often disputes over wages and benefits.
8. What I find difficult is multiple subjects and multiple verbs.
9. Math assignments are something that takes a lot of my time.
10. The reason I didn't finish the assignment is my little brother's constant interruptions.

## Exercise 4

1. were
2. is
3. is
4. are
5. are
6. is
7. were
8. cause

## Exercise 5

1. is
2. works
3. is
4. is
5. tricks
6. wants
7. is
8. is

## Exercise 6

1. was
2. was
3. believes
4. is
5. seems
6. is
7. is
8. dares

## Exercise 7

1. deserves
2. is
3. interests
4. hopes
5. works
6. is
7. wants
8. is

## Exercise 8

1. is
2. prefers
3. provide
4. fight
5. Has
6. was
7. gives
8. was

## Exercise 9

1. seems
2. is
3. seems
4. is
5. seems
6. is
7. is
8. is

## Exercise 10

1. The whole committee is . . . .
2. Anybody who really wants to . . . .
3. correct
4. Every one of the listed topics bores . . . .
5. correct
6. If there are . . . .
7. Neither Peter nor I am . . . .
8. The lack of things to write about causes . . . .
9. Farrah Fawcett, along with Lily Tomlin and Dolly Parton, has . . . .
10. It's not only the cost but also the time wasted that makes . . . .

## Exercise 11

1. The cause of all the noise and confusion was . . . .
2. correct
3. Neither the university nor the community colleges appeal . . . .
4. Only three hours of his lecture was . . . .
5. Everybody but witches loves . . . .
6. correct

7. Every one of the applicants looks . . . .
8. This afternoon the class is . . . .
9. Neither the cat nor the dog was . . . , but everybody was . . . .
10. Speculation does not occur when the balance of payments is . . . .

---

## Exercise 12

1. A handful of companies dominates . . . .
2. The loss of men and materials was . . . .
3. Has either . . . ?
4. Experience in programing, . . . is required.
5. correct
6. Ten years in prison seems . . . .
7. . . . there is bound to be a handful . . . .
8. Absolutely everyone . . . has advised me . . . .
9. It is not necessarily true that statements . . . apply with equal validity to the other.
10. . . . Disneyland, in California, and Disney World, in Florida, link . . . .

---

## Exercise 13

1. singular
2. singular
3. plural
4. singular
5. singular
6. singular
7. singular
8. singular
9. singular
10. singular

---

## Exercise 14

1. could be singular or plural
2. singular
3. singular
4. plural
5. singular
6. singular
7. singular
8. plural
9. singular
10. singular

---

## Exercise 16

1. The comical antics of the Muppets capture . . . .
2. The multitude of choices that are offered is . . . .
3. Everyone I know except my parents adores . . . .
4. The cost of new homes is . . . .
5. My sense of fear and foreboding was . . . .

6. Every one of us, at one time or another, has expressed . . . .
7. Some people believe that violence and sex are evil.
8. For the dieter, all those luscious and fattening desserts on display are . . . .
9. There seem . . . .
10. The variety of shows . . . is practically limitless.
11. The controversy surrounding these matters leads . . . .
12. A free press is one of the most important rights the people of a democratic society possess.
13. When the channels . . . disappear, . . . .
14. High mortgage rates, high real-estate prices, and low interest in gardening are . . . .
15. But nobody . . . is happy about these latest reforms.

---

## Chapter 11: Pronoun-Antecedent Agreement

---

### Exercise 1

1. Is this the dog that bit the mail carrier who carries a squirt gun?
2. The path that I took led me past the home of a hermit, who lived all alone in the forest that surrounded our town.
3. The goal that came at 15:45 of the third period was scored by a player (whom) I used to know at high school.
4. That can't be Janice O'Toole, the little girl (whom) I used to bounce on my knee!
5. The building that we entered next was owned by the company that employed my father.
6. He is the man (whom) I turn to whenever I feel depressed because of something my sister has said or done.
7. correct
8. The four tests that we wrote today would have defeated anyone who wasn't prepared for them.
9. The wind whistled around the cabin, against which they had propped their skis while waiting to see whether the skiers (whom) they had passed earlier could catch up.
10. . . . It also allows you to spot women (whom) you'd like to meet.

---

### Exercise 2

1. his
2. herself
3. his
4. his
5. their, their
6. they, his

7. his
8. itself
9. himself, he, he
10. they, them

---

## Exercise 3

1. Max is good at skating, which he practices daily.
2. Because he was wearing earplugs, he didn't hear her cry for help.
3. It never occurred to Mr. Cohen that he would be Stephen's teacher.
4. It seemed that the donkey brayed every time he looked at it.
5. Management's refusal to allow a cost-of-living clause caused the union to walk out.
6. "You'll soon get a job," he told his brother.
7. Whenever Ann and Carol met, Ann acted in a very friendly way so that no one would suspect that she hated Carol.
8. Joe told Henry that Henry was losing his hair.
9. Matthew dented his calculator by throwing it on the floor.
10. This letter is in response to your ad for a waitress and bartender, male or female. Being both a waitress and a bartender, I wish to apply for the position.

---

## Exercise 4

1. Anyone who has finished all his homework by now can't have done it properly.
2. correct
3. Everybody I know is going, even if he can't get a date.
4. Each of my roommates finally left to find an apartment of his own.
5. I'd like to meet someone who is tall, dark, handsome, and rich; in fact, he doesn't even have to be tall, dark, or handsome.
6. Here everybody is allowed to find his own path to success, according to what he considers success to be.
7. The book tries to prove that nobody can rise above his own level of ability without the help of friends.
8. Constant nagging would make anyone lose his mind unless he learned to ignore it.
9. Somebody who has many friends will have to go; he will need friends if he hopes to return.
10. Everyone likes to think that he is unique, but each of us is his own idea of perfect, so in fact we are all the same.

---

## Exercise 5

1. Each of the cars has its own faults, but nobody else wants this one, so I'll take it.

2. Every child is a product of his environment as well as his parentage.
3. correct
4. The men who made up the team agreed that everybody would have to complete his assignment.
5. Writing articles is what he does best, although he hasn't been able to complete one lately.
6. She'll put her baby to bed now because the infant is short-tempered.
7. Everyone must get in his place for the game to begin.
8. Anybody who is without a partner will have to be sure she finds one who is about her height.
9. Neither the jacket nor the pants fit the way they should.
10. He said that Dave wasn't trying hard enough and that anyone who said he was would get a punch on his nose.

---

## Chapter 12: Tense Agreement

---

### Exercise 1

1. He goes home and *tells* her what happened.
2. He was so successful that he *was* offered a promotion.
3. The plane was chartered, the bags were packed, and the champagne *was* on ice.
4. The referee stands there, blinking, unable to believe what he *is* seeing.
5. correct
6. As Castro stepped forward to speak, the crowd *began* to clap, stamp, and whistle.
7. First you will fry the onions; then you *will* brown the meat.
8. Mount Rushmore, South Dakota was the site that Gutzon Borglum *selected* . . .
9. "Safety colors" are bright and *attract* immediate attention.
10. It was not until the sixteenth century, when Leonardo *designed* his flying machine, that flight *began.*

---

### Exercise 2

1. Drill the holes for the speakers; then you *cut* a hole in the dashboard.
2. The coach went over the game and carefully analyzed the plays.

3. The Peter Principle states that every person *rises* to his or her level of incompetence.
4. The couple next door had a boa constrictor that *kept* getting loose.
5. He began by asking a rhetorical question that he *proceeded* to answer.
6. First he buys me chocolates when he knows I'm on a diet; then he *embarrasses* me by kissing me in front of everyone.
7. While our team suffered one defeat after another, the other teams *rejoiced.*
8. correct
9. The new employee was too inexperienced to do the job in the time she *was* given.
10. If a player hits another player or knocks him down, he *gets* a warning.

## Exercise 3

1. Prejudice is learned and *is* hard to outgrow.
2. I studied so hard for that test, and look at the reward I *got*!
3. If you will just keep your eyes and ears open, you *will* learn something new every day.
4. After I had already put the car away, I *realized* Ann *was* still waiting for me at school.
5. The guard didn't say anything. He just *stood* there and *stared* at us.
6. If you would include an example here, the explanation *would be* much easier to follow.
7. He kept trying to reach me for weeks, but he didn't know *I'd* moved.
8. Her argument became silly when she *went* on to suggest that watching television weakened the genes.
9. In the belief that playing pool was somehow good for his health, he *played* at least two hours every day.
10. In the dead of night, while coyotes howled in the distance, someone—or some*thing*—*was* prowling in the dark recesses of the cave.

## Exercise 4

The first time I began to sneeze, a friend *told* me to go and bathe my feet in hot water and go to bed. I did so. Shortly afterward, another friend *advised* me to get up and take a cold shower. I *did* that also. Within the hour, another friend *assured* me that it was policy to "feed a cold and starve a fever." I had both. So I thought it best to fill myself up for the cold, and then let the fever starve awhile.

I ate pretty heartily [I went to the restaurant of a man who *had* just opened for business that morning]; he waited near me in respectful silence until I *had finished* feeding my cold, when he *inquired* if the people about Virginia City *were* much afflicted with colds. I *told* him I thought they were. He then *went* out and *took* in his sign.

I started down toward the office, and on the way *encountered* another bosom friend, who *told* me that a quart of salt-water, taken warm, would come as near curing a cold as anything in the world. I hardly thought I had room for it, but I *tried* it anyhow. The result was surprising. I believed I had thrown up my immortal soul. . . . If I *had* another cold in the head and no course left me but to take either an earthquake or a quart of warm salt-water, I would take my chances on the earthquake.

---

### Exercise 5

The fisherman *returned* after his day's outing with his two friends whom he *had* taken out for the day, to his summer cottage. They *carried* with them their rods, their landing net, and the paraphernalia of their profession. The fisherman *carried* also on a string a dirty looking collection of little fish, called by courtesy the "Catch." The fisherman's wife and his wife's sister and the young lady who *was* staying with them *came* running to meet the fishing party, giving cries of admiration as they *got* a sight of the catch. In reality they would *have refused* to buy those fish from a butcher at a cent and a half a pound. But they fell into ecstasies, and they *cried,* "Oh, aren't they beauties! Look at this big one!" The "big one" *was* about eight inches long . . . and *looked* . . . as if it had died of consumption.

---

## Chapter 13: Person Agreement

---

### Exercise 1

1. he
2. he
3. she
4. you
5. one
6. his
7. she, she
8. it
9. we
10. you

---

### Exercise 2

1. You mustn't upset the instructor if you wish to leave class on time.
2. Anyone going to the class party can pick up his tickets now.
3. Men who don't think women are their equals may have to get used to living on their own.
4. Americans don't seem to realize that the situation may get out of hand if they don't vote wisely.

5. You must try to control your temper when you feel frustrated or angry.
6. correct
7. Everyone is going to get what he deserves.
8. If one is convicted on that charge, a fine is the least of one's worries.
9. After we had driven about 300 miles, we could feel the sleepiness begin to weight our eyelids.
10. correct

---

## Exercise 3

1. A great way to develop your skills is to push yourself to the limit.
2. Everyone who wants more from life must stand up and shout his name as loudly as he can.
3. Americans who travel abroad should remember they're representing their country.
4. Following one's hunch can lead to disaster—or to an easy solution to one's problem.
5. Once you have been elected to the Senate, you should always remember that you are in the public eye.
6. In this country, you receive more acclaim as a baseball player than you do as a symphony conductor.
7. Anyone who drives one of those things should be aware of the risk he's taking.
8. correct
9. Can one really be happy if he doesn't own an electric pencil sharpener?
10. Why must people always want something they don't have, even when they have more than they'll ever need?

---

## Exercise 4

1. I enjoy living in the country, because there I don't have to deal with traffic or pollution, and I can always get to the city if I want to.
2. You never really know whether she's joking or not, do you?
3. I collect art because I can always get my money back on the investment, and I can sometimes make a killing.
4. No one can help him, because if one tries, one is quickly and rudely rebuffed.
5. Americans who vacation in Canada should take the opportunity to add to their collection of china at bargain prices.
6. A high school graduate who can't construct a proper sentence ought to be ashamed of himself.

7. You can't go around picking up after your sloppy relatives all day, can you?
8. When we left the hotel's air-conditioned comfort, the heat knocked us over.
9. correct
10. An expert wine taster will find this a very acceptable vintage, and even one who knows little about wine will enjoy himself with a bottle or two.

---

## Exercise 5

1. When you're bright, talented, and rich, you don't really have to try very hard to impress your elders, especially if you are also handsome.
2. . . . We were amazed by the beauty of the country, especially the spectacular mountains. We learned quickly why many artists have found inspiration there.
3. You can't beat a charcoal grill for preparing great hamburgers in the summertime. You get so tired of pan-fried meat patties all winter long.
4. . . . We really didn't get out as much as we should have when it was cold, but we are going to make up for that now.
5. . . . How can you understand the game unless you know what's going on?
6. You mustn't push him too far, because he will either lose his temper or become hysterical, and that isn't what you want.
7. . . . We get good service, which we don't find very often, and we find the bill tolerable as well.
8. . . . suddenly we all got the idea. We couldn't wait to get our hands in the air to tell the others what we had discovered.
9. . . . Years of hard work and sacrifice had left us tired and somewhat bitter, but the feeling of accomplishment at that moment made us feel it was all worth it.
10. . . . Often I got so tired that I wanted to give up.

---

## Exercise 6

1. they're
2. their
3. they
4. their
5. themselves
6. their
7. her
8. his
9. they are
10. their

11. his or her
12. themselves
13. they

---

## Chapter 14: The Question Mark

---

### Exercise 1

1. incorrect
2. incorrect
3. correct
4. correct
5. correct
6. incorrect
7. incorrect
8. correct
9. correct
10. correct

---

### Exercise 2

1. correct
2. correct
3. incorrect
4. incorrect
5. correct
6. correct
7. incorrect
8. incorrect
9. incorrect
10. incorrect

---

### Exercise 3

1. period
2. period
3. question mark
4. period
5. question mark
6. period
7. period
8. question mark
9. question mark
10. period

---

## Chapter 15: The Exclamation Mark

---

### Exercise 1

1. question mark
2. exclamation mark or period
3. exclamation mark
4. question mark
5. exclamation mark or period
6. question mark

7. period
8. exclamation mark or period
9. question mark
10. exclamation mark

### Exercise 2

1. question mark
2. exclamation mark
3. exclamation mark, question mark
4. period
5. question mark, exclamation mark
6. exclamation mark
7. period
8. question mark, exclamation mark
9. exclamation mark, exclamation mark
10. question mark, question mark

## Chapter 16: The Colon

### Exercise 1

1. correct
2. incorrect
3. correct
4. incorrect
5. correct
6. incorrect
7. correct
8. incorrect
9. incorrect
10. incorrect

### Exercise 2

1. incorrect
2. incorrect
3. incorrect
4. correct
5. correct
6. incorrect
7. correct
8. incorrect
9. correct
10. correct

### Exercise 3

1. correct
2. They finally realized there was only one course open to them: obedience.
3. Gary had trouble with his canoe: it tipped over and then sank.
4. There is someone who can save us, though: Captain America!
5. He tossed and turned all night and found the same images recurring in his dreams: a river and a wolf.

6. His body was beyond the point of exhaustion, but he tried to force himself on by thinking of one thing: victory.
7. correct
8. I have a very large garden, but it grows only two things: tomatoes and weeds.
9. She has one goal that she is determined to achieve: the world record.
10. Two issues remained to be settled: wages and benefits.

---

### Exercise 4

2. Only one thing was needed: a boat.
4. On the list we must include chips, mix, ice, and peanuts.
6. Three qualities of a good quarterback are leadership, intelligence, and physical strength.
8. The pond is deep and cold.
9. Dogs have many qualities that make them superior to cats: loyalty, intelligence, working ability, and friendliness.
10. Let me give you an example: Abraham Lincoln.

---

### Exercise 5

1. I'd like to help, but I can't.
2. I'll take the following volunteers: John, Susan, David, and Colin.
3. We'll have to go back to get tent poles, matches, and paddles.
6. No one wants to go with him, for two very good reasons: money and time.
8. My boss is so mean she must be bitter or crazy.

---

## Chapter 17: The Comma

---

### Exercise 1

1. Careful investment of money and time can lead to wealth, fame, and happiness.
2. correct
3. Does anyone fail to remember John, Paul, George, and Ringo?
4. correct
5. Cutting the lawn, washing the dishes, and doing the shopping are my least favorite activities.

6. Cleopatra, Casanova, Rasputin, and Brigitte Bardot are four dissimilar people who have at least one thing in common.
7. He is an all-around athlete who enjoys many sports: skating, skiing, cycling, riding, and hunting.
8. She has strong ambition, a cool head, good health, and an inquiring mind; everyone hates her.
9. correct
10. Many Americans see Canada as a land where only French is spoken, ice and snow are year-round hazards, and violent hockey is the only pastime.

---

## Exercise 2

1. He is, you know, one of our best teachers.
2. If my favorite team wins, football is the sport I like best.
3. You'll have to do better than that, Steve, if you want to join us.
4. Despite her reputation, she is, we have found out, fairly bright.
5. correct
6. Where will you go now, Heather?
7. Baseball games, despite the huge increases in seat prices, are still always sold out in my home town.
8. The bride, in a departure from tradition, wore a yellow pants suit.
9. We tried, all of us, to be of some help.
10. One of my favorite writers is Tom Wolfe, the man who wrote the book, *The Electric Kool Aid Acid Test.*

---

## Exercise 3

1. He and I are good friends, yet we sometimes argue.
2. Now we'll have to try bribery, or we can resort to force.
3. We can't win this game, nor can we afford to lose it.
4. The car swerved wildly, but it narrowly missed the crossing guard.
5. She tried and tried, and soon her efforts paid off.
6. I'd like to buy a house as an investment, but I can't afford the down payment right now.
7. My part-time job isn't very rewarding, so I'm coming back to school next fall.
8. There are not many dangers, so we must conquer our fear of failure.
9. This is her last semester, so she's concentrating on school for a change.
10. Clutching his wounded shoulder, he fell through the air, but he managed to land on his feet.

---

## Exercise 4

1. In the end, quality will win.
2. John, if you don't quiet down, you'll have to leave.
3. If there were any justice, I'd have been rewarded for what I did.
4. Well, I don't believe it!
5. When the sun came up in a clear blue sky, we all sighed with relief.
6. Adorned with blue bows, her shoes clashed with her green outfit.
7. Moved beyond words, he was able only to gesture his thanks.
8. Carefully placing one foot in front of the other, she managed to walk along the white line for several feet.
9. Falling, staggering to his feet, then falling again, he stumbled painfully toward the finish line.
10. Where a huge hardwood forest had stood, now there was only blackened ground.

## Exercise 5

1. The job interview isn't so bad if you're prepared, relaxed, and confident.
2. With a shout of glee, the boys ran to the heavily laden Christmas tree.
3. There is something wrong here, but I haven't yet determined what it is.
4. In the end, they'll be caught, so all we have to do is wait.
5. George Washington, the first President of the United States, was an officer in the British army before the American Revolution.
6. Clam chowder, baked beans, and Indian Pudding are typical New England recipes found in my *Fannie Farmer Cookbook.*
7. Well, Mrs. O'Hara, if that's the best you can do, it's out of my hands.
8. correct
9. A good dictionary, used properly, can be an important tool for developing a mature vocabulary.
10. If there were any point in complaining, I would have protested long ago, but I don't think anything can change their course of action now.

## Exercise 6

1. My world is made up of handsome men, fast cars, loud music, expensive clothes, and other dreams.
2. The movie, despite some excellent action sequences, was a failure because of the terrible script.

3. If starvation and lack of recognition made great artists, many of my friends would be Picassos.
4. The letter of application is the most important document you will ever write, yet you have spent only an hour composing it.
5. Wrapping the watch in a handkerchief, he produced a mallet and smashed the expensive timepiece to smithereens, or so it appeared.
6. The retirement of Bobby Orr from hockey was the end of an era for the game, but those who saw him play will never forget it.
7. In the 1960s, blue jeans became a uniform for the young, but today jeans are popular only as very casual attire, and a much more fashionable look has emerged.
8. Despite some early problems, the Golden Gate Bridge has become one of the most interesting and exciting sights in North America, don't you think?
9. There, you've gone and broken it again!
10. correct

---

## Exercise 7

1. Your fall order, which we received last week, has been filled.
2. An excellent pool is available for those who like to swim, and, for those who play golf, there is a beautiful eighteen-hole course.
3. John, realizing his position, resigned.
4. Inside, the piano was going at full blast.
5. What you hear, what you read, and what you think all help to form your intellectual background.
6. Quickly, girls, or we'll be late.
7. Ever since, I have been a regular theatergoer.
8. A few days after they sailed, the boat sprang a leak.
9. A fine fellow, a member of the yacht club, was drowned.
10. Antonio's grandmother was very short, black-haired, and extremely thin.

---

## Exercise 8

1. When you enter the store, go to the counter on your left, ask for Ms. Bertrand, and tell her that you want to see the latest prints.
2. These cold, wet, gray days are not good for the crops.
3. The thick syrup boiled over and spilled on the stove, on the table, and on the floor.
4. correct
5. Conflicts have occurred between students and faculty, students and administration, and faculty and administration.

6. However capable he was, he failed miserably in this case.
7. Oh, excuse me. I didn't hear you come in.
8. Nearby, an old oak lifted its gaunt limbs to the sky.
9. Mr. Smith, the head of the department, despite his vast knowledge of his subject, couldn't change a light bulb if his life depended on it.
10. I dressed, you will be amazed to learn, in two minutes flat and was out the door before his knock had stopped echoing.

---

## Exercise 9

1. For the last ten years, oil-consuming nations have been struggling with the "energy crisis," or, more specifically, the "oil crisis."
2. Everyone is familiar with the problems the crisis has created: ever-increasing prices, higher taxes, and political conflict, to name only a few.
3. Many solutions, ranging from the practical to the fantastic, have been proposed. Almost every magazine or newspaper we read contains at least one article on the exciting possibilities of solar power, tidal power, biomass, or wind power.
4. Despite the optimism of the writers, however, most readers do not find such articles very reassuring. All the solutions proposed are realizable only in the future; the problem confronts us now, today.
5. correct
6. The ideal fuel would be, first, one that could be manufactured from an inexhaustible American resource.
7. Second, the ideal fuel would be one that could be used to power existing cars, trucks, buses, planes, and other transit vehicles without major mechanical alterations.
8. Third, the ideal fuel must be safe, powerful, and nonpolluting.
9. One possible fuel that meets these requirements is hydrogen, the most abundant element in the universe.
10. According to Roger Billings of Independence, Missouri, who is the leading expert in hydrogen-powered automobiles, almost any internal combustion engine that runs on gasoline can be converted inexpensively to run on hydrogen.

---

## Exercise 10

1. "The world is changing," my friends in data processing told me. They warned me that I, a naive English teacher, would not be able to keep up with my students unless I learned some basic computer skills.

2. They assured me that machines with nonthreatening names like PET and Apple would do a better job than I could in teaching students about commas, colons, semicolons, and spelling.
3. Then I would be free, my friends maintained, to teach the things that *really* mattered. In the cybernetic world of the future, computers would take care of the details of grammar, spelling, and punctuation, and I had better prepare myself for the revolution.
4. Furthermore, they told me, silicon chips would soon be doing my cooking, balancing my checkbook, and even going shopping for me. If a computer could do all that, I thought dreamily, perhaps it could even be programmed to sort socks.
5. Curiosity finally outweighed my lifelong distrust of machines, and I enrolled in a course called "Your Friendly Computer."
6. I must admit the little demon seemed friendly at first. It quickly established itself on a first-name basis with me, but the mass of information about inputs, outputs, modems, disks, bits, and bytes soon left me dazed and bewildered.
7. Recognizing a rank amateur when it saw one, my friendly computer attempted to win my trust and inspire my confidence by allowing me to pick off PacMans, blast Rasters, and incinerate Invaders. Dots, gobblers, and rocketships appeared and disappeared on the screen with dazzling speed.
8. Ever cheerful, the computer tried to console me for my pitiful scores. "Not bad," it blinked, but my hand-eye coordination was obviously unequal to the demands of video games.
9. Thinking I would feel more comfortable in the slower world of punctuation exercises, I tried a program on exclamation marks, question marks, and periods. Nothing, I thought, could possibly go wrong now.
10. To my surprise, the machine, no longer friendly, flashed "GIGO—GIGO—GIGO" at me. Even I, ignorant and inexperienced as I was, knew what GIGO meant: "Garbage In, Garbage Out." So I left the blinking computer behind me and went home to sort socks.

---

## Chapter 18: The Semicolon

---

### Exercise 1

1. correct
2. incorrect
3. correct
4. incorrect
5. incorrect
6. incorrect

7. incorrect
8. correct
9. correct
10. correct

## Exercise 2

1. correct
2. incorrect
3. correct
4. correct
5. incorrect
6. correct
7. incorrect
8. correct
9. incorrect
10. incorrect

## Exercise 3

2. He sat down near a refreshing stream, for he was very tired.
4. It's a beautiful day, just right for a long walk.
5. Six of the Indian nations joined together in a loose union; they were called Iroquois.
6. The lawn needs to be cut; the hedge needs to be trimmed; the flowers need to be watered; and, not least of all, the gardener needs to be paid.
7. I'd like to help; however, I'm supposed to rest all day.
2. There are only a few who could catch him, and I'm sure she isn't one of them.
5. We'll have to go soon, for it's getting late.
7. If ever there were a time to act, it is now.
9. She disobeyed the rules, so she will have to be punished.
10. She is always late; however, she's worth waiting for.

## Exercise 4

1. There seems to be no end to the work that must be done; furthermore, there isn't enough time in which to do it.
2. There must be a way, or we're finished before we've begun.
3. I can't afford a Porsche; therefore, I drive a Volkswagen.
4. Shirley is one of my favorite people; she can always cheer me up.
5. There will be ample time to finish your homework, but right now I need your help.
6. The flooring was all knotty pine, yellowed with age; the walls and furniture were of such design and color as to blend with it.
7. Mark Twain made a fortune as a writer, but he lost it as an unsuccessful inventor.

8. Killer whales at Marineland look very dangerous; however, their high intelligence makes them relatively tame and easy to train.
9. John has gone away to become a teacher; Martha now has twin baby girls; Kevin is unemployed; Julie is a lawyer or stockbroker (I forget which); and Paul is, as usual, drifting from job to job.
10. When the rain started, they were trapped in the open; nevertheless, they stayed where they were until it let up and then watched the game with enjoyment, despite being a little wet.

---

### Exercise 5

1. I have grown fond of semicolons in recent years. The semicolon tells you that there is still some question about the preceding full sentence; something needs to be added.
2. It is almost always a greater pleasure to come across a semicolon than a period. The period tells you that that is that; if you didn't get all the meaning you wanted or expected, anyway you got all the writer intended to parcel out and now you have to move along.
3. But with a semicolon there, you get a pleasant little feeling of expectancy; there is more to come; read on; it will get clearer.
4. Colons are a lot less attractive, for several reasons: firstly, they give you the feeling of being rather ordered around, or at least having your nose pointed in a direction you might not be inclined to take if left to yourself; and, secondly, you suspect you're in for one of those sentences that will be labeling the points to be made: firstly, secondly, and so forth, with the implication that you haven't enough sense to keep track of a sequence of notions without having them numbered.
5. correct

---

## Chapter 19: Capital Letters

---

### Exercise 1

1. Henry Smith wants to be a prince when he grows up.
2. The Queen of England visited Australia last winter.
3. Confident of victory, we marched on Paris, led by our heroic captain.
4. correct
5. Laurie tries hard, but she'll never be as good at typing as Frank.

6. *Santa Claus Conquers the Martians* was a film that featured a cute little Martian named Dropo.
7. Do you think Fords are better than Chevies in the middle price range?
8. correct
9. High school is a time of growing and development for young people, a time for them to find a direction for the rest of their lives.
10. Office supplies are in great demand, so, if you need pens or paper, you'd better see Ms. Carlo in Supplies right away.

### Exercise 2

1. Sue Ellen rode down Grant Avenue every day in the fall to look at the leaves.
2. I went with my English professor to the Newport Jazz Festival.
3. Alan goes to the city on weekends to see French films.
4. correct
5. I want to grow up to be a movie star, or at least a company president.
6. Jane studied cooking, art history, and French in Europe last summer.
7. The committee we had elected deprived us of our human rights.
8. He considers himself liberal on matters such as the dress code.
9. Jim works for the phone company, which has an office on a street near his home.
10. correct

## Chapter 20: Finding Something to Write About

### Exercise 1

1. Not specific. What war? What about it?
2. Not supportable. There is no evidence to show what space travel will be like years from now.
3. Not significant. Every child knows what they are.
4. Not supportable. No one can prove Shakespeare did or did not have a guilt complex.
5. Not single.
6. Not significant.
7. Not specific enough.
8. Not single and not specific.

9. Not specific. Whole books have been written on this topic.
10. Not significant.

## Exercise 4

1. acne (not significant)
2. more dates (not significant)
3. good visual impact (overlaps with *neat appearance*) neat signature (not significant)
4. unemployment (overlaps with *economic difficulties*) adultery (overlaps with *sexual incompatibility*)
5. spouse would benefit (overlaps with *family would benefit*)
6. warning (overlaps with *safety*) fluorescent paint (not related to subject; it's not a *use*)
7. requires southern exposure (not related; it's a disadvantage) three main kinds (not related; the *kinds* are not an advantage)
8. to decriminalize prostitution (not related; it means exactly the same thing as subject)
   to ensure regular health checkups for prostitutes (overlaps with *to control spread of venereal disease*)

# Chapter 21: Writing the Thesis Statement

## Exercise 1

1. There are four kinds of patients whom doctors hate to treat : clingers, demanders, help rejecters, and deniers.
2. The most prolific producers of unnecessary jargon are politicians, sportswriters, advertising copywriters, and educators.
3. The principles of good child care include understanding the development of the child, accepting his need to regress as well as progress, and encouraging him to become independent.
4. Seventy-five percent of Americans over twenty suffer from cardiovascular disease because we eat too much, we eat the wrong kinds of food, and we exercise too little.
5. According to Aaron Copland, people listen to music on three planes simultaneously : the sensuous plane, the expressive plane, and the "sheerly musical" plane.
6. Standardized examinations should be introduced in all college courses in order to force students to learn the work and to ensure a fair assessment of each student's ability.

7. Since children are expensive, time-consuming, and often ungrateful, young couples should think carefully before deciding to become parents.
8. Three passions, simple but overwhelmingly strong, have governed my life: the longing for love, the search for knowledge, and unbearable pity for the suffering of mankind. (Bertrand Russell, "What I Have Lived For")
9. Supermarket people take us for fools, presuming that we know nothing about food, that we shop impulsively and irrationally, and that we can be cheated with impunity. (John Keats, "Rip-Off at the Supermarket")
10. Several subtle aspects of the relationship between population growth and environmental degradation operate to make man's predicament even more perilous than superficial analyses indicate. Four to be considered here are synergisms, threshold effects, trigger effects, and time-lag effects. (Paul R. Ehrlich and John P. Holdren, "Hidden Effects of Overpopulation")

---

## Exercise 2

1. The chief characteristics of good writing are clarity, brevity, simplicity, and accuracy.
2. Two features of the semester system are flexibility and economy.
3. The elderly deserve more attention: they have valuable knowledge to offer, time to spare, and the desire to be useful.
4. To win, a team needs discipline, determination, and cooperation.
5. The cost of eating out has increased enormously because we're paying for more than food: we're paying for décor, service, and entertainment.
6. There are three ways to find a job: by reading the want ads, by consulting an employment agency, and by writing letters to company personnel managers.
7. Basic principles to be observed in caring for the premature infant include maintaining body temperature, maintaining adequate oxygen intake, protecting the infant from infection, and maintaining adequate fluid and calorie intake.
8. Individual communities can no longer cope with our state's garbage-disposal crisis because disposal sites are so hard to find, the costs are so high, and new technologies are not yet fully developed.
9. A high level of motivation, experience in dealing with all sorts of problems, and confidence in your decisions are necessary if you hope to run a successful business.

10. Two questions about battery-operated vehicles need answering: how soon are practical models likely to become available, and what role might the government play in their production?

---

## Chapter 22: Writing the Outline

---

### Exercise 1

A good business letter is concise, clear, and courteous.

I. Conciseness
  A. Don't waste time with irrelevant personal details.
  B. Cut out all unnecessary words.
II. Clarity
  A. Use an accepted business-letter format.
  B. Include all information your reader might need.
    1. Include file number or other reference number, if possible.
    2. Include specific information such as names, dates, product numbers.
III. Courteousness
  A. Avoid sarcasm and insults.
  B. Politely request what action you want the reader to take.

Notice that we've omitted number 6, "Always type your letter." It isn't relevant to any of our main points (nor is it always possible).

---

### Exercise 2

"The Dimensions of a Complete Life"

Introduction
  *Attention-getter:* paragraphs 1 and 2
  *Statement of subject:* paragraph 3
I. (paragraphs 5 to 8)
  A. paragraph 5
  B. (paragraphs 6 and 7)
    1. paragraph 6
    2.
      a. } paragraph 7
      b. }
  C. paragraph 8
II. (paragraphs 9 to 13)
  A. paragraph 9
  B. (paragraphs 10 to 13)
    1. paragraphs 10 and 11

2.
a. } paragraph 12
b.

3.
a.
b. } paragraph 13
c.

III. (paragraphs 14 to 18)
A. paragraph 14
B. paragraph 15
C. (paragraphs 16 and 17)
1.
2. } paragraph 16
3.
4. paragraph 17
D. paragraph 18

Conclusion
*Summary:* paragraph 19
*Memorable statement:* paragraph 20

---

### Exercise 3

II. Supermarket managers view us as impulsive and unthinking shoppers.
A. They design floor plans and displays to trap us.
1. They put juvenile junk food where it will attract children.
2. They lay out the store so shoppers come to high-profit items first.
3. They put "impulse items" at the ends of aisles or close to the check-out counters.
4. They display "go-togethers" next to loss-leaders.
B. They use advertising to try to mislead us.
1. They advertise a regular-price item as a "special."
2. They put a sale placard advertising one brand over a different, more expensive brand.

---

## Chapter 23: Writing the Paragraphs

---

### Exercise 1

Paragraph 2: I have sought love,
Paragraph 3: With equal passion I have sought knowledge.
Paragraph 4: But always pity brought me back to earth.

---

### Exercise 2

1. examples
2. specific details
3. definition
4. comparison and quotation
5. examples
6. examples
7. examples
8. specific details
9. definitions and examples
10. specific details: numerical facts

### Exercise 4

Anyone who enjoys baseball must be a masochist! It is the dullest game ever invented. Let me give you some examples of how boring baseball is. First, the batter actually swings at every third pitch, on average, which means that the fielders are totally inactive for the greater part of the game. Secondly, the fielding team does come to life when there's a hit . . . an event that occurs about fifteen times per game. Allowing thirty seconds of action per hit, this means that the players actually do something for seven and one half minutes out of an entire afternoon. Even home runs are dull: one man trots around the bases while everyone else stands still and watches. I've come to the conclusion that anyone who enjoys baseball must be a pretty boring person!

## Chapter 27: Wordiness

### Exercise 1

1. Basically, I prefer the genuine article to an imitation.
2. Although small and an ugly yellow, the car was, in fact, identical to his last one.
3. The conclusion wasn't known until he was free to announce himself elected.
4. I will repeat, for those who disappeared, that we are now free.
5. They circled behind the enemy and, at four A.M. on July twelfth, surrounded them and eliminated the threat of an invasion.
6. There was nothing they could do except repeat the facts.
7. In my opinion, this innovation won't see the light of day.
8. There comes a time of final reckoning, and you reach a conclusion.
9. Although his ideas seem unique, we must be positive that we don't repeat the mistake.
10. I think she is pretending to be sick so she won't have to go to work.

## Chapter 28: Abusages

### Exercise 1

1. I could have done many things, but I chose to become rich and powerful very quickly.
2. Regardless of what you say, I think the media are generally reliable.
3. The reason Dennis came home was that he couldn't do anything more to help at the hospital.
4. They teach us many irrelevant things at this school.
5. correct
6. Mark was supposed to be in the race, but he fell off his bike during practice.
7. I should have stayed home, but I went anyway.
8. The reason you are failing is that you don't do any homework.
9. The police department was accused of prejudice against minority groups.
10. correct

### Exercise 2

1. She and I did a really stupid thing.
2. He is a better cook than she, although she plays snooker better than he.
3. correct
4. We and they are not the best of friends anymore.
5. In fact, they and we are now enemies as you and he used to be.
6. No one is happier than I that this is the last exercise in this book.
7. She and I are so glad to see the end that we are going to celebrate with them and their friends.
8. I can't believe that you and she got higher marks than I!
9. correct
10. She and I approve of Ralph and her joining them and us.